Europe and Europeanness in Early Modern Latin Literature

Latinity and Classical Reception in the Early Modern Period

Editor-in-Chief

Gesine Manuwald (*University College London*)

Associate Editors

Valéry Berlincourt (*University of Geneva*)
Sarah Knight (*University of Leicester*)
Marianne Pade (*Aarhus University*)
Raija Sarasti-Wilenius (*University of Helsinki*)

Volumes published in this Brill Research Perspectives title are listed at *brill.com/rplcs*

Europe and Europeanness in Early Modern Latin Literature

Fuitne Europa tunc unita?

By

Isabella Walser-Bürgler

BRILL

LEIDEN | BOSTON

Library of Congress Control Number: 2021900289

Typeface for the Latin, Greek, and Cyrillic scripts: "Brill". See and download: brill.com/brill-typeface.

ISSN 2772-3852
ISBN 978-90-04-45954-0 (paperback)
ISBN 978-90-04-45972-4 (e-book)

Contents

Editorial Note

This is the first volume of *Brill Research Perspectives in Latinity and Classical Reception in the Early Modern Period*. This series aims to address important themes connected with the re-shaping and re-imagining of material inherited from classical antiquity, primarily the Latin language and Latin writing conventions, but also the creative adaptation of Greek and Roman traditions in other languages and media. Issues will consist of individual contributions by leading scholars from different disciplinary backgrounds, providing up-to-date overviews on contexts, key texts, fundamental and controversial questions, existing scholarship, current methods, theories and approaches as well as avenues for further research concerning particular topics and ideas.

These surveys are designed to give scholars new to the specific area and advanced students an introductory overview of the sources, approaches, scholarly history and existing research in the respective field. Thus, readers will be able to use these articles as starting points for researching the subject, using the bibliography to identify the most important primary and secondary sources.

It is hoped that the launch of this series will enable a greater number of researchers to engage with the important and rich material from the early modern period and thus to facilitate further work.

Europe and Europeanness in Early Modern Latin Literature

Fuitne Europa tunc unita?

Isabella Walser-Bürgler
Ludwig Boltzmann Institute for Neo-Latin Studies, Innsbruck, Austria
isabella.walser@neolatin.lbg.ac.at

Abstract

The history of European integration goes back to the early modern centuries, when Europeans tried to set themselves apart as a continental community with distinct political, religious, cultural, and social values in the face of hitherto unseen societal change and global awakening. The range of concepts and images ascribed to Europeanness in that respect is well documented in Neo-Latin literature, since Latin constituted the international *lingua franca* from the fifteenth to the eighteenth centuries. This investigation examines the most prominent concepts of Europe as expressed in Neo-Latin sources. It is aimed at both an interested general audience and a professional readership from the fields of Latin studies, early modern history, and the history of ideas.

Keywords

European identity – early modern Europe – discourse of Europe – European history – Europeanness – European integration

1 Introduction

Est Europa nunc unita
et unita maneat;
una in diversitate
pacem mundi augeat.

Semper regant in Europa
fides et iustitia
et libertas populorum
in maiore patria.

Cives, floreat Europa,
opus magnum vocat vos.
Stellae signa sunt in caelo
aureae, quae iungant nos.

Europe is united now and united may it remain. May our unity in diversity contribute to world peace.

May there therefore reign in Europe faith and justice and freedom for its people in a greater homeland.

Citizens, may Europe flourish, a great task calls you on. Golden stars in the sky are the symbols that are to unite us.

The anthem of Europe is a piece of Latin literature from modern times, the text of which was composed by the former Viennese school principal, founder of the *Europa-Akademie* in Vienna, and project manager of the international training course *Examen Europaeum*, Peter Roland.[1] Despite the text's unofficial status and modern origin, it serves as an exemplary illustration of how the Latin language can be utilised to propagate ideas of European unity and shared identity. During the early modern centuries (i.e. from roughly 1400 to 1800), Latin had performed precisely this function, defining, describing, and promoting the slowly evolving sense of Europeanness in many genres and texts of Neo-Latin literature. Roland's Latin text of the European anthem clearly takes after this early modern Latin tradition. After all, according to the statements made on his homepage, he chose Latin as the language of the hymn in order to avoid giving preference to any of Europe's national languages on the one hand, and to emphasise Europe's common ground on the other. Moreover, the text reveals insights into Roland's own understanding of Europe and Europe's

---

1 The Latin text and English translation – the latter with slight modifications – are taken from Peter Roland's website "Hymnus Latinus Europae": https://www.hymnus-europae.at/ hymnus-europae/ (accessed 8 January 2021). The instrumental version of the hymn (based on Beethoven's *Ode to Joy* from the final movement of the ninth symphony) was accepted as an expression of 'Europeanness' by the Council of Europe in 1972 and by the European Community in 1985. Text suggestions – among them Roland's Latin version as the first and most prominent one – have since then been rejected by arguing in favour of the universality of music. For more information on the history and context of the anthem, see Esteban Buch, 'Parcours et paradoxes de l'hymne européen', in *Figures d'Europe – Images and Myths of Europe*, ed. by Luisa Passerini (Brussels: Lang, 2003), pp. 87–98; Albrecht Riethmüller, 'Die Hymne der europäischen Union', in *Europäische Erinnerungsorte. Bd. 2: Das Haus Europa*, ed. by Pim den Boer and others (Munich: Oldenbourg, 2012), pp. 89–96.

customary self-characterisation. As will be shown in this study, all these aspects were crucial to Neo-Latin discussions of Europe.

With particular regard to the latter aspects of an author's understanding of Europe and continental self-characterisation in general, Roland's contribution to what could be considered the modern discourse of Europe[2] expresses a set of values that the members of the European Union and those striving to become integrated perceive as typically and originally European: the mention of diversity hints at the appreciation of Europe's multi-national and multi-cultural consistence; the mention of peace renders Europe a place of friendly cohabitation in which individual and collective ventures can thrive; the mention of faith refers to religion as an essential ingredient of Europe's viability; the mention of justice signals the establishment of the rule of law and human rights on the continent; the mention of liberty voices notions of personal autonomy and political independence, and so on.

The antecedent of these present-day deliberations on what typified Europe constituted a pervasive early modern phenomenon. From the end of the Middle Ages to the beginning of the nineteenth century, politicians, scholars, and ordinary people were pondering extensively over what made Europeans

---

2　The phrase 'discourse of Europe' is indispensable to any study on Europe as an imagined community, viz. notions of Europeanness, and will thus also play a central role in the present study. To clarify its meaning, one needs to turn to Michel Foucault's general discourse analysis. According to Foucault, a discourse designates a group of statements which determine the use of language, behaviours, and mindsets of a given group of people at a given time. They define how something (in our case: Europe) is spoken about. As such, discourses not only dictate the objects of discourse (in our case: Europe) but also its subjects (in our case: the Europeans). Within the experienced field of discourse, both objects and subjects are permanently redefining themselves. The terms 'image', 'idea', 'concept', 'vision', or 'construction of Europe' are integral parts of the discourse and constitute a means to describe and observe Europeans trying to become aware of themselves and the environment they live in. In addition, they enable references to a plural meaning of Europe, i.e. to multiple 'Europes'. This is crucial given that it would be methodologically wrong to surmise the existence of only one form or perception of continental communality. A concise overview of Foucault's discourse analysis is provided in Michael Arribas-Ayllon and Valerie Walkerdine, 'Foucauldian Discourse Analysis', in *The SAGE Handbook of Qualitative Research in Psychology*, ed. Carla Willig and Wendy Stainton-Rogers (Los Angeles, CA: SAGE Publications, 2008), pp. 91–108. On the plurality of meanings tied to the discourse of Europe, see Florian Kläger and Gerd Bayer, 'Introduction: Early Modern Constructions of Europe', in *Early Modern Constructions of Europe: Literature, Culture, History*, ed. by Florian Kläger and Gerd Bayer, Routledge Studies in Renaissance Literature and Culture, 29 (New York: Routledge, 2016), pp. 1–23 (p. 1): "[...] clearly, there is no one perennial Europe but a multiplicity of historical versions of it." Indicative of this conclusion is also the title of J.G.A. Pocock's article: 'Some Europes in Their History', in *The Idea of Europe: From Antiquity to the European Union*, ed. by Anthony Pagden (Cambridge: Cambridge University Press, 2002), pp. 55–71.

distinctly European and by what factors the continent and its community were defined. Of key interest in this respect were questions of geography (what and where exactly are Europe's borders; which nations form part of the main body of the continent); of political amalgamation (how could Europe best be joined to one system; which form of rule would be most appropriate for unification); of cultural belonging (are there certain customs and traditions that have grown over the course of the centuries, demarcating Europe from the rest of the world; if so, what exactly are they); of religious cohesion (does Christianity bear potential for association beyond the various confessional splits and schisms; or does Europe rather constitute a melting pot of different beliefs as there are Christians, Jews, and Muslims scattered over the different nations); and of intellectual connection (can Europe be considered the engine of human progress; does the supranational scholarly and scientific exchange within Europe justify the continent's salient superior position in the world). The scrutiny into these questions mainly took place in the Latin language, leading to the production of an altogether inconceivable quantity of texts in all kinds of genres.

1.1   The Discourse of Europe in Neo-Latin Literature

When talking about the combined implications of the terms 'Latin' and 'Europe', usually three major lines of reference come up: the legal, administrative, intellectual, and literary legacy of the ancient Roman Empire; the Romance languages as successors of ancient Latin or linguistic variations of ancient vulgar (i.e. colloquial) Latin; and the tradition of Western Christianity based on Latin as the liturgical language. Yet while all these issues are legitimate in their own right, Europe and the Latin language are bound by an even more intricate relationship that has received only scant attention so far, namely the analysis of Europe and Europeanness in Neo-Latin literature. This issue lacks representation both within and without the narrower realms of scholarship. Even the most noteworthy recent contributions to the history of Europe and the discourse of Europe in early modern times tend to show a striking ignorance regarding the Neo-Latin source material.[3]

This ignorance means that the significance of Neo-Latin language and literature in creating European identity and in envisioning different forms of

---

3 Cf., for example, Wolfgang Schmale and others, *Studien zur europäischen Identität im 17. Jahrhundert: Mit 28 Abbildungen und 72 Tabellen*, Herausforderungen, 15 (Bochum: Winkler, 2004); Michael Gehler, *Europa – Ideen – Institutionen – Vereinigung* (Munich: Olzog, 2010); or Florian Kläger and Gerd Bayer (eds.), *Early Modern Constructions of Europe: Literature, Culture, History*, Routledge Studies in Renaissance Literature and Culture, 29 (New York: Routledge, 2016).

European integration is either downplayed or – more frequently – decidedly overlooked. Apart from a few texts by central figures like Enea Silvio Piccolomini (1405–1464) or Erasmus of Rotterdam (1466–1536), which more often than not are cited in translation only and without any reference to the original Latin works, Latin texts are excluded from the historical examination of Europe. Instead, most of what we know about the development of 'Europe' as a term and the formation of Europe as an ideological entity still relies on vernacular sources.[4] This is problematic for two reasons: On the one hand, as Klaus Oschema already rightly observed twenty years ago, the textual canon of vernacular Europe literature has not been expanded since the first studies on European history came out in the first half of the twentieth century.[5] Time and again the same texts have been treated in studies discussing the early modern discourse of Europe. Yet how is a field of study to progress, if there is no new input coming from empirical data? On the other hand, by focusing solely on vernacular sources, historians of Europe run into the danger of rendering a distorted and partial image of the process of early modern European integration.[6]

This is all the more concerning considering the dimension and impact of Latin literature between 1400 and the middle of the eighteenth century. During that period, Latin was the *lingua franca* of Europe (and even beyond, in those parts of the world that were colonised or proselytised by Europeans). As such, it outdid all European vernaculars in use and reach many times over.[7] All

---

4   Isabella Walser, '*Unitas multiplex*: John Barclay's Notion of Europe in His *Icon animorum* (1614)', *History of European Ideas*, 43 (2017), 533–46 (p. 533) <https://doi.org/10.1080/01916599 .2017.1309673>.

5   Klaus Oschema, 'Der Europa-Begriff im Hoch- und Spätmittelalter: Zwischen geographischem Weltbild und kultureller Konnotation', *Jahrbuch für europäische Geschichte*, 2 (2001), 191–235 (pp. 191–92). Nicolas Detering introduced the phrase "from Dante to Leibniz" for this repetitive pattern, thus referring to the subtitle of Werner Fritzemeyer's groundbreaking (yet by now obsolete) survey from 1931: Werner Fritzemeyer, *Christenheit und Europa: Zur Geschichte des europäischen Gemeinschaftsgefühls von Dante bis Leibniz*, Historische Zeitschrift. Beihefte, 23 (Munich and Berlin: Oldenbourg, 1931); Nicolas Detering, *Krise und Kontinent: Die Entstehung der deutschen Europa-Literatur in der Frühen Neuzeit* (Cologne: Böhlau, 2017), p. 42. One of the few exceptions is Winfried Böttcher's edited volume, which includes about sixty forgotten visionaries of Europe from twelve countries over the last 700 years: Winfried Böttcher (ed.), *Europas vergessene Visionäre: Rückbesinnung in Zeiten akuter Krisen* (Baden-Baden: Nomos, 2019). However, Böttcher does not always strictly distinguish between figures and texts actually addressing Europe as a subject and others generally discussing topics like the law of nations that would later become integrated into European policies.

6   Walser, '*Unitas multiplex*', p. 534.

7   An in-depth investigation of Latin's scope as an international language will follow in part 2.

across the European nations, scholars, scientists, politicians, noblemen, teach-
ers, priests, and poets wrote all sorts of texts in Latin if they wanted to be heard
and understood by a big international audience and if they aimed at winning
fame and receiving attention outside their local or national community. This
all-encompassing approach naturally also involved writings about the state
and future of Europe as a continental entity – especially since the topic per se
transcended national borders, addressing the international community living
on the continent.

There is no doubt that Neo-Latin literature was the major early modern
player when it came to defining, shaping, and propagating concepts of Europe
as a continental community on multiple levels from the political to the cultural.
While the vernacular output on the matter seems to be relatively manageable
(at least according to what the research on Europe suggests)[8] and frequently
looked at the creation of European identity from a paradoxical national point
of view, the quantity of Neo-Latin texts dealing affirmatively with Europe and
Europeanness abounds beyond any easy estimations.[9] In all probability, there
are tens of thousands of texts processing ideas and representations of Europe
in the Latin language. This sheer quantity of texts can only be partly explained
by the status of early modern Latin as a *lingua franca*. It also has to do with the
circumstances of early modern Latin literature on the one hand, and the strat-
egies chosen by Latin authors for discussing Europe on the other.

After all, to start with the latter, Europe could either be treated in an overt
and explicit way by approaching the subject directly, naming and configuring
Europe; or it could be treated in an obscure and implicit way, in which case the
continental framework was merely revealed between the lines.[10] In terms of
literary circumstances, the discourse of Europe had a lot of space to flourish at
a time when, in particular, political thinking had not yet been institutionalised

---

8   For a comprehensive study of the vernacular Europe literature in early modern Germany
       and France, for example, see Detering, *Krise und Kontinent*, and Niall Oddy, '"Europe" in
       Renaissance France: The Word, Its Uses and Contexts (*c.* 1540–1620)' (unpublished doc-
       toral thesis, University of Durham, 2017).

9   On the paradoxical nature of expressing affirmative supra-national ideas in national lan-
       guages, see Isabella Walser-Bürgler, '*Europa Exultans*: The Personification of Europe as
       a Representation of the Habsburg Universal Monarchy in Johann Lauterbach's Pastoral
       Poem *Europa Eidyllion* (1558)', *Lias. Journal of Early Modern Intellectual Culture and Its
       Sources*, 45 (2018), 1–43; on the quantity of Neo-Latin Europe literature, see Walser, '*Unitas
       multiplex*', p. 534.

10   Klaus Oschema's firm opinion that a text cannot illustrate the discourse of Europe when
       the term 'Europe' is not used has the discourse of Europe fall short in many of its central
       aspects (in the case of Christianity, for instance). Klaus Oschema, *Bilder von Europa im
       Mittelalter* (Ostfildern: Thorbecke, 2013), pp. 16–17.

and scientific investigations or cultural deliberations were prone to transgress the conventional boundaries of genre.[11] Instead of confining as broad an issue as the discourse of Europe to particular genres, it would come up in practically every genre of Neo-Latin literature. Ideas of continental unification are therefore found in belletristic genres (e.g. novels, dramas, poems), in pragmatic genres (e.g. political treatises, mirrors for princes, peace treaties, legal textbooks), journalistic genres (e.g. pamphlets, leaflets, journals), scientific genres (e.g. dissertations, geographical treatises and travelogues, cosmographies), private media (e.g. letters, diaries), and all sorts of scholarly writings (e.g. orations, literary histories, chronicles, theological and philosophical treatises).[12] This generic overview shows that in contrast to today, early modern Europe as an entity was not conceived in the offices of politicians and diplomats but on the desks of poets, scholars, and intellectuals.

Given these considerations, conquering the mountain of Neo-Latin Europe literature is by no means a feasible task for the foreseeable future. So far, the ascent has only just begun in recent years with a couple of selected case studies.[13] However, during this short period of time, the examination of

---

11   Just think of the didactic poem, for example, which is science in hexameters. The missing literary institutionalisation of political thinking is mentioned in Martin Korenjak, *Geschichte der neulateinischen Literatur: Vom Humanismus bis zur Gegenwart* (Munich: Beck, 2016), p. 176.

12   Walser, '*Unitas multiplex*', p. 534.

13   Cf. Johannes Helmrath, 'Enea Silvio Piccolomini (Pius II.) – Ein Humanist als Vater des Europagedankens?', in *Europa und die Europäer: Quellen und Essays zur modernen europäischen Geschichte*, ed. by Rüdiger Hohls, Iris Schröder, and Hannes Siegrist (Stuttgart: Steiner, 2005), pp. 361–69; Ronny Kaiser, 'Antiketransformationen in Enea Silvio Piccolominis *Clades*-Rede (15. Oktober 1454)', in *Europa, das Reich und die Osmanen: Die Türkenreichstage von 1454/55 nach dem Fall von Konstantinopel*, ed. by Marika Bacsóka, Anna-Maria Blank, and Thomas Woelki, Zeitsprünge. Forschungen zur Frühen Neuzeit, 18 (Frankfurt a.M.: Klostermann, 2014), pp. 87–109; Detering, pp. 63–76; Walser, '*Unitas multiplex*'; Isabella Walser-Bürgler, 'Europa und europäische Identität(en) in der neulateinischen Literatur: Neue Wege und Perspektiven in Forschung und Unterricht', *Ianus. Informationen zum Altsprachlichen Unterricht*, 38 (2017), 56–72; Marc Fumaroli, *The Republic of Letters*. Transl. from the French by Lara Vergnaud (New Haven, CT: Yale University Press, 2018), pp. 50–64; Walser-Bürgler, '*Europa exultans*'; Isabella Walser-Bürgler, 'Europe without the Bull? Reflections on the Absence of the Ancient Myth of Europa in the Neo-Latin Discourse on Europe', *Medievalia et Humanistica*, 44 (2018), 81–103; Nicolas Detering and Dennis Pulina, 'Rivalry of Lament: Early Personifications of Europe in Neo-Latin Panegyrics for Charles V and Francis I', in *Contesting Europe: Comparative Perspectives on Early Modern Discourses on Europe, 1400–1800*, ed. by Nicolas Detering, Clementina Marsico, and Isabella Walser-Bürgler, Intersections, 67 (Leiden: Brill, 2019), pp. 13–38; Ronny Kaiser, '*Tota caduca et dehiscens* – Europe's Critical Condition in Andrés Laguna's *Europa* (1543)', in ibid., pp. 39–53; Isabella Walser-Bürgler, 'Geopolitical Instruction and

Neo-Latin texts has already contributed to a revaluation of prior assumptions (mostly based on vernacular sources). Among this revaluation is the supposed inception of the early modern discourse of Europe. While in 1980 Peter Burke – less provocatively than factually – raised the question "Did Europe exist before 1700?" and ended his investigation with the long-lasting statement that "by the year 1700, European consciousness was still weak",[14] the study of Neo-Latin Europe literature has proven otherwise. The first attempts at bringing together the European nations under imagined terms go back to around 1400. In the fifteenth century, the Latin term *Europa* was used to such an extent already that speaking of coincidence would no longer mean simply to underestimate the European cause, but to undermine the historical reality of living. The sixteenth and seventeenth centuries eventually saw a true explosion of Latin writings bearing *Europa* in their titles or main bodies of text.[15]

Another positive result the scrutiny into the Neo-Latin text material has yielded is the expansion of the canon of early modern Europe literature. The uncovering of various hitherto unknown Latin texts on Europe complements the existing text base of both vernacular and Latin literature, thus not only enriching the field of study in general, but also complying with the urgent request for more empirical research in the field.[16]

---

the Construction of Europe in Seventeenth-Century Neo-Latin Texts', in ibid., pp. 317–46; Isabella Walser-Bürgler, 'Andrés Laguna, *Europa heautentimorumene* (1543): Europas Klage im Kontext europapolitischer Bewusstseinsbildung', *Latein Forum*, 97/98 (2019), 6–24; Isabella Walser-Bürgler, 'Continuities of Historical Crises and Discourses of Europe from the Neo-Latin Past to the 21st Century', *International Relations and Diplomacy*, 7 (2019), 549–63 <https://doi.org/10.17265/2328-2134/2019.12.001>; Isabella Walser-Bürgler, 'Staging Oratory in Renaissance Germany: The Delivery of Andrés Laguna's *Europa heautentimorumene* (1543)', *Rhetorica. A Journal of the History of Rhetoric*, 38 (2020), 84–117 <https://doi.org/10.1525/rh.2020.38.1.84>; Isabella Walser-Bürgler, 'Reflections of "Europe" and Continental Thinking? The Language of Inclusion in the *Instrumenta Pacis Westphalicae* (1648)', *The Seventeenth Century*, 36 (2021), 3–31 <https://doi.org/10.1080/0268117X.2019.1704852>.

14   Peter Burke, 'Did Europe Exist before 1700?', *History of European Ideas*, 1 (1980), 21–29 (pp. 21 and 27). Burke did not come to this conclusion himself, but he only stood in a tradition of thinking dating back to the post-war period (cf. Helmut D. Schmidt, 'The Establishment of "Europe" as a Political Expression', *The Historical Journal*, 9 [1966], 172–78). Unfortunately, this opinion continues to be cited in many historical works up to this date.

15   On this development, see part 4 in this study.

16   Cf. Achim Trunk, *Europa, ein Ausweg: Politische Eliten und europäische Identität in den 1950er-Jahren*, Studien zur Internationalen Geschichte, 18 (Munich: Oldenbourg, 2008), p. 55. The main heuristic methods applied to find new texts on Europe pertain to the nominalist approach on the one hand and the realist approach on the other. While the former denotes a search procedure by which texts are collected that bear the name 'Europe' (or its derivative adjective 'European') in their titles, the latter traces concepts of Europe by

1.2   A Short History of the Research into Europe

The ignorance surrounding the Neo-Latin discourse of Europe is deeply rooted in the history of the research on Europe. The early publications formed such a strong tradition, on the sole ground that they reflected the anti-nationalist attitudes of the post-war period, that taking new paths was often considered in the scientific community as going against the European cause as such. At the same time, the dimensions of Neo-Latin literature had not been known to twentieth-century historians at all before Neo-Latin studies were established as a field of their own a few decades ago. Denys Hay, one of the doyens of the early modern discourse of Europe, had referred to the potential value of Latin texts in the context of the formation of Europe by citing the example of fifteenth-century Latin historiography, but no one really took the idea any further (including Hay himself).[17] When Neo-Latin was finally institutionalised towards the end of the twentieth century, many historians either could no longer read Latin as well as the generations before them, or they no longer perceived it as their duty to unveil Latin sources, given that specialists of their own kind were now to arise.

The research into the history of Europe emerged in the twentieth century and has since its beginnings become part of the research agenda of the disciplines of history (and its various subdisciplines like contemporary history, early modern history, intellectual history, and art history), the political sciences, and various national philologies (among them German, Italian, and Russian studies). Despite minor disciplinary distinctions, it mainly comprises questions regarding the origin and meaning of the name, investigations of all sorts of continental concepts, ranging from affirmative pan-European to depreciating nationalist deliberations, as well as general thoughts on mechanisms and behaviours of inclusion and exclusion.

The first studies discussing Europe as a central category of collective interpretation were published between the two World Wars, that is, at a time when Europe experienced a phase of transition and change. The old monarchies had disintegrated, and new party systems and ideologies had evolved, competing

---

the close reading of texts dealing with Europe despite a lack of respective indication in the title. A comparison between the nominalist and the realist approach, their benefits and downsides, is briefly featured in Kläger and Bayer, 'Introduction', pp. 3–6, and Walser, 'Unitas multiplex', pp. 534–35. Special criticism of the nominalist approach is expressed in Eric-Oliver Mader, 'Das Europabild in der politischen Theorie des 16. und 17. Jahrhunderts', in *Departure for Modern Europe: A Handbook of Early Modern Philosophy (1400–1700)*, ed. by Hubertus Busche (Hamburg: Meiner, 2011), pp. 823–39.

17   Walser, 'Unitas multiplex', p. 534 n. 5; Denys Hay, *Europe: The Emergence of an Idea* (Edinburgh: Edinburgh University Press, 1957).

for power and the public's voice. In the face of this zeitgeist, scholars found themselves emphasising the western culture and linking it to an appeal for a 'new' Europe: Oswald Spengler in his monumental two-volume *Der Untergang des Abendlandes* (1918–1922) reacted to the events of contemporary Europe by evoking the flourishing culture of previous centuries; Fritzemeyer's afore-mentioned work *Christenheit und Europa* (1931) investigated Europe through the lens of Christianity; Christopher Dawson's *The Making of Europe* (1932) preached the harking back to late ancient and mediaeval culture to lead Europe out of the present crises; Paul Hazard explicitly conjured the European con-science for the first time in *La crise de la conscience européenne* (1935).[18] During the 1930s and 1940s, the term Europe was also frequently used as a propaganda item with racist tendencies.[19]

Despite the abuse of the term 'Europe' by the fascists and the Nazis, render-ing it a charged word, it quickly advanced to become a popular code for deline-ating history past and present after the Second World War. Already towards the end of the 1940s, but especially during the two following decades, publications relating to Europe as a historical category, endowed with visions of a prom-ising future for the entire continent, literally flooded the European nations. Today the authors' names and the titles of their works are legion: Armando Saitta, *Dalla Res Publica Christiana agli Stati Uniti di Europa* (1948); Helmut Gollwitzer, *Europabild und Europagedanke* (1951); Jürgen Fischer, *Oriens, Occidens, Europa* (1957); Denys Hay, *Europe: The Emergence of an Idea* (1957); Carlo Curcio, *Europa: storia di un idea* (1958); Denis de Rougemont, *Vingt-huit siècles d'Europe* (1961); Jean-Baptiste Duroselle, *L'idée d'Europe dans l'histoire* (1965).[20] All these studies were but an answer to the disconcertion deriving

---

18   Oswald Spengler, *Der Untergang des Abendlandes: Umrisse einer Morphologie der Weltgeschichte*, 2 Bde. (Vienna: Braumüller, 1918, and Munich: Beck, 1922); Fritzemeyer, *Christenheit und Europa*; Christopher Dawson, *The Making of Europe: An Introduction to the History of European Unity* (New York: Sheed & Ward, 1932); Paul Hazard, *La crise de la conscience européenne (1680–1715)* (Paris: Boivin et Cie, 1935).

19   A representative list of studies from these years is provided in Oschema, *Bilder von Europa*, pp. 41–51.

20   Armando Saitta, *Dalla Res Publica Christiana agli Stati Uniti di Europa: sviluppo dell'idea pacifista in Francia nei secoli XVII–XIX* (Rome: Storia e Letteratura, 1948); Helmut Gollwitzer, *Europabild und Europagedanke: Beiträge zur deutschen Geistesgeschichte des 18. und 19. Jahrhunderts* (Munich: Beck, 1951); Jürgen Fischer, *Oriens, Occidens, Europa: Begriff und Gedanke 'Europa' in der späten Antike und im frühen Mittelalter*, Veröffentlichungen des Instituts für Europäische Geschichte Mainz, 15 (Wiesbaden: Steiner, 1957); Hay, *Europe*; Carlo Curcio, *Europa: storia di un idea* (Florence: Valecchi, 1958); Denis de Rougemont, *Vingt-huit siècles d'Europe: La conscience européenne à travers les textes – d'Hésiode à nos jours* (Paris: Bartillat, 1961); Jean-Baptiste Duroselle, *L'idée d'Europe dans l'histoire* (Paris: Denoël, 1965). Some offer a more idealistic view of Europe (like Curcio and Rougemont),

from the catastrophe of the two World Wars and the failure of the nationalist principle.[21] The collective trauma of destruction and suffering all over the
continent resulted in the birth of modern European integration as a deliberate
averting of the immediate past. The analysis of post-war polls from the late
1940s clearly reveals the then-existing European-wide desire to close ranks in
some form or another.[22] A prominent figure in the contemporary rebuilding of
Europe, Winston Churchill, gave voice to and fuelled this awakened European
sense of community in his famous speech delivered at the University of Zurich
in September 1946.[23] With a view to Europe's degenerating relationship with
the United States of America and the Soviet Union, he called for the formation
of the 'United States of Europe' – even if he did so from his British (and indeed
national) and economically self-serving perspective (which today is often forgotten when referring to Churchill's pointed claim).

To conclude, Europeanness was given a real chance in discourse after the
Second World War. Starting with the Marshall Plan in 1948, the research on
Europe constantly received new stimuli from ongoing political, economic, and
social developments. In particular, arrangements and events from the context of
European integration played a major part in this (e.g. the Treaty of Brussels in
1948, the foundation of the Council of Europe in 1949, the establishment of the
European Coal and Steel Community in 1951, the institution of the European Eco-
nomic Community in 1957, the creation of the European Free Trade Association

---

others regard the European cause from a more pragmatic point of view (like Gollwitzer
and Hay). A comprehensive overview of studies on Europe in the twentieth century can
be found in Heinz Duchhardt, 'Europa-Diskurs und Europa-Forschung: Ein Rückblick auf
ein Jahrhundert', *Jahrbuch für Europäische Geschichte*, 1 (2000), 1–14. Oschema (*Bilder von
Europa*, pp. 51–60) and Detering (pp. 23–35) present a highlight reel of the most important studies from the previous century. A critical examination of the research on Europe
from the Second World War to the present provides David Blanks, 'Europeans before
Europe: Modernity and the Myth of the Other', in *Early Modern Constructions of Europe:
Literature, Culture, History*, ed. by Florian Kläger and Gerd Bayer, Routledge Studies in
Renaissance Literature and Culture, 29 (New York: Routledge, 2016), pp. 27–40.

21   Richard Swedberg, 'The Idea of "Europe" and the Origin of the European Union – A
Sociological Approach', *Zeitschrift für Soziologie*, 23 (1994), 378–87; Oschema, *Bilder von
Europa*, p. 51.

22   Ludger Vielemeier, 'European Union in Public Opinion Polls, 1945–50', in *Documents of
the History of European Integration: Vol. 4: Transnational Organizations of Political Parties
and Pressure Groups in the Struggle for European Union, 1945–1950*, ed. by Walter Lipgens
and Wilfried Loth (Berlin: de Gruyter, 1991), pp. 574–626 (p. 581).

23   For more details on the speech, its content, its rhetorical tricks, and its current political context, see Justin D. Lyons, 'The Temple and the Tower: Winston Churchill on the
Political Language of Peace', *Perspectives on Political Science*, 33 (2004), 30–39. Lyons also
presents extracts from the original speech.

in 1960, the end of the Cold War and the fall of the Berlin Wall in 1989, the formation of the European Union and the Maastricht Treaty in 1992, the Eastern Enlargement of the European Union in 2004 and 2007, and, lately, with the refugee crisis, Brexit, and the nationalist updraft). All these circumstances have served as triggers for the periodic appearance of new studies.[24] In the twenty-first century, the research on Europe has finally also reached the field of Neo-Latin studies.

1.3   Scope and Aim of This Study

The following parts will outline the most popular concepts of Europe as expressions of Europeanness in the Latin language from the late mediaeval period to the eighteenth century. The source coverage will include genres of all sorts of stripes, whose authors come from different European nations. This way, the scope and reach of Latin as a supranational medium of communication on the one hand, and the ubiquity of the Europe discourse on the other, will become recognisable. In addition, the variegation of Neo-Latin literature can be savoured to the fullest and in compliance with the broad literary concept encompassed by Neo-Latin literature (i.e. both factual and fictional texts).[25]

The main choice of text samples has been dictated by the exclusivity with which Europe and Europeanness are discussed. In other words, the Neo-Latin texts presented mostly involve texts negotiating Europe in their entirety or dedicating a substantial number of chapters or larger segments to its discourse. When reading, however, it is important to keep in mind that the texts cited constitute merely a tiny section of Neo-Latin Europe literature. They serve as representative examples of a great quantity of similar texts, which in many cases were strongly influenced by the representative examples chosen. With regard to the corpus used for the present study, the aim was to find a good mixture between edited and unedited, as well as already known and as yet unknown, texts.[26] Thus, the readers should be treated to an easy access

---

24   Lists of books reacting to these integrative moments (with a focus on the years following the end of the Cold War) are presented in Swedberg, p. 380, and Christof Dejung and Martin Lengwiler, 'Einleitung: Ränder der Moderne. Neue Perspektiven auf die Europäische Geschichte', in *Ränder der Moderne: Neue Perspektiven auf die Europäische Geschichte (1800–1930)*, ed. by Christof Dejung and Martin Lengwiler (Cologne: Böhlau, 2016), pp. 7–35 (pp. 12–14).

25   The same approach is in any case known from the study of ancient Greek and Latin. More explicitly on the nature of 'literature' with reference to Neo-Latin text corpora, see Korenjak, pp. 12–13.

26   All translations from Latin to English are exclusively mine, unless stated otherwise. In the case of editions containing an English translation, the existing English translations are reproduced. If the editions cited comprise a translation in another language than English, I have provided a translation into English following the vernacular translation.

to the texts and their interpretation if needed, while at the same time their curiosity should be incited as to what is still out there awaiting investigation. From the panorama of texts and concepts of Europe offered, two main effects are intended to proceed.

Firstly, the genesis and development of the early modern Europe discourse based on Neo-Latin source material should for the first time become traceable for the beneficial use of scholars and students of Neo-Latin literature, early modern historians, and historians of ideas. Similarly, anyone interested in the history of Europe will hopefully find some expedient information, as well as come across some findings which complement the existing narrative of European integration based on vernacular sources. In order to show what early modern people understood as 'Europe' in Neo-Latin literature, the focus of the investigation will be on the discursive context. After all, it is more revealing to look at the fields of application of the term 'Europe' and its synonyms – along with the reasons for their application – instead of simply noting "how frequently the term cropped up in discourse and how important were the authors who used it".[27] This undertaking will be a matter neither of determining the character of Europe nor of contributing to the – according to Hayden White – "ill-fated" mythologisation of European identity, which was on the agenda of so many studies of the twentieth century.[28] Rather, the study will offer an analytical description of early modern discourses of Europe, free from any underlying political ideologies of Europe (whether past or present).[29]

In the second instance, this study should yield a better understanding of the foundations which underlie modern Europe and the ways in which certain factors tied to them still influence our modern thinking about Europe and European identity. In his monumental survey of Latin as a world language, Jürgen Leonhardt accentuates the importance of history as imparted by means of Latin literature as follows:

---

27 Timothy Reuter, 'Medieval Ideas of Europe and Their Modern Historians', *History Workshop*, 33 (1992), 176–80 (p. 177).

28 Hayden White, 'The Discourse of Europe and the Search for a European Identity', in *Europe and the Other and Europe as the Other*, ed. by Bo Stråth (Brussels: Lang, 2000), pp. 67–86 (p. 70). A typical study in this respect is Jörg A. Schlumberger and Peter Segl (eds.), *Europa – aber was ist es? Aspekte seiner Identität in interdisziplinärer Sicht*, Bayreuther historische Kolloquien, 8 (Cologne: Böhlau, 1994).

29 Disclaimer: any concepts related to European exceptionalism, ethnic superiority, or religious racism that might turn up in the course of the investigation are not endorsed by the author in any way whatsoever. As most people are aware, history is unforgiving in that it shows us the defects of human action in the past, for which historical analyses ought not to be held accountable.

[...] history speaks to us more clearly when we understand where it antic-
ipated our problems and conversely it sharpens historical distance and
our view of the present. Here, Latin has something to offer [...].[30]

The Neo-Latin discourse of Europe has a lot to offer in historical terms. Many
notions of European values or European identity show a strong continuity from
the early modern Latin past to the present day; certain political and cultural
ideals and symbols of Europe have prevailed for centuries, going back to the
earliest Neo-Latin negotiations of Europe.[31] Yet – as we will see in the subse-
quent investigation – there are even more parallels between Europe then and
now that call for a proper historicisation of continental thinking (such as the
omnipresence of the term 'Europe', political and cultural target sets directed
at the entire continent, or questions of centralisation, nationalism, and xen-
ophobia).[32] Getting in touch with history, therefore, in order to understand
how exactly European integration has been carried out, might lead to a better
assessment of present European achievements and exigencies beyond mere
populist phrases. If the act of historicisation is not driven by teleological ends,
there is hardly any reason to doubt its benefit. To quote Richard Swedberg:

While the literature on the European idea may not be ultimately con-
vincing in its claim that the European Union has indeed its origin in the
very distant past, it does prove one very important point: that our knowledge about the birth of major social institutions – such as the European
Union – can be complemented and enriched by insights into the role that
ideas, ideals and cultural symbols do play in history.[33]

---

30   Jürgen Leonhardt, *Latin: Story of a World Language*. Transl. by Kenneth Kronenberg
       (Cambridge, MA: Belknap Press of Harvard University Press, 2013), p. 14.
31   On this matter, cf. Swedberg, p. 378 and his reference to the sociological theory of Emile
       Durkheim, according to which society is determined by symbols and other collective
       representations. The development of a society or social values, hence, can always be
       traced by means of the continuity or discontinuity of collective representations. Emile
       Durkheim, *Sociology and Philosophy*. Transl. by David F. Pocock. With an Introduction by
       John G. Peristiany (New York: The Free Press, 1974 [1898]).
32   Oschema, *Bilder von Europa*, p. 11. To state that continental crises are a phenomenon
       of modern-day Europe is a fundamental misconception of the history of Europe. Such
       a statement is issued, for example, by Poul F. Kjaer and Niklas Olsen, 'Introduction:
       European Crises of Public Power from Weimar until Today', in *Critical Theories of Crisis in
       Europe: From Weimar to the Euro*, ed. by Poul F. Kjaer and Niklas Olsen (London and New
       York: Rowman & Littlefield, 2016), pp. xi–xx (p. xi). A compact overview of the continuity
       of European crises concerning the discourse of Europe and extending over six hundred
       centuries is provided in Walser-Bürgler, 'Continuities of Historical Crises'.
33   Swedberg, p. 386.

The present contribution from the field of Neo-Latin studies to complementing and enriching the existing knowledge of European integration will be realised in three major steps: in a first step, the nature of Latin as a European language, in its role as the main language for the discourse of Europe, will be revealed; in a second step, a brief discussion of 'Europe' in Antiquity and the Middle Ages will follow – not so much because the early modern Latin discourse harked back to earlier notions of Europe very often, but rather because this 'prelude' facilitates a better understanding of the turning point the Early Modern Period provided regarding the discourse of Europe; in the third and final step, the most important concepts of Europe in Neo-Latin literature will be expounded in thematic order.

2   Early Modern Latin: A European Language and a Language for 'Europe'

As the socio-linguistic studies of Peter Burke have shown, language always serves as both a reflector and an indicator of social and cultural occurrences at a given time in a given place. Unsurprisingly, therefore, it is also one of the crucial tools involved when it comes to the construction or reconstruction of communities.[34] In the case of early modern Europe, it was the Latin language that presided over any prevailing sense of supranational communality. The desire for a European identity was inevitably linked to the convention and tradition of communicating with each other in Latin.[35] Since language and identity are, by socio-linguistic definition, inseparable and since especially voluntary group affiliations often "involve linguistic features of great depth and importance",[36] this part will dive into the interaction between the Latin language and the European community. In addition to this socio-linguistic approach, ideas surrounding the linguistic turn of the 1960s will also play a role in the examination – most importantly, the idea that languages influence

34   Peter Burke, *Languages and Communities in Early Modern Europe* (Cambridge: Cambridge University Press, 2004), pp. 1 and 6.
35   Helpful references regarding the role of Latin as the early modern language of Europe might come from Tore Janson, *A Natural History of Latin*. Transl. and adapted into English by Merethe Damsgård Sørensen and Nigel Vincent (Oxford: Oxford University Press, 2004), pp. 145–76; Leonhardt, pp. 122–244; Korenjak, *Geschichte der neulateinischen Literatur*. Despite these general efforts in shedding light on the diverse uses of Latin between 1400 and 1800, the field of Neo-Latin studies still lacks an investigation exclusively dedicated to Latin as the language of early modern Europe.
36   John R. Edwards, *Language and Identity: An Introduction* (Cambridge: Cambridge University Press, 2009), p. 3.

the sort of conceptualisation taking place in the mind.[37] In other words, the main line of argument will be dictated by the premise that the Neo-Latin discourse of Europe took on a unique quality precisely due to the fact that it was expressed in Latin.

The Italian philosopher and ardent republican Carlo Cattaneo (1801–1869) famously stated in 1835 that Europe had forever been characterised by four uniting forces: imperial authority, Roman law, Christianity, and the Latin language.[38] But Latin was more than just a language within the borders of early modern Europe. It was "the carrier of European culture par excellence, conveying common values and beliefs",[39] thus creating a sense of mutuality and unification permeating all social classes.[40] In contrast to modern-day Europe, which has since the 1950s been brought together in economic or political unions yet not by a common language, it was exactly the other way round in early modern times. The plurilingual population of Europe, which knew between forty and seventy different mother tongues in the centuries

---

37   On this matter, see Stephen C. Levinson, 'From Outer to Inner Space: Linguistic Categories and Non-Linguistic Thinking', in *Language and Conceptualization*, ed. by Jan Nuyts and Eric Pederson (Cambridge: Cambridge University Press, 1997), pp. 13–45.

38   Anthony Pagden, 'Europe: Conceptualizing a Continent', in *The Idea of Europe: From Antiquity to the European Union*, ed. by Anthony Pagden (Cambridge: Cambridge University Press), pp. 33–54 (pp. 43–44); Carlo Cattaneo, *Sulle interdizioni israelitiche*, ed. by Giulio A. Belloni (Rome: Sestante, 1944), pp. 56–58.

39   Jan Bloemendal, 'Introduction: Bilingualism, Multilingualism and the Formation of Europe', in *Bilingual Europe: Latin and Vernacular Cultures. Examples of Bilingualism and Multilingualism c. 1300–1800*, ed. by Jan Bloemendal (Leiden: Brill, 2015), pp. 1–14 (p. 1).

40   On the use of Latin in the contexts of theology, education, law, diplomacy, science, and scholarship, see Jozef IJsewijn, *Companion to Neo-Latin Studies. Part I: History and Diffusion of Neo-Latin Literature*, Supplementa Humanistica Lovaniensia, 5, 2nd edn (Leuven: Leuven University Press, 1990), p. 30; Françoise Waquet, *Le Latin ou l'empire d'un signe: XVIe–XXe siècle* (Paris: Albin Michel, 1998), pp. 17–55; Burke, *Languages and Communities*, p. 54; Janson, pp. 148–49; Leonhardt, pp. 3 and 219–27; Per P. Aspaas, 'The Use of Latin and the European Republic of Letters: Change and Continuity in the Seventeenth and Eighteenth Centuries', *Nordlit. Tidsskrift i litteratur og kultur*, 33 (2014), 281–95 (p. 284); Korenjak, pp. 14–17. The knowledge and use of Latin in peasantry circles is outlined in Wilhelm Kühlmann, Robert Seidel, and Hermann Wiegand (eds.), *Humanistische Lyrik des 16. Jahrhunderts: Lateinisch und deutsch*, Bibliothek der frühen Neuzeit, I.5 (Frankfurt a.M.: Deutscher Klassiker Verlag, 1997); Aspaas, p. 289; István G. Tóth, *Literacy and Written Culture in Early Modern Central Europe* (New York: Central University Press, 2000), pp. 130–45; and Burke, *Languages and Communities*, pp. 46–47. An overview of Latin women's writing is provided in Jane Stevenson, *Women Latin Poets: Language, Gender, and Authority from Antiquity to the Eighteenth Century* (Oxford: Oxford University Press, 2005).

from 1400 to 1800,[41] which was living in different nations of different sizes and histories and under different forms of government, intentionally chose to employ Latin, a language without native speakers, as their means of international conversation. In fact, Latin was even used quite frequently as an intranational language, that is, as a functional language of exchange within nations in which either dialects predominated or the vernaculars lacked standardisation.[42] If it is true that "a language is a dialect with an army and navy",[43] then Latin definitely constituted an unbeatable force simply through the massive community it had subjugated. While Peter Burke indirectly refutes the view (held particularly by mediaevalists) that Latin dwelled in a state of 'communitylessness' since its last native speakers had disappeared in the seventh and eighth centuries CE with the provocative chapter title "Latin in search of a community" (signalling that the search was successful), Anthony Grafton explicitly summarises the scope of Latin in the following words:[44]

> Individuals across Europe and beyond knew Latin as intimately, loved it as passionately, and rolled it off the tongue as easily as they did their native languages.

When it came to talking about Europe specifically, one could compare the role of the Latin language from the fifteenth to the eighteenth centuries to the role the vernaculars attained in the nationalist strife of the nineteenth century. For similarly to how the different vernacular languages turned into tools of national self-definition in the age of nationalism,[45] Latin had served as the

---

41   Burke's estimates range from conservative to rather optimistic numbers (Burke, *Languages and Communities*, p. 8; a full list of native languages spoken in Europe at the time in question is provided on pp. 173–75).

42   The terms 'international' and 'intranational *lingua franca*' are expounded in Christiane Meierkord, 'Lingua Franca Communication in Multiethnic Contexts', in *Handbook of Intercultural Communication*, ed. by Helga Kotthoff and Helen Spencer-Oatey, Handbooks of Applied Linguistics, 7 (Berlin: de Gruyter, 2007), pp. 199–218 (p. 199).

43   This saying is derived from Yiddish "A shprakh iz a dialekt mit an armey un flot", uttered by a listener at a Max Weinreich lecture in the 1940s. Aspaas, p. 292 n.30.

44   Cf. Burke, *Languages and Communities*, p. 44 (and the entire chapter, pp. 43–60); Anthony Grafton, *Worlds Made by Words: Scholarship and Community in the Modern West* (Cambridge, MA: Harvard University Press, 2009), p. 151. A modern-day tribute to Latin as the engine of early modern Europe was paid by Finland during the nation's EU council presidency in 1999 and 2006, when the news was regularly read in Latin on national radio (Leonhardt, pp. 1–2).

45   This matter is discussed in Fania Oz-Salzberger, 'Languages and Literacy', in *The Oxford Handbook of Early Modern European History. Vol. 1: 1350–1750: Peoples and Place*, ed. by Hamish Scott (Oxford: Oxford University Press, 2015), pp. 192–213 (pp. 207–208).

engine of the supranational European self-discovery in the previous centuries. In other words, the national languages forged national identities and national consciousness, whereas Latin fostered an awareness of European interna- tionality and of a European public. What ultimately made the discourse of Europe thrive in Latin was the early modern notion of the connection between nation and language.[46] The well-known saying that 'the language makes the people' (*gentem lingua facit*) goes back to the Middle Ages and underpinned the discourse of Europe from its earliest stages.[47] The congruence between territory and language was deemed imperative for the unification of Europe. Accordingly, it had to be Latin that 'made' Europe. Its use provided an actual statement about the speaker's identity, as Latin "bec[ame] an instrument of thought, of feeling and belonging".[48] To express oneself in Latin about a mat- ter such as Europe was as much an act of identity as the deliberate choice of a Frenchman to write a poem in French, signalling his belonging to the French nation and its literary tradition. In this sense, the writers discussing Europe in the Latin language formed not only a language community but also a European community (even if the term 'community' misleadingly suggests that this European community was a homogeneous group of people).[49] Latin turned into a symbol of participation in European affairs.

On that account, many influential thinkers of the Early Modern Period promoted Latin as Europe's universal language.[50] The Bohemian pedagogue Johan Amos Comenius (1592–1670), the German scholar Daniel Georg Morhof

---

46   The interaction between the two is pointedly outlined in Benedict Anderson, *Imagined Communities: Reflections on the Origin and Spread of Nationalism*, 2nd edn (London: Verso, 2006), p. 84; Burke, *Languages and Communities*, p. 161, presents an illustrative example pertaining to the Hungarian politics of Ferdinand of Austria, the later emperor Ferdinand I (1503–1564).

47   Contrary to popular belief, Johann Gottfried Herder (1744–1803) was not the inven- tor of this notion. Even though he would later become famous for defining a nation as a community of people bound by a common language in his *Abhandlung über den Ursprung der Sprache* (Treatise on the Origin of Language, 1769), his theoretical deliber- ations had already been century-old. For more information on that matter, see Michael Townson, *Mother-Tongue and Fatherland: Language and Politics in German* (Manchester: Manchester University Press, 1992), pp. 80–102.

48   William F. Mackey, 'Conflicting Languages in a United Europe', *Sociolinguistica. Inter- national Yearbook of European Sociolinguistics*, 15 (2001), 1–17 (p. 6).

49   The predicament concerning the concept of community in the face of different social groups using the 'same' language is touched upon in Burke, *Languages and Communi- ties*, p. 5.

50   Both a list and an overview of Latin texts arguing in favour of Latin as a universal language can be found in Jozef IJsewijn and Dirk Sacré, 'The Ultimate Efforts to Save Latin as the Means of International Communication', *History of European Ideas*, 16 (1993), 51–66.

(1639–1691), and the Spanish priest Miguel Maria Olmo (*c.* 1770–?) even went as far as to propose the foundation of a Latin city-state right in the middle of Europe, whose inhabitants were meant to mingle with people from all European nations in order to institutionalise Latin as the new (old) European mother tongue.[51] Yet probably the most pointed statement regarding the promotion of Latin as a universal language was voiced by the German polyhistor Gottfried Wilhelm Leibniz (1646–1716). In his programmatic German treatise *Kurzes wohl gemeyntes Bedencken vom Abgang der Studien und wie denenselben zu helffen* (Short and Well-Meaning Considerations about the Decline of the Studies and How to Help them Recover, 1711), which was densely interspersed with Latin phrases and formulas, he celebrated Latin as "the European universal language, enduring to posterity" ("lingua Europaea universalis et durabilis ad posteritatem"; p. 441).[52] For Leibniz, Latin was the solution to all problems of continental discord. And indeed, "Latin as the early modern supranational language of choice transgressed national belonging, separation, and demarcation by nature".[53] Since it had lost its status as a mother tongue along with native speakers in late Antiquity, it belonged in a levelling way to no one and everyone, to no place and every place at the same time. Without implying any national hierarchy, confessional order, or ethnic preference, it gave equal voice to everybody. The Croatian Marco Faustino Gagliuffi (1765–1834) briefly touched on this topic in his *Specimen de fortuna Latinitatis* (A Specimen of Latin's Fortune, 1833), when talking about the advantages of the "linguae communis adoptio" ("adoption of the common language"; p. 14).[54] In the end, he concluded assertively: "latina est societas nostra" ("our [European] society is a Latin society"; p. 29).

Concrete historical examples testifying to the early modern understanding of Latin's neutrality and supranationality abound. To cite just a few prominent cases: The majority of peace treaties between European powers from

51   Johan Amos Comenius, *Latium redivivum: Hoc est de forma erigendi Latinissimi Collegii, ceu novae Romae Civitatulae*, in *J.A. Comenii Didacticorum operum pars IV* (Amsterdam: Cunradus and van Rot, 1657), coll. 75–80; Daniel Georg Morhof, *Polyhistor litterarius, philosophicus et practicus*, 4th edn (Lübeck: Boeckmann, 1747), pp. 425–26; Michael Olmo, *De Lingua latina colenda et civitate latina fundanda liber singularis. Accedit epistola auctoris ad Barberium Vemars, cum responsione Barberii* (Toulouse: Douladoure, 1816).

52   Gottfried Wilhelm Leibniz, *Kurzes wohl gemeyntes Bedencken vom Abgang der Studien und wie denenselben zu helffen*, in *Die Werke von Leibniz gemäß seinem handschriftlichen Nachlasse in der Königlichen Bibliothek zu Hannover: Bd. 10*, ed. by Onno Klopp (Hannover: Klindworth, 1877), pp. 435–42.

53   Walser-Bürgler, 'Europe without the Bull', p. 82.

54   Marco Faustino Gagliuffi, *Specimen de fortuna Latinitatis. Accedunt poemata varia meditata et extemporalia* (Turin: Favale, 1833).

the fifteenth to the eighteenth centuries – among them the *Instrumenta pacis Westphalicae* (the Westphalian Peace Treaties) of 1648 – were composed in the Latin language as a signal of impartiality.[55] Yet even non-European powers failing to agree on the matter of which party's language should be used for making peace sometimes chose Latin to bridge language barriers and express neutrality. The Treaties of Nerchinski (1689) and Kyakhta (1727) between China and Russia followed this policy.[56] When in 1725 the Academy of Sciences in St Petersburg was founded, its members decided to instate Latin as the language of publication, in order to reach every European regardless of nationality or confession.[57] The supranational character of Latin devoid of any national tendency was invoked also in strict political terms in Hungary and the associated kingdom of Croatia. There, Latin prevailed as the official language until well into the 1840s, after the estates had voted for its adoption as a reaction to Emperor Joseph II (1741–1790) and his attempts to introduce German as Hungary's official language. To avoid having to use the language of the Austrian 'conqueror', the Hungarian and Croatian nobility chose Latin as an alternative.[58] Similarly, Latin had served as the official language in Denmark, as a strategy to evade the use of German, as well as in Finland, in order to evade Swedish, until the end of the eighteenth century.[59]

Overall, Latin bore two more advantages when it came to discursively scrutinising Europe. First, owing to its authoritative qualities derived from its continuity, the pure use of Latin could grant prestige to a challenging topic such as the all-encompassing integration of an entire continent. As we know from early modern medical reports, Latin automatically increased the importance

---

55   Greater detail on the prime role of Latin in peace treaties is provided in Walser-Bürgler, 'Reflections of "Europe"', pp. 9–13.

56   Gerd Flemming has investigated the special role of Latin in the Chinese-Russian context of making peace: Gerd Flemming, 'Latein in Fernost: Die Verträge von Nerčinsk (1689) und Kjachta (1727)', in *Weltbild und Weltdeutung*, ed. by Peter Neukam and Bernhard O'Connor, Dialog Schule – Wissenschaft. Klassische Sprachen und Literaturen, 36 (Munich: Bayerischer Schulbuch-Verlag, 2002), pp. 7–48.

57   Burke, *Languages and Communities*, p. 53; Aspaas, pp. 287–88.

58   Anderson, p. 78; Gábor Almási and Lav Šubarić, 'Introduction', in *Latin at the Crossroads of Identity: The Evolution of Linguistic Nationalism in the Kingdom of Hungary*, ed. by Gábor Almási and Lav Šubarić, Central and Eastern Europe, 5 (Leiden: Brill, 2015), pp. 1–26 (pp. 3–4 and 8–10). On the general political convergence of Latin and the vernaculars in the eighteenth and nineteenth centuries, see Oz-Salzberger, p. 194.

59   Burke, *Languages and Communities*, p. 59; the Finnish situation in particular has been studied by Iiro Kajanto, 'The Position of Latin in Eighteenth-Century Finland', in *Acta Conventus Neo-Latini Amstelodamensis: Proceedings of the Second International Congress of Neo-Latin Studies, Amsterdam, 19–24 August 1973*, ed. by Eckhard Kessler, Peter Tuynman, and Gerdina C. Kuiper (Munich: Fink, 1979), pp. 93–106.

of a given issue. Whenever doctors would switch from the vernaculars to some sort of fake Latin, their patients, though deceived, seemed almost to start abruptly confiding in the doctors.[60] In the case of the propagation of Europe as an entity, the discourse was given weight simply by the fact that it was phrased in Latin. A second advantage of Latin in relation to the discussion of Europe was that Latin was literally famous for expressing outrageous things that were either hard or impossible to express in the vernaculars. Examples of this tendency range from pornographic and masochistic topics to all kinds of offensive texts entering the realms of literature for the first time in the Early Modern Period.[61] The discourse of Europe in some way belonged to this category, since the concept of a united Europe constituted a completely new approach to contemporary life, or rather something previously unheard of.

3   Antecedents of the Early Modern Discourse of Europe

3.1   *Europe in Antiquity*
The civilisations of Greece and Rome have exerted an immense influence on Europe as we know it today. Their legacies are traceable in both institutional and intellectual life: Greek philosophy, political formats like monarchy and democracy, Hellenistic culture, Roman law, maxims of a unified economic area, multi-territorial administration, and Christendom have shaped Europe for centuries.[62] However, this does not mean by inversion of the argument that an awareness of Europe, European identity, or any form of Europeanness already existed in Antiquity. Such assumptions amount to nothing more than projections of subjective and speculative views on to ancient literature, which do not withstand objective examination.[63] Neither were any notions of Europe

---

60   The association between Latin and prestige is expounded in greater detail in Burke, *Languages and Communities*, p. 46.

61   Waquet, *Le Latin*, pp. 125–43 and 273–302 is very explicit on the matter; examples and references can also be seen in Karl A.E. Enenkel, 'Neo-Latin Erotic and Pornographic Literature (*c.* 1400–*c.* 1700)', in *Brill's Encyclopaedia of the Neo-Latin World. Vol. 1: Macropaedia*, ed. by Philip Ford, Jan Bloemendal, and Charles Fantazzi (Leiden: Brill, 2014), pp. 487–501.

62   Jürgen Malitz, 'Imperium Romanum und Europagedanke', in *Blicke auf Europa: Kontinuität und Wandel*, ed. by Andreas Michler and Waltraud Schreiber (Neuried: ars una, 2003), pp. 79–103 (pp. 79 and 93–94).

63   Olaf Asbach, *Europa – Vom Mythos zur Imagined Community? Zur historischen Semantik 'Europas' von der Antike bis ins 17. Jahrhundert*, Europa und Moderne, 1 (Hannover: Wehrhahn, 2011), p. 41. This approach was typical of the enthusiastic studies of Europe following the Second World War, overcompensating for decades of nationalism gone wrong (such as de Rougemont's *Vingt-huit siècles d'Europe*).

as a continental entity, or as a uniform cultural system, or as a community of destiny prevalent in ancient Greece and Rome. In the few cases where the name 'Europe' came up, it was mainly used in geographical terms, frequently overlaid with political stereotypes.[64]

Yet far from providing any precise data, ancient geographical mentions of Europe were confined to the simplest and most ambiguous definitions. As is evident from the sources, the borders were not clearly determined and changed often. In the earliest written geographical instantiation of Europe, the third *Homeric Hymn to Apollo* (*c.* seventh or sixth century BCE), Europe was listed as one of the places where people could offer sacrifices to Apollo alongside the Peloponnese and the Greek islands (v. 247–53).[65] Hence, Europe was equated with a territory on the Greek mainland of approximately the same size as the Peloponnese and the catchment area of the islands included.[66]

In his account of the Greek-Persian wars, Herodotus was the first to coherently call all people living on the mainland west of the Bosporus, the Sea of Marmara, and the Dardanelles 'Europeans' (7.73).[67] His geographical outline

---

64   Asbach, p. 38, and Reuter, p. 176. The exact origin and etymology of the word 'Europe' are unclear to the present day. Essentially, there are four interpretive approaches: derivations from Greek, derivations from Semitic languages, derivations from Greek city names, and derivations from the ancient myth of Europa and the bull. For a theoretical overview, see Danielle Jouanna, *L'Europe est née en Grèce: La naissance de l'idée d'Europe en Grèce ancienne* (Paris: L'Harmattan, 2009), pp. 30–32, and Oschema, *Bilder von Europa*, p. 82. Despite the obscurity surrounding Europe's etymology, neither ancient nor mediaeval nor early modern scholars seem to have been too concerned about the literal meaning of the term 'Europe'. Not even an author like Isidore of Seville (*c.* 560–636), whose main work was entitled *Etymologiae* (Origins of Words) and dedicated to uncovering the underlying notions behind an immense wealth of knowledge, took appropriate charge of explaining 'Europe'. He contented himself with a brief retelling of the myth of Europa and the bull (XVI.4.1): Isidore of Seville, *Etymologiarum sive Originum Libri XX*, ed. by Wallace Lindsay (Oxford: Clarendon Press, 1911). No wonder, then, that early modern scholars like the Frenchman Guillaume Postel (1510–1581) nonchalantly suggested renaming Europe as *Japetia* after the biblical progenitor of the continent, Japheth (cf. Genesis 10. 1–31): Guillaume Postel, *De cosmographica disciplina et signorum coelestium vera configuratione libri III*, 3rd edn (Leiden: Maire, 1636), p. 56: "[...] repetatur, eam partem terrae, quam fabulae Europam dixere, Japetiam debere dici, ob primum illum Japetum [...] principem institutum." – "[...] it is repeatedly demanded that the very part of the earth which has been commonly named Europe, should be called Japetia due to its first ever ruler Japheth."
65   Jouanna, p. 28. The text has been edited in *The Homeric Hymns*, ed. by Thomas W. Allen, 2nd edn (London: Oxford University Press, 1980 [1936]).
66   Andreas Hartmann, 'Im Osten nichts Neues: Europa und seine Barbaren seit dem V. Jahrhundert v. Chr.', in *Blicke auf Europa: Kontinuität und Wandel*, ed. by Andreas Michler and Waltraud Schreiber (Neuried: ars una, 2003), pp. 31–69 (pp. 37–38).
67   Herodotus, *Historiae*, 2 vols., ed. by Nigel G. Wilson (Oxford: Oxford University Press, 2015).

of Europe also enclosed the land of the barbarians along the Danube, leading up all the way to the Atlantic Ocean (3.115), as well as the Scythian lands north of the Black Sea, stretching to the river Don (4.45). The exact size and borders of Europe, however, Herodotus failed to expound. At the same time, his insufficient knowledge of particularly the western and northern parts of what he claimed to be Europe was exposed in the mythical elements he attached to the people inhabiting the north (Herodotus explained, for example, that the Hyperborean people only had one eye; cf. 3.116 and 4.16).[68] It was only with the voyage of exploration undertaken by Pytheas of Massalia (fourth century BCE) that the continent was given sharper contours. According to his report, indirectly transmitted in the *Histories* of Polybius (34.52.55) and Strabo's *Geography* (2.4.1–2), Pytheas had reached the coasts of Scotland, Iceland, Norway, and Germany via the Straits of Gibraltar all the way down to the Don.[69] The unfamiliarity with these regions during Polybius' and Strabo's lifetimes in the second and first centuries BCE, however, is revealed in the ridicule with which they discarded Pytheas' account as follies.[70]

As far as the issue of communality was concerned, the ancient Greeks never knew any form of European identity. In fact, they did not even know a common Greek identity, because the concept of Panhellenism was merely based on an Athenocentric view of Hellas which was introduced when Athens tried to reconfigure Greek culture after the Persian wars. Identity in ancient Greece basically came down to not more than a local or regional sense of affiliation, defined by the intra-Greek ethnic antagonisms growing in the course of the Peloponnesian War (e.g. Athens vs. Sparta or Ionia vs. Doris).[71] Whenever the term Europe came up, it was partly used synonymously with Hellas during and after the Persian wars (e.g. in Hdt. 1.209 and 7.5, as well as in many places in Isocrates' early writings, such as *Helena* or *Panegyricus*), partly with reference to single regions of Greece at the time of the intra-Greek conflicts (the poet Eumelus, for example, supposedly wrote an epic entitled *Europia* at the end of

---

68   Jouanna, pp. 157–58.

69   Polybius, *Historiae*, 5 vols., ed. by Ludwig Dindorf and Theodorus Büttner-Wobst (Leipzig: Teubner, 1882–1904); Strabo, *Geographika*, 10 vols., ed. by Stefan Radt (Göttingen: Vandenhoeck & Ruprecht, 2002–2011).

70   Jouanna, pp. 248–49. For a realistic overview of the actual knowledge of the Greeks and Romans of what geographically is Europe today, see Raymond Chevallier, 'L'Europe dans les textes géographiques grecs et latins', in *D'Europe à l'Europe. Vol. 1: Le mythe d'Europe dans l'art et la culture de l'antiquité au XVIIIe siècle. Actes du colloque tenu à l'ENS, Paris (24–26) avril 1997*, ed. by Rémy Poignault and Odile Wattel-De Croizant (Tours: Centre Piganiol, 1998), pp. 39–54.

71   An intriguing picture of Hellenic identities is painted in Jonathan M. Hall, *Hellenicity: Between Ethnicity and Culture* (Chicago: Chicago University Press, 2002).

the eighth century BCE, dealing with Theban local myths; in 6.43.4 and 7.8.1,
Herodotus refers to Europe, meaning the area of Thrace and Macedonia).[72]
The campaigns of conquest by Alexander the Great, whose empire stretched
from the Adriatic Sea to Persia, eventually put an end not only to the dichotomy between Europe and Asia but also to 'Europe' as a term of reference for
the Greeks.[73] Europe as a category became entirely obsolete.

During the time of the Roman Empire, Europe was never given any more of
a chance. Roman imperialism inhibited any form of European thinking, since
the Imperium Romanum spanned all three known continents and was therefore equated with the *orbis terrarum*, the entire world (Polyb. 1.6.3–6).[74] This
might also have been a reason why so many Roman authors had such a hard
time defining Europe.[75] The power of the Romans over the world and their
constant expansion was so extensive that Horace could without hesitation
call Rome the *princeps urbium* ("head of all cities") in carm. 4.3.13, while Vergil
referred to the Roman Empire as a world state solely bounded by the ocean
in Aen. 1.286–87.[76] Likewise, many coins from the later period of the Roman
Republic displayed the globe as a symbol of the world-spanning rule of Rome.[77]

---

72   Herodotus' inconsistency in denoting Europe has been explained by the changing per-
       spectives he took: whenever he talked about the Greeks from the Persian perspective
       (meaning that the Greeks needed to defend themselves), he used 'Europe' as a synonym
       for all of Greece; whenever he described actions on the part of the Greeks directed against
       Persia (meaning that Greece was on the military offensive), he equated 'Europe' with sin-
       gle regions or *poleis* (Jouanna, pp. 169–70). On Eumelus, see Hartmann, p. 38; on Isocrates,
       see Renate Müller, 'Europa in der Antike: Mythos und Toponym', *Traverse. Zeitschrift für
       Geschichte / Revue d'histoire*, 3 (1994), 195–210 (p. 202; including a list of illustrative quota-
       tions from his Greek texts), and Jouanna, pp. 217–24.

73   Müller, 'Europa in der Antike', p. 203.

74   Burke, 'Did Europe Exist', p. 23; Malitz, p. 80.

75   In the most vague manner, Sallust (first century BCE) reported that only a few people
       would consider Africa a part of Europe (Iug. 17.3); Lucan (first century CE), on the other
       hand, confidently made Africa a part of Europe (Civ. 9.411–20); Marcus Aurelius (second
       century CE) described Europe as an uncouth piece of land of unknown size and form,
       with unknown borders, in his *Meditationes* (§33). Cf. Hartmann, p. 40. Editions of the
       texts are available in: Sallust, *Catilina, Iugurtha, Historiarum Fragmenta Selecta. Appendix
       Sallustiana*, ed. by Leighton D. Reynolds (Oxford: Oxford University Press, 1991); Lucan,
       De bello civili libri X, ed. by David R. Shackleton Bailey, 2nd edn (Stuttgart: Teubner,
       1997); Marcus Aurelius, *Meditations with Selected Correspondence*, ed. by Robin Hard and
       Christopher Gill (Oxford: Oxford University Press, 2011).

76   Pagden, p. 42. For texts of Horace and Vergil, see Horace, *Opera*, ed. by David R.
       Shackleton Bailey (Berlin: de Gruyter, 2008), and Vergil, *Aeneis*, ed. by Gian Biagio Conte
       (Berlin: de Gruyter, 2009).

77   Malitz, p. 80.

The term 'Europe' further deteriorated in Roman times compared to the age of Greek predominance. It was still used sporadically, but never in a self-descriptive fashion and never in an ideological sense that would have gone beyond merely vague geographical notions.[78] Even though the knowledge of the very part of the world that the Romans termed 'Europe' grew with the imperial expansion into modern-day Spain, France, Belgium, Germany, Britain, and Eastern Europe, the descriptions of Europe remained strikingly conservative. Polybius, for example, in his history of Rome, followed Herodotus' explanations when it came to outlining the three parts of the world and admitted that no one really knew their complete area or borders (3.37–38). Despite the fact that book 34 contained a comprehensive description of Europe – which is, however, only indirectly handed down through Strabo's criticism of Polybius in Geogr. 2.4 – Danielle Jouanna observes that the world according to Polybius appears to be less known than that of Herodotus.[79]

The same held true for Strabo, who already lived under the impression of Caesar's and Augustus' imperialist endeavours. While he paid at least some attention to Gaul and Brittany on the Atlantic coast, his description focused on the peoples living in regions adjoining the Mediterranean Sea (which was, not coincidentally, called *mare nostrum* ["our sea"] by the Romans), namely the Greeks, the Macedonians, the Thracians, the Iberians, the Sicilians, and the Romans (books 3–10). The rest of the continent was ignored; new geographical insights beyond the Greek patterns of knowledge were completely absent.[80] A look at later sources from the third and fourth centuries CE reveals that 'Europe' was increasingly downgraded, instead of receiving an upgrade to a greater continental scope: when Diocletian, for example, divided the province of Thrace into four parts at the end of the third century, one of these four units – the small area stretching from the Gallipoli peninsula to the Bosporus – was assigned the name *Europa*.[81]

---

78   For a detailed overview of the Romans' employment of the term 'Europe', see Malitz, pp. 82–85.

79   Jouanna, p. 258.

80   For illustration, Jouanna (p. 262–63) refers the reader to Geogr. 2.5.26. This passage is almost overrun by commonplaces relating to the argument that Europe has been particularly favoured by nature, endowing the continent with civilised people and an abundance of fruit.

81   Malitz, pp. 85–86. Lat. Ver. 4.2 (= Theodor Mommsen, *Gesammelte Schriften, Bd. 7: Philologische Schriften* (Berlin: Weidmann, 1909), p. 655.

3.2   *Europe in the Middle Ages*

In late Antiquity and the early Middle Ages, the perception of what supposedly was 'Europe' slowly shifted from the Mediterranean region to the northern parts of the Alps east and west of the river Rhine. Nevertheless, 'Europe'
as a term still referred to a reduced entity, only now the geographical reach
included Italy, Germany, France, and Spain.[82] From the sixth century onwards,
the term 'Europe' was steadily pushed into the background, while a range of
substitutional expressions emerged. Apparently, then, the term 'Europe' had
been anything but established as a designation for supranational-related matters. People preferred to use expressions that reflected not so much a continental but a more context-bound sense of belonging within the continental frame.

In historiographical writings such as chronicles or annals delineating the
history of the western area of Europe, *Hesperia* or *Hesperia terra* ("the western lands") was most frequently used; the people living in these lands were
likewise called *Hesperii* ("westerners").[83] The Roman-Gothic historiographer
Jordanes (sixth century CE) spoke of "res publica Hesperiae plagae" ("the
republic of the western realms") in his *De origine actibusque Getorum* (On
the Origin and Deeds of the Getae) when referring to the western part of the
Roman Empire.[84] For him, clearly, *Hesperia* signified a collective term for the
people inhabiting Italy, Spain, France, and parts of Germany and Britain. In
the context of the Latin Christian tradition of the Western Roman Empire, the
terms *ecclesia* (the Church), *imperium* (empire), or *gens Latina* (Latin people)
prevailed most frequently as a demarcation from non-Christians.[85] Following
the biblical tradition of contrasting the east (*oriens*) with the west (*occidens*),
further Latin expressions denoting the Western World, such as *occidens, pars*

---

82   Cf., for example, Isid., Orig. 14.4. Manfred Fuhrmann, *Europa: Zur Geschichte einer kulturel-
      len und politischen Idee*, Konstanzer Universitätsreden, 121 (Konstanz: Universitätsverlag,
      1981), p. 8 n. 8. A broad overview of the history of the meanings of 'Europe' between
      Antiquity and the Middle Ages is offered in Oschema, *Bilder von Europa*, pp. 101–31.

83   An exception can be seen in many universal histories of the time, whose authors kept
      employing the term 'Europe' in retrospective relation to ancient geographers. See, for
      example, the histories of William of Tyre (*c.* 1130–1186) and Rodrigo Jiménez de Rada
      (*c.* 1170–1247), as discussed in Oschema, *Bilder von Europa*, pp. 232–37.

84   Jordanes, *Romana et Getica: Monumenta Germania historica, Bd. 5.1*, ed. by Theodor
      Mommsen (Berlin: Weidmann, 1882), p. 108. Siegfried Epperlein, 'Zur Bedeutungsge-
      schichte von *Europa, Hesperia* und *Occidentalis* in der Antike und im frühen Mittelalter',
      Philologus, 115 (1971), 81–92 (p. 84).

85   Unfortunately, this part of the history of Europe is not very well known. The most rele-
      vant studies still stem from the twentieth-century post-war period (e.g. Gollwitzer, p. 163;
      Epperlein, pp. 82–83).

occidentis, populi occidentalis, or *imperium occidentale,* emerged in the course of the mediaeval centuries.[86]

In the centuries which saw the Carolingian dynasty dominate the western part of the continent, the Latin term *Europa* received new stimuli: it was deliberately applied for the first time in history to designate a larger coherent area governed by the same ruler, the same institutions, and the same (namely western) values, dissociating this area from the Greek-Byzantine sphere of influence. The expanding hegemonic empire of the Carolingians apparently required a denomination that could encompass both the State and the Church and that went beyond the rather restrictive terms *Francia* or *Gallia*.[87] In other words, the altered power relations within Europe led to a change in the perception of 'Europe' as a category; the term shifted from its centuries-old, exclusively geographical meaning to a geographical meaning with a strong political undertone.[88] As the frequent use of the term in the context of dynastic policies and military campaigns reveals, 'Europe' was to be naturalised as a concept of reference within the Carolingian lands and the competing dominions.

To cite three examples from two different centuries: Already around 775 CE the Franconian cleric Catwulf considered Charlemagne (*c.* 747–814), who at the time was busy fighting the Saxons, "gloria regni Europae" ("the glory of the European empire") in one of his letters to the Franconian king himself.[89] On the occasion of Charlemagne's receiving Pope Leo III (*c.* 750–816) in Paderborn in 799, an anonymous writer celebrated Charlemagne in a fragmentary epic poem as "Europae veneranda pharus" ("the venerable beacon of Europe"; v. 12), "Europae venerandus apex" ("the venerable crown of Europe"; v. 93), and "pater Europae" ("the father of Europe"; v. 504).[90] The attribute of 'father of Europe'

---

86   Gollwitzer, p. 164; Epperlein, p. 82. According text samples from the astrological-prophetic literature of the Middle Ages are presented in Oschema, *Bilder von Europa,* pp. 418–19.

87   Gollwitzer, p. 165; Oschema, *Bilder von Europa,* p. 133. The latter also offers a comprehensive overview of the use of 'Europe' during the Carolingian age (pp. 133–60).

88   Epperlein, p. 86; cf. also Kläger and Bayer, 'Introduction', p. 4.

89   Catwulf, *Cathwulfius Carolo I Francorum regi prosperitatem gratulatur eumque ad virtutem sequendam admonet,* in *Monumenta Germaniae historica: Epistolae Karolini aevi, Bd. 4,* ed. by Ernst Dümmler (Berlin: Weidmann, 1895), pp. 501–505 (p. 503). A profound analysis of Catwulf's letter to Charlemagne can be found in Franz Kampers, 'Rex et sacerdos', *Historisches Jahrbuch,* 45 (1925), 495–515.

90   Anon., *Karolus magnus et Leo papa: Ein Paderborner Epos vom Jahre 799,* ed. by Helmut Beumann, Franz Brunhölzl, and Wilhelm Winkelmann, Studien und Quellen zur Westfälischen Geschichte, 8 (Paderborn: Bonifatius, 1966). The text was reprinted in unaltered form as an appendix to Wilhelm Hentze's study of Charlemagne's meeting with Leo III: Wilhelm Hentze (ed.), *De Karolo rege et Leone papa: Der Bericht über die Zusammenkunft Karls des Großen mit Papst Leo III. in Paderborn 799 in einem Epos*

is particularly interesting. It is the very reason why Charlemagne has – often uncritically – been declared the founder of the idea of Europe in scholarship.[91] Yet while it is true that the epithet carried some weight as an adaptation of the Roman imperial title *pater patriae* ("father of the fatherland") on the one hand, and as a telling alteration of Venantius Fortunatus' description of Martin of Tours as a *Gallica pharus* ("Gallic beacon") on the other,[92] one must be cautious about drawing hasty conclusions regarding Charlemagne's role in the formulation of the concept of Europe. For neither was the Carolingian Empire an early version of Europe – not even in geographical terms, because it only comprised a small proportion of the continent – nor was Charlemagne interested in creating 'Europe' in progressive terms. His aim was rather to re-erect the Roman Empire in a backwards-looking vision.[93]

When Charlemagne's empire crumbled after the death of his successor Louis the Pious (778–840) and was subsequently divided between Louis' three sons, Erchanbert, the bishop of Freising, kept up the European frame of reference in his *Breviarium regum Francorum* (Short Account of the Franconian Kings) by referring to the division as the 'division of Europe': "[...] tres filii eius [...] Europam [...] diviserunt" ("his three sons divided Europe among themselves"; p. 329).[94] Similarly, the son of Louis, the poet Ermoldus Nigellus (first half of the ninth century CE), understood that Louis would eventually leave behind a significant legacy when he praised the emperor a few years earlier with the words: "Tu pius Europae regna potenter habes" ("You, Pius, have got the realms of Europe firmly under your control"; v. 2.272).[95] However, with the death of Louis the Pious, the term 'Europe' as a political category of hegemonic superiority disappeared again. Apparently, it had not successfully settled outside the

---

      für Karl den Kaiser, Studien und Quellen zur westfälischen Geschichte, 36 (Paderborn: Bonifatius, 1999).

91   Most recently again by Alessandro Barbero, *Carlo Magno: un padre dell'Europa* (Rome and Bari: Laterza, 2004).

92   Gollwitzer, p. 165, highlights the modification of the epithet *Gallica* in connection with Charlemagne's symbolic expansion of his hegemonic area. General observations on the phrase *pater patriae* are found in Fuhrmann, p. 10.

93   Peter Segl, 'Europas Grundlegung im Mittelalter', in: *Europa – aber was ist es? Aspekte seiner Identität in interdisziplinärer Sicht*, ed. by Jörg A. Schlumberger and Peter Segl, Bayreuther historische Kolloquien, 8, (Cologne: Böhlau, 1994), pp. 21–43 (pp. 24–25); Asbach, pp. 69–70.

94   Erchanbert, *Breviarium regum Francorum*, in *Monumenta Germaniae historica: Scriptores, Bd. 2*, ed. by Georg Heinrich Pertz (Hannover: Hahn, 1829), pp. 327–30.

95   Ermoldus Nigellus, *Carmina*, in *Monumenta Germaniae historica: Poetae Latini medii aevi, Bd. 2*, ed. by Ernst Dümmler (Berlin: Weidmann, 1884), pp. 5–93. Further examples of poets making use of the term 'Europe' at the time are discussed in Epperlein, p. 85.

academic-literary context of the Carolingian court. At least for some decades, though, it had served as the ideal term to accommodate notions of authority, owing to its classical connotations and its geographical vagueness devoid of any previous political meaning.[96]

Despite the Carolingian foray in the direction of a politically underpinned notion of Europe, along with the preceding religious ideas of a western realm of distinct characteristics, a comprehensive notion of Europe never evolved in the Middle Ages. In a way, it is paradoxical that new denominations came up and novel qualities were given to the term 'Europe' in Carolingian times, bespeaking certain reflections on Europe as a category, but then those new denominations and novel qualities proved only feignedly integrative.[97] Moreover, if the very term 'Europe' was used at all before and after the Carolingian era, it usually pertained to the geographical context.[98] The ancient view of Europe as extending from Gibraltar to the river Don was widely spread until the advent of the Renaissance and was held, for example, by as influential a contemporary of Charlemagne as the encyclopaedist Rabanus Maurus (c. 780–856).[99] In the *Gesta Treverorum* (The Deeds of the Trevians), the founding history of the city of Trier from around 1100, Europe was mentioned many times – among others, Trier was even explicitly called the "capital of Europe" ("capud Europae", p. 131).[100] Nevertheless, what Klaus Oschema slightly overinterpreted as moments of "creating identity",[101] in the end proves to be nothing more than

---

96 Reuter, p. 179.
97 Asbach, pp. 65–66.
98 Indicative of this trend is the fact that there is no article in the German reference work for mediaeval studies, the *Lexikon des Mittelalters*, specifically dedicated to the term 'Europe'. Under the respective lemma in volume four, the reader is merely referred to the lemma 'Kontinente' ('continents') in the fifth volume, which, in turn, refers the reader to the lemma 'Welbild, geogr.' ('geographical world view') in volume eight. Here, Europe is briefly expounded in geographical demarcation from Asia and Africa in no more than eighteen lines (Rudolf Simek, 'Weltbild, geogr.', in *Lexikon des Mittelalters, Bd. 8*, ed. by Robert-Henri Bautier [Munich and Zurich: Artemis, 1997], coll. 2159–65; the paragraph on Europe is located in col. 2164). On this issue, see Walser-Bürgler, 'Europa und europäische Identität(en)', p. 65, and Wolfgang Behringer, 'Einführung: Das frühneuzeitliche Europabild als Forschungsaufgabe', in *Departure for Modern Europe: A Handbook of Early Modern Philosophy (1400–1700)*, ed. by Hubertus Busche (Hamburg: Meiner, 2011), pp. 781–803 (p. 781). On mediaeval Europe in geographical context, see Ingrid Baumgärtner and Hartmut Kugler (eds.), *Europa im Weltbild des Mittelalters: Kartographische Konzepte*, Vorstellungswelten des Mittelalters, 10 (Berlin: Akademie Verlag, 2008).
99 Oschema, *Bilder von Europa*, p. 169.
100 *Gesta Treverorum: Pars prior usque ad a. 1101*, ed. by Georg Waitz, in *Monumenta Germaniae historica: Scriptores, Bd. 8*, ed. by Georg Heinrich Pertz (Hannover: Hahn 1848), pp. 111–200.
101 Oschema, *Bilder von Europa*, p. 167 ("identitätsstiftend"). Despite his pioneering work on the mediaeval use of the term 'Europe', Oschema at times is prone to ascribe a symbolism

geographical commonplaces popular since Antiquity (such as the demarcation of the continent from Asia and Africa, p. 130).

Not even during the time of the crusades (eleventh to thirteenth centuries)
was 'Europe' of great importance, even though various European peoples went
to war against the common Muslim enemy. In this context, it was customary
instead to speak of *ecclesia occidentalis* or *Christianitas* instead of *Europa*. If
anything, 'Europe' served as a vague geographical point of reference, simply
bearing the meaning of having many different princes living in Europe turning
against the east – yet not in a collective endeavour, but separately for the sake
of their own interests.[102] So when the (otherwise unknown) eleventh-century
chronicler Albericus de Tribus Fontibus, for instance, spoke of an "expeditio
Asiaca, quam Europa contra Turcos movit" ("an expedition to the east, which
Europe launched against the Turks"; p. 821),[103] a formula typical of the crusading age, he did not refer to the feudal entities of continental Europe as a unity;
after all, they were all competing against each other in the strife for military
glory, fame, and prey.

In fact, it is very likely that not even religious feelings of togetherness played
a significant role among the 'Europeans' going east. This is best illustrated by
the often-cited *Continuatio Hispana* (Spanish History, 754 CE), composed by
an anonymous Christian chronicler from Al-Andalus. In describing the ongoing Muslim stampede, he designated the soldiers fighting for Charles Martel
and defeating the Muslims in the Battle of Tours and Poitiers (732 CE) twice as
"Europenses" ("Europeans"; p. 362).[104] While many over-enthusiastic interpret-
ers have seen in this expression an ideological meaning, it seems to have been
used merely as a pseudo-collective auxiliary term for all the different soldiers
of European origin involved.[105] This claim is supported by two observations:

---

to the term where there is none. One definitely treads on safer ground with Peter Burke
('Did Europe Exist', p. 23): "Thus for nearly two thousand years, from the fifth century BC
to the fifteenth century AD, the term 'Europe' was in sporadic use without carrying much
weight, without meaning very much to many people."

102   Fuhrmann, p. 12; Oschema, *Bilder von Europa*, pp. 266 and 270. For more general information on 'European' campaigns in the age of the crusades (including the citation of a few
texts which could perhaps be understood in a continental-symbolic way), see Michael
Mitterauer, *Warum Europa? Mittelalterliche Grundlagen eines Sonderwegs* (Munich: Beck,
2003), and Oschema, *Bilder von Europa*, pp. 263–88.

103   Albericus Trium Fontium, *Chronica a monacho Novi Monasterii Hoiensis interpolata*, ed.
by Paul Scheffer-Boichorst, in *Monumenta Germaniae Historia: Scriptores, Bd. 23*, ed. by
Georg Heinrich Pertz (Hannover: Hahn, 1874), pp. 631–950; Epperlein, p. 89.

104   *Continuatio Hispana anno DCCLIV*, in *Monumenta Germaniae historica: Auctores antiquissimi, Bd. 11*, ed. by Theodor Mommsen (Berlin: Weidmann, 1894), pp. 323–69.

105   Burke, 'Did Europe Exist', p. 23; Oschema, *Bilder von Europa*, p. 135.

first, the Muslim enemy received a similarly vague treatment, simply being called "the Arabs" ("Arabes"; p. 362); second, the anonymous chronicler did not fail to mention that after their victory, the *Europenses* "in suas se leti recipiunt patrias" ("happily returned to their [various] homelands", p. 362). Rather than propagating any form of belonging, therefore, the ethnic differences between the individual European soldiers were emphasised. Notions of a cultural, political, or ideological solidarity among the European army could not be more blatantly missing.

4   From Zero to Hero: Conceptualisations of Europe in the Early
         Modern Period

At the transition from the Middle Ages to the Renaissance, the big bang occurred, and Europe all of a sudden unfolded. Out of nothing the idea of Europe expanded and took shape throughout the early modern centuries. Sporadically, single studies still pop up treating the Early Modern Period as a mere 'incubation phase' or a prehistory of the Europe discourse along with Antiquity and the Middle Ages.[106] According to these studies, Europe eventually only turned into a category of thinking in the eighteenth century. However, in general this opinion is widely considered obsolete today.[107] The Early Modern Period was not so much an incubation phase but rather the take-off phase of the discourse of Europe, which is ultimately proven by the numerous European concepts as well as affirmations of European identity expressed in Neo-Latin literature.

It is difficult to pinpoint the exact date or year in which an increasing number of people all over the continent started to develop an awareness of each other as an interrelated international group.[108] Similarly, scholarship is confronted with the chicken-or-egg-question when it comes to deciding whether feelings

---

106   At the beginning of this research tradition, for example, stands Gollwitzer, *Europabild und Europagedanke*, later followed by Burke, 'Did Europe Exist'; Klaus Malettke, 'Europabewusstsein und europäische Friedenspläne im 17. und 18. Jahrhundert', *Francia*, 21 (1994), 63–94; Schmale and others, *Studien zur europäischen Identität*; and Asbach, *Europa*.

107   As is emphasised by Swedberg, 'The Idea of "Europe"', and by Nicolas Detering, Clementina Marsico, and Isabella Walser-Bürgler, 'Contesting Europe: Comparative Perspectives on Early Modern Discourses on Europe, 1400–1800 – an Introduction', in *Contesting Europe: Comparative Perspectives on Early Modern Discourses on Europe, 1400–1800*, ed. by Nicolas Detering, Clementina Marsico, and Isabella Walser-Bürgler, Intersections, 67 (Leiden: Brill, 2019), pp. 1–10 (p. 3).

108   Detering, p. 16.

of continental belonging, eventually put down in Latin texts, or the Latin texts propagating the feeling of continental belonging, and thus only inciting it, came first. All we know is that at some point between the Middle Ages and the Renaissance, Europeans must have come to realise that apart from the city they were living in, apart from the territory whose administration they were part of, apart from the ethnic group by which they were defined, and apart from the religious institutions that put their lives in order, there was another parameter – Europe – towards which they could feel a certain affiliation. The fact that they did feel such an affiliation, however, presented a unique trait of the European people. After all, continental identities only evolved in the nineteenth century; before, Europeans had been the only people in the world who comprehensively shared a continental identity.[109] To quote Anthony Pagden:

> Only Europeans have persistently described themselves [...] to be not merely British or German or Spanish but also European [...]. [The] sense that it might be possible to belong to something larger than the family, the tribe, the community or the nation yet smaller and more culturally specific than 'humanity' may indeed be a distinctly European conception.[110]

In the case of early modern European integration, notions of holism were driven to the extreme. As much as groups of units usually are characterised by a natural desire to form a whole, the continental extent at that time was simply mind-blowing – especially when perceived through the lens of a contemporary eye that is completely detached from any of the global schemes we are accustomed to today. In the end, this is evidence enough of the fact that the early modern European universe was largely supported by cohesive mechanisms binding its single parts together into one functioning system.

Already towards the end of the Middle Ages, an altered use of the term 'Europe' became noticeable that hinted at the development its meanings would undergo in the decades and centuries to follow. In a first step, the Latin word *Europa* increasingly appeared as a category of broad geographical reference. Dante Alighieri (*c.* 1265–1321) employed the term thirteen times in total in his Latin works, Francesco Petrarca (1304–1374) even more often.[111] The first text to carry the term in a prominent position, namely its title, was Enea Silvio

---

109   And even afterwards, the formation of the Asian, African, and American identities was largely influenced by European notions of ethnicity and compatriotism. For more information on the imprint Europe has left on other continental identities down to the present day, see Pagden, p. 53.

110   Pagden, pp. 33 (first part of the quote) and 53 (second part of the quote).

111   Burke, 'Did Europe Exist', p. 23.

Piccolomini's historico-geographical account of Europe (finished in 1458), which was part of a comprehensive yet unfinished description of the world. An incunable printed in the free imperial city of Memmingen in 1490, arranged by the cleric Michael Christan (exact life dates unknown), endowed the part on Europe with the title *Aeneas Silvius in Europam* (Enea Silvio about Europe).[112] Today, the work is most commonly referred to as *De Europa*. But not only did the term 'Europe' become more and more fashionable around 1400. It was also destined to remain popular from this time on and never to fall into desuetude again as it had done before in the course of history, particularly after the demise of Carolingian rule. Last but not least, new levels of meaning were created around the term 'Europe' beyond the geographical category transmitted from Antiquity and the Middle Ages. This traditional category was partly expurgated, partly subjoined now by many different political and cultural notions of Europe, as well as by religious, legal, economic, and social visions of continental unity (as we will see shortly).

All these developments indicate the intensification of a European consciousness – the famous *conscience européenne* Denis de Rougemont evoked in the title of his study from 1961. But on top of these, the Latin language reacted to the new representation of real and imagined Europe alike on the lexical level: the collective term *Europaei* ("Europeans") for the people inhabiting the geographical realm called 'Europe' was introduced, from which circumstance also the adjective *Europaeus* ("European") was born.[113] The originator, once again, was Piccolomini in *De Europa*. In outlining the aim of his account of Europe, which he himself considered a summary of everything that had happened under the reign of Emperor Frederick III (1415–1493), he stated (p. 27):[114]

> Que sub Friderico, tertio eius nominis imperatore, apud Europeos [!] et, qui nomine christiano censentur, insulares homines gesta feruntur memoratu digna mihique cognita, tradere posteris quam brevissime libet.

---

112 The background story behind this early edition is illustrated in Detering, pp. 61–62.

113 Burke, 'Did Europe Exist', p. 23; Oschema, 'Der Europa-Begriff', p. 226; Oschema, *Bilder von Europa*, p. 306. The Latin adjective was later adopted by most European vernaculars (cf. German: europäisch; English: European; French: européen; Spanish: europeo; Italian: europeo; Swedish: europeisk; Polish: europejski).

114 Enea Silvio Piccolomini, *De Europa*, ed. by Adrian van Heck, Studi e testi, 398 (Vatican City: Biblioteca Apostolica Vaticana, 2001). Although several translations into both English and German, as well as commentaries, have been published since van Heck's edition, his edition still constitutes the only critical edition of Piccolomini's *Europa*. All other editions are merely based on his pioneering work.

Everything that took place during the reign of Emperor Frederick III among the Europeans and the Christian people on the islands that is worthy to be remembered and that is known to me, I will hand down to posterity as briefly as possible.

Piccolomini employs the term 'Europeos' in the most natural manner, as if it had always existed and been used. And even though he might have had a secret precursor, a work possibly known to him – the *Strategicon adversum Turcos* (Stratagems against the Turks; conceived before 1455) by the Lombard humanist Lampo Birago (1390–1472), who had put the *Asiani* in opposition to the *Europaei*[115] – Piccolomini ended up being the one to spread the term and render it respectable among intellectuals and the broad public. All other contemporary attempts at forging an appropriate term for the people inhabiting Europe or an adjective denoting the continent failed: in *De Monarchia* (On Monarchy; conceived *c.* 1316), Dante had used the phrase "Europam colentes" ("those who live in Europe") analogously to the "Asyani et Affricani" ("Asians and Africans"); Boccaccio had created the Italian "Europico" ("European"), corresponding to the adjective "Affricano" ("African") in his commentary on Dante's *Divina Commedia* (1373–1374); the Polish humanist Maciej Miechowita invented the neologism "Europianus" ("European") in his *Tractatus de duabus Sarmatiis Asiana et Europiana et de contentis in eis* (Treatise on the Two Sarmatias, Asian and European, and What is Contained in Them, 1517).[116]

Both the failed creations and Piccolomini's successful invention serve as additional witnesses to the growing European consciousness, viz. as a reflector of the evolving discourse of Europe. After all, languages are but supplying systems operating in response to the needs of their speakers, and "if these needs change, then languages are more or less infinitely adaptable".[117] In this sense, the Latin language bent to the desire of the early modern Europeans to express themselves by means of the self-referential category *Europaei/Europaeus* and to determine their collateral environment as social agents. Apart from

---

115   Birago's potential role as a harbinger for Piccolomini is outlined in greater detail in Oschema, *Bilder von Europa*, pp. 440–43; Detering, p. 60 n. 32; Katharina N. Piechocki, *Cartographic Humanism: The Making of Early Modern Europe* (Chicago: The University of Chicago Press, 2019), p. 12.

116   The respective terms are found in: Dante Alighieri, *De Monarchia*, ed. by Maurizio Pizzica (Milan: Biblioteca universale Rizzoli, 1988), 3.13.7; Giovanni Boccaccio, *Il commento alla Divina Commedia e gli altri scritti intorno a Dante, vol. 3*, ed. by Domenico Guerri, Scrittori d'Italia, 12 (Bari: Laterza, 1918), p. 180; Maciej Miechowita, *Tractatus de duabus Sarmatiis Asiana et Europiana et de contentis in eis* (Krakow: Haller, 1517), in the title and passim.

117   Edwards, p. 5.

depicting the European consciousness, the discussions centred around the terms 'Europe', 'Europeans', and 'European' also created, reproduced, and refined the early modern European consciousness.[118] The Neo-Latin literature on Europe bespeaks this trend by the frequency and intensity with which Europe was conceptualised.[119] Heuristically, this is a simple calculation: the more texts were distributed discursively dealing with Europe at a certain time, and the more elaborately these discussions were expounded with respect to the meanings that the term 'Europe' and its derivatives evoked, the greater – we can assume – was the European consciousness.

After the initial decades, terms denoting continental togetherness and the various concepts attached to them caught on fully in the sixteenth century. As a consequence of their spread through the work of well-known and respected scholars like Erasmus, Niccolò Machiavelli (1469–1527), Juan Luis Vives (1493–1540), Philip Melanchthon (1497–1560), Luís de Camões (1524–1580), and Michel de Montaigne (1533–1592), they gained a Europe-wide prevalence that included all strata of society.[120] In the seventeenth and eighteenth centuries, the peak of this development was finally reached. During this time, the terms *Europa* and *Europaeus* (in all their declensions) turned up with a frequency both previously and subsequently unseen. It is safe to say that around 1700 there were no other words or formulas for European identity more common in Latin literature than these two.[121]

The reasons for the blooming of the term 'Europe' and the emergence of a proper discourse of Europe for the first time in history immediately after the Middle Ages are attributable to the wind of change sweeping the continent from the fifteenth to the eighteenth centuries. The striking upswing of Europe in terminology and conceptualisation coincided with the dissolution

---

118   Detering, pp. 43–44.

119   Despite this enthusiasm with which Latin authors negotiated Europe and Europeanness, it needs to be added here that none of the concepts envisaged ever came into being (maybe with the slight exception of the *res publica literaria*, which will be discussed in part 4.5.). They remained mere concepts, propagating images of what Europe could or should be. However, communities must always remain imagined to a certain degree. This is simply the result of the fact that the members of a community (at least if it is larger than a small village) will never meet, see, or know their fellow members. It is only in their imagination that they nurture the notion of a common bond based on the values upon which the members jointly define themselves. Cf. Anderson, p. 6.

120   Burke, 'Did Europe Exist', p. 24.

121   This observation complies with the suggestions made concerning contemporary vernacular literature (cf. Hay, p. 73; Fritz Wagner, 'Europa um 1700 – Idee und Wirklichkeit', *Francia*, 2 (1974), 295–308 (p. 295); Burke, 'Did Europe Exist', pp. 23–24; Malettke, p. 83; Detering, p. 43). Useful indicators in this respect are the titles of books, pamphlets, and journals.

of the existing patterns structuring the world and defining its view. In sum, Europe was characterised by a radical break with the social, political, and cultural norms of the preceding centuries.[122] In the midst of all the upheaval and uncertainty shaking all corners of the continent as well as all areas of life, Europe turned into the mainstay of the ever-evolving world order, its anchor, its opportunity for redefinition of the self and the other. In a way, the early modern European integration was the product of a period of steady crisis.

Much ink could be spilled on a comprehensive list of all early modern upheavals ultimately fostering and shaping the discourse of Europe. It will suffice here to mention only the most important ones.[123] First of all, the population of the continent grew continuously after the demographic catastrophe of the fourteenth century. The awareness of the size of Europe in terms of population also led to a revalued awareness of the qualities tied to the continent. The general economic growth in most European nations from the fifteenth century on (and then again after the Thirty Years' War) had a similar effect. Furthermore, European self-perception underwent a significant change when confronted with the world in the course of global imperialism, exploration, colonialism, trade, and navigation. In the face of the cultural pluralism encountered in overseas territories, as well as the discovery of hitherto unknown places, Europe needed to redefine itself and its role in the world. On a political level, the centralisation of government, leading away from the feudal kinship-based society towards larger territories and states, broadened the horizon of most people on the continent. Many different small communities merged into one society, allowing for more encompassing group identities. The Reformation and the Counter-Reformation, eventually, challenged prevailing human norms. The loss of authority suffered by the mediaeval institutions of the pope on the one side and the emperor on the other, caused Europe to search for a secularised identity. In scientific and intellectual terms, the invention of the printing press in particular catapulted Europe into the age of data and public communication. With every printed text – be it a travel journal, or a treatise

---

122   Asbach, pp. 96 and 99. Gollwitzer (p. 163) dramatically emphasises the formation of European communality in the context of "hours of utmost danger to the world" ("Stunden, da diese neue Welt in ernster Gefahr schwebte"). Cf. Michael Wintle, *The Image of Europe: Visualizing Europe in Cartography and Iconography throughout the Ages* (Cambridge: Cambridge University Press, 2009), p. 3.

123   In order to get a full picture of everything that was going on in the early modern centuries, it is recommendable to consult a thematic history such as Hamish M. Scott's (ed.) two-volume *Oxford Handbook of Early Modern European History, 1350–1750* (Oxford: Oxford University Press, 2015). The first volume deals with "Peoples and Place", the second with "Cultures and Power".

on gravity, or the production of coffee – the level of knowledge grew, bringing about a constant revaluation of the world and its people. Regarding the discourse of Europe, printing even served as a special catalyst for popularising and spreading deliberations on the continent and its relationship with itself and the rest of the world.

It is against this background that the following ideas of Europe in Neo-Latin literature are to be understood. These ideas will comprise the religious concept of Europe as a *res publica Christiana*, the political concepts of Europe as a universal monarchy on the one hand and as a federation of autonomous nations on the other, the concept of Europe as a continental hub of peace and balanced power, cultural concepts of European superiority and civilisational world domination, as well as the scientifically and intellectually underpinned concept of Europe as a *res publica literaria*. All these concepts combine historical, philosophical, theological, ethnological, geographical, political, commercial, and scientific aspects, which is why they are sometimes hard to differentiate clearly and more often than not interlock. They constitute the most successful and influential sketches of discourse, yet as has been pointed out in the introduction to this study, the discourse of Europe was not exclusively confined to these aspects. Smaller conceptualisations pertained, for instance, to mystical, fiscal, economic, or legal discussions of European communal life. Unfortunately, scholarship is still missing a proper processing of the respective sources, along with a better understanding of early modern mysticism, fiscal policies, international economy, and European law. Many other concepts might even await future identification.

Finally, all texts chosen for representing and illustrating the individual concepts in the next parts emerged from the inner-European context. People from outside Europe or, to be more precise, non-Europeans, hardly ever perceived Europeans in an ideological light beyond their being their colonial masters or missionaries. They tended rather to use 'Europe' (if at all) in a vague geographical sense.[124] Latin texts on Europe written from outside and applying a

---

124   An interesting study in this respect is Nabil Matar, '*Ūrubba* in Early Modern Arabic Sources', in: *Early Modern Constructions of Europe: Literature, Culture, History*, ed. by Florian Kläger and Gerd Bayer, Routledge Studies in Renaissance Literature and Culture, 29 (New York: Routledge, 2016), pp. 41–56. Matar looks at early modern Europe from the Arabian perspective and shows that although the word *Ūrubba* had existed in the eastern realms, Muslims generally had a very vague idea of what Europe was and meant apart from being Christian. Similar conclusions are drawn by Bekim Agai, who examines early modern travel reports by Muslims visiting Austria and France: 'Europa im Spiegel der Wahrnehmungen von Reisenden aus der islamischen Welt', in *Pluralistische Identität: Beobachtungen zu Herkunft und Zukunft Europas*, ed. by Dirk Ansorge (Darmstadt: Wissenschaftliche Buchgesellschaft, 2016), pp. 120–45.

non-Eurocentric view of the world are not known so far. If they ever existed, they would certainly shed new light on the dichotomy between European self-perception and external perception.

4.1   *Notions of Christianity United: The* Res Publica Christiana

Between 1300 and 1450 the Ottoman Empire grew into a serious world power owing to a combination of aggressive policies and geopolitical fortune. After the fall of Constantinople in 1453 and the ensuing advance of the Ottomans towards the West, religion was made a compelling argument when trying to define Europe and Europeanness in the face of the Muslim threat. Christianity in this respect implied the sharing of the same values regardless of the confessional split between Protestants and Catholics on the one hand, and the opposition between the Roman Latin and the Greek orthodox Church on the other.[125] The common Muslim enemy brought together Protestants, Catholics, and orthodox Christians alike, and the unspoken amnesty regarding their former conflicts fostered a renewed feeling of solidarity among them.[126] This tendency even reached a point where *Europa* was frequently equated or used synonymously with *Christianitas* (Christianity).[127] The conclusion drawn from this was quite clear: if Europe was the home of the Christians, then everything that was not Christian simply was not Europe. Given that the military power of the Ottomans required the cooperation of the European leaders, the religious understanding of Europe was, in a way, also connected to the political discourse of Europe and overlapped with it.

The notion of Europe as the home of Christianity has proven the most durable continental concept of all times. While it already served as a means to prevent the breaking apart of the ethnic groups assembled under the roof of the Western Roman Empire after it had come to an end in 476 CE, its significance as an 'identity creator' has stretched to the present day. This is manifest both in the public treatment of the EU accession negotiations Turkey has been involved in since 1999 and in the heated discussions about the incorporation of the Christian inheritance in the preamble to the Lisbon Treaty or the Christian symbolism in the flag of Europe.[128] The remarkable weight of Christianity as

---

125   The concept of the *res publica Christiana* is pointedly outlined in Asbach, pp. 100–108.

126   Cf. Pärtel Piirimäe, 'Russia, the Turks and Europe: Legitimations of War and the Formation of European Identity in the Early Modern Period', *Journal of Early Modern History*, 11 (2007), 63–86 (p. 75): "No matter how serious the divisions within Christendom, the antagonism to the Turks was even stronger."

127   Hay, p. 87.

128   General observations on the success of Christianity confronted with the Muslim faith have been made in Oschema, *Bilder von Europa*, p. 13, and Michael Wintle, 'Islam as Europe's

a sign of common European identity can be traced to the continuity of the Christian religion. Christianity has managed over the centuries not only to preserve its original coating since Antiquity but also to expand its sphere of influence to European regions originally untouched by the campaigns of the Roman Empire.[129]

Along with the category of Christian-European as a symbol of demarcation from the Ottomans, the opposition of western civilisation and eastern barbarity emerged. Instead of referring to the Muslim enemy as 'Ottomans', the 'Turk' (*Turca*) was introduced as a purely pejorative antonym – and less a political or ethnic-cultural expression as it is today. What Benedict Anderson has found to be a driving force behind the formation of nationalist tendencies is valid in the case of the formation of early modern continentalism as well: Anderson defines the so-called 'othering', that is, the fear and hate of other nations or groups, as the ultimate catalyst for emotional attachment to one's favoured imagined community.[130] One could also speak of patriotism and racism in that respect, even if it puts the early modern formation of Europe based on religious notions in a somewhat bad light. Yet as a matter of fact, both the term 'Europe' and the notion of European identity were massively promoted particularly from around 1400 to 1600 by means of the Christian dissociation from the Turks.[131] In this way, Europe came to be formed *ex negativo*, driven by the creation of xenostereotypes as well as autostereotypes. Given that the struggle between the West and the East had been a prolific theme in history and literature since Antiquity (e.g. in the fifth century BCE the Greeks fought the Persians and the Parthians; in the Middle Ages East Central Europe fought the

---

"Other" in the Long Term: Some Discontinuities', *History*, 101 (2016), 42–61. The topicality of the notion of Christianity in European politics on both an international and a national level (in the context of the latter especially in conjunction with nationalist approaches) is reviewed in Walser-Bürgler, 'Continuities of Historical Crises', pp. 553–54. The conflict surrounding references to the European Christian heritage in the preamble to the Treaty of Lisbon has received special attention in Sergei A. Mudrov, 'Religion in the Treaty of Lisbon: Aspects and Evaluation', *Journal of Contemporary Religion*, 31 (2016), 1–16.

129   James Hankins, 'Renaissance Crusaders: Humanist Crusade Literature in the Age of Mehmed II', *Dumbarton Oaks Papers*, 49 (1995), 111–207; Hartmann, p. 32.

130   Anderson, p. 141; cf. also Wintle, 'Islam as Europe's "Other"', p. 43.

131   There is a broad consensus of certainty regarding this finding in modern scholarship. See, for instance, Swedberg, p. 379; Hankins, pp. 111–146; Bo Stråth, 'Introduction: Europe as a Discourse', in *Europe and the Other and Europe as the Other*, ed. by Bo Stråth (Brussels: Lang, 2000), pp. 13–44 (p. 15); Asbach, p. 100; Oschema, *Bilder von Europa*, p. 299; Detering, p. 63.

Mongols and the Huns), it seemed to settle well with early modern continental contemporaries as a feature of western self-assertion.[132]

Although the European wars against the Ottomans lasted until the seventeenth and eighteenth centuries (there was, for example, of the Siege of Vienna in 1683 or the Seventh Ottoman-Venetian War from 1714 to 1718), the concept of the *res publica Christiana* reached its heyday in the fifteenth and sixteenth centuries. This had to do with the circumstances of the Ottoman military campaigns: the period of relentless expansion – which involved the victory over the Christians at Kosovo in 1389, at Nicopolis in 1396, at Varna in 1444, the conquest of Constantinople in 1453, the capture of Athens (1459), Otranto (1480), Belgrade (1521), Rhodes (1522), Buda (1541), and Cyprus (1570), as well as the victory at the Battle of Mohács (1526), the near-conquest of Vienna in 1529 and Malta in the 1560s – was followed by a phase of relative peace after the death of Suleiman the Magnificent (1494–1566) in 1566 and the ensuing truce between the Ottoman leadership circle and Emperor Maximilian II (1527–1576) in 1568. But during the entire time the discourse of Europe as a *res publica Christiana* flourished, it was strongly pervaded by the idea of crusading. The age of crusades had not simply ended with the Middle Ages. As the sources suggest, its practice was still widely considered in the fifteenth (and partly still in the sixteenth) century.[133] The literary output in that respect took the form of either offensive or defensive policies, the latter aiming to maintain what was left of Christian Europe, the former aiming to regain the territories lost to the Ottomans. At any rate, both forms stipulated the proposition to establish a European league of princes and nations.

In 1438, *Europa* was for the first time mentioned in the context of the *res publica Christiana*, more specifically, in an equating sense.[134] Since the successful campaigns of the Ottomans in the eastern parts of the continent, as well as the *Reconquista* on the Iberian Peninsula, had resulted in the approximate congruence of Europe with Christianity, Pope Eugene IV (1383–1447) expressed the urgency of a joint European offensive against the Turks in his official letter to Albrecht II of Germany (dated 30 March 1438) after his election as King of the Romans: "[...] speramus te eum esse futurum, qui partes Europe liberes ab infidelium dominatu [...]." – "[...] let us hope that you will be the one who

---

132   Hartmann, pp. 33–34 and 62; Jouanna, pp. 109–71 (on the Greek conflicts in particular).
133   On that matter, see the various contributions in Norman Housley's collected volume *Crusading in the Fifteenth Century: Message and Impact* (Basingstoke: Palgrave Macmillan, 2004).
134   Oschema, 'Der Europa-Begriff', p. 222.

delivers the [lost] parts of Europe from the tyranny of the infidels [...]."[135] Enea Silvio Piccolomini followed this path, exploiting the categories of *Christianitas* and *Europa*.

Piccolomini's significance with regard to the early modern Europe discourse cannot be stressed enough. He was among those Italian humanists who worked in political offices but developed an interest in European matters beyond their immediate affairs. For them, Europe offered an ideal projection surface for a more effective and peaceful cohabitation on a grander scheme.[136] Unfortunately, a comprehensive investigation of Piccolomini's life and works still constitutes a big research desideratum.[137] For our purpose it suffices to say that throughout all stages of his political career, Piccolomini was almost obsessed with the idea of organising a European crusade against the Ottomans to recapture what had been lost to the enemy, to Christianise the world beyond the Ottoman borders, and to protect Europe's cultural heritage (not just in the sense of the Christian faith but in a broader sense, meaning extant historical sites, art, and literature).[138] Already before and during his time as a secretary to the Emperor Frederick III, for whom he began to work in 1443, he expressed his crusading ideas in various letters directed towards Pope Nicholas V (1397–1455), Pope Calixtus III (1378–1458), his fellow humanist Nicholas of Cusa (1401–1464), and Frederick himself. This tendency amplified in the years preceding his election as Pope Pius II in 1458 and finally culminated in his organisation of an international conference in Mantua (1459–1460) where he tried to oblige the European leaders to join in a crusade. In 1463 he issued the famous bull *Vocavit nos pius* (Pius Called Us), which "was promulgated throughout Western

---

135   *Deutsche Reichstagsakten unter König Albrecht II.: Bd. 13.1: 1438*, ed. by Gustav Beckmann (Göttingen: Perthes, 1957), p. 236.

136   On crucial figures such as the Florentine chancellor Coluccio Salutati (1331–1406), the Milanese scholar Andrea Biblio (c. 1395–1435), and the later secretary of the papal court, Flavio Biondo (1392–1463), see Margaret Meserve, 'Italian Humanists and the Problem of the Crusade', in *Crusading in the Fifteenth Century: Message and Impact*, ed. by Norman Housley (Basingstoke: Palgrave Macmillan, 2004), pp. 13–38 (pp. 16–25). A broad range of humanists and their attitude towards the advancing Ottomans is discussed in Hankins (including an appendix of unedited Latin texts on crusading measures: pp. 147–207).

137   A first step in this direction has been taken by Volker Reinhardt, *Pius II. Piccolomini: Der Papst, mit dem die Renaissance begann. Eine Biographie* (Munich: Beck, 2013). For a more concise overview, see Stefan Bauer, 'Enea Silvio Piccolomini', in *Enciclopedia italiana di scienze, lettere ed arti: Appendice 8.5: Il contributo italiano alla storia del pensiero*, ed. by Giuseppe Galasso and others (Rome: Istituto della Enciclopedia Italiana, 2013), pp. 137–43.

138   As Nancy Bisaha shows, these goals are evident from his letters: 'Pope Pius II and the Crusade', in *Crusading in the Fifteenth Century: Message and Impact*, ed. by Norman Housley (Basingstoke: Palgrave Macmillan, 2004), pp. 39–52 (p. 41).

Europe, drawing in volunteers from as far afield as the Netherlands, Spain, and Scotland".[139]

Even though all his efforts were doomed to failure, Piccolomini's line of thought remained influential until the end of the Early Modern Period. In the service of the Emperor Frederick III, he attracted far-reaching attention for the first time with his so-called 'Turkish speeches' (*Türkenreden*) at the German Diets of Regensburg (given on 16 May 1454), Frankfurt (held on 15 October 1454), and Wiener Neustadt (one speech given on 25 February, another on 23 March 1455). As these German imperial assemblies were dedicated almost exclusively to the European issue of the Turkish advance and how the German Empire and its surrounding states could contribute to protecting the continent,[140] Piccolomini took his chance and delivered his personal thoughts on the issue.

In the fashion of both a true politician and a true humanist, Piccolomini particularly pushed the limits of European thinking at the Frankfurt meeting in 1454. In his legendary opening address entitled *Constantinopolitana clades* (The Fall of Constantinople),[141] he performed a rhetorically outstanding oration of undeniable political significance for the entire continent. With regard to content and structure it drew on Cicero's speech *Pro lege Manilia*, delivered in 66 BCE before the Roman senate, and it entertained an international audience of diplomats, princes, scholars, and envoys from all over Christian Europe.[142]

---

139   Noel Malcolm, *Useful Enemies: Islam and the Ottoman Empire in Western Political Thought, 1450–1750* (Oxford: Oxford University Press, 2019), p. 12. For more information on Piccolomini's ardent support for a crusade, see Bisaha, pp. 39–41, and Johannes Helmrath, 'Pius II. und die Türken', in *Europa und die Türken in der Renaissance*, ed. by Bodo Guthmüller and Wilhelm Kühlmann, Frühe Neuzeit, 54 (Tübingen: de Gruyter, 2000), pp. 79–137.

140   On the concrete measures taken during these meetings, such as drawing together lists of the existing resources and first proposals for campaigning on both land and water, see Heribert Müller, 'Europa, das Reich und die Osmanen: Die Türkenreichstage von 1454/55 nach dem Fall von Konstantinopel, oder: Eine Hinführung zu Großem und Kleinem im Spiegel der *Deutschen Reichstagsakten*', in *Europa, das Reich und die Osmanen: Die Türkenreichstage von 1454/55 nach dem Fall von Konstantinopel*, ed. by Marika Bacsóka, Anna-Maria Blank, and Thomas Woelki, Zeitsprünge. Forschungen zur Frühen Neuzeit, 18 (Frankfurt a.M.: Klostermann, 2014), pp. 9–29 (pp. 12 and 26).

141   Enea Silvio Piccolomini, *Constantinopolitana clades*, in *Deutsche Reichtagsakten unter Kaiser Friedrich III.: Bd. 19.2: Reichsversammlung zu Frankfurt 1454*, ed. by Johannes Helmrath (Munich: Oldenbourg, 2013), pp. 463–565.

142   The audience is not known in full detail, but at least some renowned figures could be named by Johannes Helmrath, 'The German *Reichstage* and the Crusade', in *Crusading in the Fifteenth Century: Message and Impact*, ed. by Norman Housley (Basingstoke: Palgrave Macmillan, 2004), pp. 53–69 (p. 60), and Jörg Feuchter, 'Der Reichstag im 15. Jahrhundert – ein europäisches Forum?', in *Europa, das Reich und die Osmanen: Die Türkenreichstage von 1454/55 nach dem Fall von Konstantinopel*, ed. by Marika Bacsóka, Anna-Maria Blank,

The power that radiated from his speech is ultimately traceable in Piccolomini's autobiographical comments conceived five years later (pp. 83–84):[143]

> oravit ille duabus ferme horis, ita intentis animis auditus, ut nemo unquam screaverit, nemo ab orantis vultu oculos suos averterit, nemo non brevem eius orationem existimaverit, nemo finem non invitus acceperit.

> He spoke for nearly two hours and his listeners were so captivated that no one ever harrumphed, no one averted their eyes from the speaker's face, no one considered his speech long-winded, no one accepted its end without dismay.

The success of Piccolomini's speech was not confined to its immediate reception. The general idea of Europe as a *res publica Christiana* eventually became incredibly popular as a result of his efforts at spreading his message. From all the copies he must have sent all over the continent, fifty are still extant – not even to mention later copies by foreign hands, and not including later printings.[144] This made *Constantinopolitana clades* one of the best-known orations of the fifteenth and sixteenth centuries.

Piccolomini's idea of Europe, dictated by the principle of Christian values and morals, is evident right from the start of his oration. The initial description of the atrociousness of the Turks is followed by the forceful picture of a Europe doomed. Its climax is reached with the outcry (pp. 495–96):

> retroactis namque temporibus in Asia atque in Affrica, hoc est in alienis terris, vulnerati fuimus, nunc vero in Europa, id est in patria, in domo propria, in sede nostra percussi cesique sumus.

> We have been wounded in times past in Asia and Africa – that is, in foreign places – but now we are executed and slaughtered in Europe, that is, in our homeland, in our own house, in our abode.

With the metaphor of Europe as *patria*, *domus*, and *sedes*, Piccolomini created a strong formula of European identity whose scope was unmatched by

---

and Thomas Woelki, Zeitsprünge. Forschungen zur Frühen Neuzeit, 18 (Frankfurt a.M.: Klostermann, 2014), pp. 30–43 (p. 32).

143   Enea Silvio Piccolomini, *Pii commentarii rerum memorabilium que temporibus suis contigerunt, vol. 1*, ed. Adrian van Heck, Studi e testi, 312 (Vatican City: Biblioteca Apostolica Vaticana, 1984).

144   Helmrath, 'The German *Reichstage*', p. 62.

anything that had been said about Europe previously. In addition, it seems to
have marked the first instance of referring to Europe as the 'House of Europe'.[145]
What Piccolomini actually understood as 'Europe' eventually becomes clear a
few moments later when he describes the crusade against the Turks as a just
war: Europe is the "totality of Christians" ("Christiana communitas"; p. 507)
stretching from Constantinople to the utmost western lands (p. 496) – thus
joining the Western Latin Church and the Eastern Greek Church.[146] Piccolomini
defines the joint goal of Christianity in the face of the Ottoman threat as being
"to protect the religion, to save the homeland [Europe], and to preserve the
[Christian-European] fellows" ("pro tuenda religione, pro salvanda patria,
pro conservandis sociis"; p. 505). The term 'fellows' (*socii*) is not just used in
the sense of 'allies' here; it also implies a common bond tying together all
Christian states. In this sense, Piccolomini admonishes the European leaders
and their people to come together as one, as only by means of joint Christian
power could the "damage awaiting the entirety of Christians" ("damna, quae
toti Christianismo imminent"; p. 522) possibly be averted. Cohesion would be
required across and beyond borders if Christianity, if Europe, is to be liberated
(pp. 524–46):

> pugnandum est vobis omnino, principes, si liberi, si Christiani vitam
> ducere cupitis. existimatote nunc, an salvis et integris sociis, an fractis
> atque amissis id agere magis expediat. [...] et vos ergo, Theutones, si –
> quemadmodum spero – sapientes eritis, maiores vestros imitabimini, qui
> remota semper a domo bella gerere ac vicinorum fines non minus quam
> suos tueri consueverunt. quod si vos, Germani, hoc tempore Hungaros
> neglexeritis, non erit denique, cur vos ex Gallis auxilia prestolamini, nec
> rursus illi apud Hispanos opem invenient. [...] neque vos soli, Theutones,
> inquam, pugnabitis! ex Italia, ex Gallia, ex Hispania multi concurrent;
> nec Hungari deerunt nec Bohemi, fortissime gentes, Rasciani, Bulgari,
> omnes Illirienses, omnes Greci sumpta occasione consurgent.

It is on you to fight, you princes, if you want to be free and if you want to
carry on leading your lives as Christians. Just think about whether this
might be better achieved with the help of allies safe and sound or broken

---

145   Asbach, pp. 106–107; Georg Kreis, 'Das Europäische Haus', *in Europäische Erinnerungsorte.
       Bd. 2: Das Haus Europa*, ed. by Pim den Boer and others (Munich: Oldenbourg, 2012),
       pp. 577–85 (p. 577).
146   This reunion had been an impossibility during the Middle Ages and constituted
       another of the many revolutionary aspects of Piccolomini's notion of Europe (Kaiser,
       'Antiketransformationen', p. 95).

and battered. [...] Therefore, you Teutons, if you are prudent – as I hope – you are going to imitate your ancestors, who were used to waging war outside their own lands and to protecting their neighbours' borders as their own. If you, you Germans, let down the Hungarians now, then there will be no reason for you to ask the French for help, and the French in turn will not find support from the Spaniards. [...] But you will not fight alone, you Teutons, I say. Many will join from Italy, from France, from Spain; and neither the Hungarians nor the Bohemians – very brave people – will be absent, and the Serbians, the Bulgarians, all inhabitants of the Balkans, all Greeks will take the occasion and rise.

A similar appeal is expressed in Piccolomini's *Epistola ad Mahumetem* (Letter to Mehmed II, 1461).[147] While it is highly improbable that Piccolomini intended to send the letter off to the sultan, the former conqueror of Constantinople, there is way more to be gained from the text when understanding it as a provocation directed at the European leaders.[148] The main purpose of the letter was to convert Mehmed (1432–1481) to the Christian faith by providing him with theological arguments on the one hand (§39–149) and by threatening him with the joint strength of Europe on the other (§1–38).[149] The latter part in particular was of great importance in relation to the discourse of Europe.

Already at the beginning of the letter, Piccolomini points out to the sultan the military strength of Christian Europe as a closed system (§2.3):

> Nos non ita ignarum te credimus nostrarum rerum, quin scias, quanta est Christianae gentis potentia, quam valida Hispania, quam bellicosa Gallia, quam populosa Germania, quam fortis Britannia, quam audax Polonia, quam strenua Hungaria, quam dives et animosa et bellicarum perita rerum Italia.

> We do not hold you to be so ignorant of our situation that you do not know how great the power of Christianity is, how strong Spain, how bellicose France, how populous Germany, how brave Britain, how bold Poland, how energetic Hungary, and how rich, courageous, and veteran Italy are.

---

147   Enea Silvio Piccolomini, *Pius II. Papa Epistola ad Mahumetem. Einleitung, kritische Edition, Übersetzung*, ed. by Reinhold F. Glei and Markus Köhler, Bochumer Altertumswissenschaftliches Colloquium, 50 (Trier: Wissenschaftlicher Verlag, 2001).

148   Helmrath, 'Pius II.', p. 126.

149   Piccolomini expounds his aim explicitly in §9.

Rather than denoting individual strengths of the nations mentioned, Piccolomini perceives them as the most powerful parts of a bigger whole. They do not signify the entirety of the continent, but rather serve as its representatives, as prime examples of authority and resistance among the Christians. And indeed Piccolomini does not need to cite all European nations, since "a quarter of all nations would be more than enough" to defeat Mehmed's troups anyway ("una ex quattuor nationibus satis fuerit superque satis [tuas copias profligare]"; §5.5). In sum, Piccolomini's preferred use of the word *provincia* ("province"; e.g. in §5.3 or 17.1) when denoting specific European nations or territories hints at his understanding of Europe as one all-encompassing continental empire subdivided merely into ethnic groups – similar to the organisation of the Roman Empire. Yet in contrast to *Constantinopolitana clades*, Piccolomini's appeal to the European Christians to stand together as one and shake off their internal European conflicts is less direct than manipulatively implicit by disguising it as an address of warning to Mehmed (§5.4):

> Nec Christiana discidia desiderio tuo conducere putes aut in his confidas: unientur Christiani omnes, si quando te audient interiora Christianitatis accedere. [...] cessabunt privata odia, ubi publica senserint, et coniunctis viribus adversus communem hostem arma sumentur.

> Do not expect the quarrels among the Christians to be conducive to your desire and do not rely on them. For all Christians will unite as soon as they learn about your advance into their core areas. [...] They will settle their internal disputes the moment they notice danger coming from outside, and with joint forces they will take up arms against the common enemy.

This citation marks a key passage of the *Epistula* with respect to the Europe discourse. For not only does Piccolomini refer to Europe as *Christianitas* here, but the underlying message he conveys is that of unquestionable unity in the face of the external threat caused by the Ottoman expansion. Despite the brevity of this passage, the vocabulary of union is highly representative and densely used ("unientur", "Christiani omnes", "coniunctis viribus", "communem hostem"). This is typical of Piccolomini's rhetorical strategy and was subsequently picked up by many authors.

One of them might have been George of Podiebrad (1420–1471), King of Bohemia from 1458 until his death and the first king of the Early Modern Period to turn his back on Rome and to support the Hussite confession. Podiebrad was the initiator and co-designer of a European peace plan entitled *Tractatus pacis toti christianitati fiendae* (Treaty on the Establishment of Peace throughout

Christendom, 1464), the intention of which was to unite all European leaders in a Christian league against the Turks and thus put the continent to peace.[150] Already in 1455 Podiebrad, at the time official administrator of Bohemia by vote of the Bohemian estates, had announced that he would go on a crusade against the Ottomans as soon as Bohemia had made peace with the rest of Europe.[151] In addition, Podiebrad had become known from the beginning of his reign for his predilection for interterritorial contracts.[152] Apparently, he regarded them as the ideal tool for joint policies on the continent, guaranteeing peace for longer periods of time.

Unsurprisingly, therefore, the *Tractatus* features many characteristics of contemporary peace treaties and constitutes, in fact, nothing less than a preconceived peace treaty. Podiebrad's peace plan ultimately never came to be enacted, because as a follower of the Hussite confession, he was officially declared a heretic by Pope Paul II (1417–1471) and excommunicated in 1466, which forbade the Christian leaders of Europe to conduct any further negotiations with the Bohemian king.[153] Despite having been shelved, the *Tractatus* still tells the story of Podiebrad's affirmative pan-Europeanism underpinned

---

150   Podiebrad presumably was not the sole author, as has often been wrongly suggested owing to an ambiguous note in the extant manuscripts. The majority of the text was in all likelihood written by the German jurist Martin Mair (*c.* 1420–1480) who was part of Podiebrad's court for several years. Since the main ideas and the power support came from Podiebrad, I will refer to the text in what follows as Podiebrad's treatise for pure practicality. On Mair, see Rainer Hansen, 'Martin Mair: Ein gelehrter Rat in fürstlichem und städtischem Dienst in der zweiten Hälfte des 15. Jahrhunderts' (unpublished doctoral thesis, University of Kiel, 1992); on Podiebrad's private and political life, see Magda Schusterová, *Der Friedensvertrag Georgs von Podiebrad von 1464 vor dem Hintergrund der spätmittelalterlichen Vertragspraxis*, Osnabrücker Schriften zur Rechtsgeschichte, 17 (Göttingen: v&r unipress, 2016), pp. 41–84. The Latin text of the *Tractatus* is appended ibid. on pp. 195–204; it is based on the Czech edition *Všeobecná mirova organizace podle návrhu českého krále Jiřího z let 1462/1464* by Václav Vaněček (Prag: Nakl. Československé akademie věd, 1964). As the latter was not available, the following quotations are taken from Schusterová's reprint.

151   Schusterová, p. 66.

152   Among them ranked the hereditary alliances arranged with several German dynasties (such as the influential House of Wittelsbach and the House of Brandenburg), a series of pacts made in connection with his attempts at seizing the Bohemian throne, as well as plans for a reconciliation between himself, Emperor Frederick III, and the hostile German princes. These interterritorial alliances are all expounded in greater detail from Podiebrad's perspective in Schusterová, pp. 48–65.

153   Paul Michael Lützeler, 'The European Imaginary in the Discourse on Peace', in *Early Modern Constructions of Europe: Literature, Culture, History*, ed. by Florian Kläger and Gerd Bayer, Routledge Studies in Renaissance Literature and Culture, 29 (New York: Routledge, 2016), pp. 194–210 (p. 200).

by the notion of common Christian kinship and inter-continental peace. As becomes evident from the preamble and the total of twenty-three articles of the *Tractatus* (especially art. 19), Podiebrad's Christian Europe consists of the German Empire and all its principalities, the Kingdom of France and its appendages, the Kingdom of Spain, Castile, and the remaining parts of the Iberian Peninsula, the Kingdoms of Poland, Hungary, and Bohemia, and Venice and the rest of the Italian city-states. The way Podiebrad looks at Europe, it appears discharged of the feudal structures, representing an interrelated federation of autonomous Christian states.[154]

Even though Podiebrad does not once apply the term 'Europe' and instead sticks with *nationes christianorum* or *christianitas*, Piccolomini's equation of *Europa, Christianitas, patria, domus*, and *sedes* from *Constantinopolitana clades* is unmistakably present in Podiebrad's justification of why a Christian league needs to be founded (preamble): "At nunc quantum lacerata, confracta, cassata atque omni nitore splendoreque pristino enudata sit, omnes agnoscimus." – "But now everybody knows to what degree we are lacerated, defeated, crushed, and stripped of any reputation and former glory." The Ottomans would penetrate further and further into Europe, threatening to devastate the Christian continent (preamble). In telling fashion, the virtuous Christians of the occident are set in opposition to *perfidus* [...] *Maumetus* ("the infidel Mehmed"; preamble) and *spurcissimi* [...] *Teurcri* ("the filthy Turks"; preamble). Therefore, it is necessary "quod vera, pura et firma pax, unio et caritas inter cristianos fiat" ("that a true, honest, and firm peace, a sense of union and appreciation among the Christians be established"; preamble). The preamble, emphasising the joint venture of Christian Europe, eventually ends on a pointed note of perpetual peace and solidarity:

> [...] nos de certa sciencia, matura deliberacione prehabita, invocata ad hoc Spiritus Sancti gracia, prelatorum, principum, procerum, nobilium et iuris divini et humani doctorum nostrorum ad hoc accedente consilio et assensu, ad huiusmodi connexionis, pacis, fraternitatis et concordie inconcusse duraturam ob Dei reverenciam fideique conservacionem devenimus in unionem in modum, qui sequitur, pro nobis heredibus et successoribus nostris futuris, perpetuis temporibus duraturam.

> [...] we have decided based on our reliable knowledge, after some careful considerations, the respective invocation of the grace of the holy spirit, after the advice and consent of our prelates, princes, magnates,

---

154   Schusterová, p. 133.

noblemen, doctors of divine and human law, to create a covenant in
the following manner for the purpose of a perpetual and steadfast connection, peace, fraternity, and concord, for the glory of God and for the
protection of faith, which is to remain binding for our heirs and future
successors for all time.

Some attentive readers might find in the formulas expressing eternal peace
and solidarity typical building blocks of mediaeval and early modern contractual writing. And it is certainly true that Podiebrad's *Tractatus* draws heavily
on contractual vocabulary which particularly revolves around ideas of *amicitia* ("friendship").[155] After all, it is a draft for a real peace contract meant to
be decreed. However, as Randall Lesaffer points out, if terms of friendship,
kinship, and togetherness are used slightly excessively, they ought to be taken
as deliberate reactions to international conflicts.[156] As far as Podiebrad's
Tractatus is concerned, the corporate elements are so densely employed that
it is actually hard to ignore or downplay the notions of supranational communality expressed. Considering that the text itself makes for a comparatively
short contemporary treaty, the conspicuous accumulation of cooperation and
solidarity within an overarching continental system could almost be understood as satirical if the context did not suggest otherwise.

To give a few illustrative examples: the Christian league itself is, among
other terms, alternately called a *fraternitas* ("brotherhood"; art. 4, 5, 12, 19),[157] a
collegium ("association"; art. 16), a *congregacio* ("federation"; art. 4, 9, 11, 12, 14,
15, 16, 17, 18, 20, 22, 23), and a *unio* ("union"; art. 12, 13, 19) – more often than not in
conjunction with the possessive pronoun *nostra/nostrum* ("our"). In addition,
the descriptive words *amicitia, caritas* ("charity"), *pax* ("peace"), *concordia*
("harmony"), and *socii* ("companions") are omnipresent throughout the twenty-
three articles; sometimes they take the form of sequences (as in art. 12: "nostrum pacem, unionem, caritatem et fraternitatem"). Decisions that need to

---

155   The term *amicitia* and related expressions such as *fraternitas* ("brotherhood") have often
       been applied since the Middle Ages to signal legal equality and the equal status between
       contracting parties. As a term denoting a mutual agreement on peace it had been
       used already in Antiquity in the context of interstate relations. Randall Lesaffer, 'Peace
       Treaties from Lodi to Westphalia', in *Peace Treaties and International Law in European
       History: From the Late Middle Ages to World War One*, ed. by Randall Lesaffer (Cambridge:
       Cambridge University Press, 2007), pp. 9–44 (p. 36). Complementary information on the
       idea of 'friendship' in mediaeval treaties and how it was strongly influenced by Christian
       values is given in Schusterová 2016, pp. 152–59.

156   Lesaffer, p. 37.

157   In art. 23 the author even speaks emphatically of a *vinculum fraternitatis* ("fraternal
       bond"), tying together the Christian territories.

be made in terms of the duration and expenses of military campaigns against the Turks, the sending of auxiliary troops, the use of armed forces, the exact time for attacking the common enemy, the scale of the tax burden, the members' jurisdiction, the rotating presidency of the league, and other aspects of political integration are exclusively endowed with the phrasing *unanimiter* ("unanimously"), *communi sentencia* ("by common resolution"), or *unanimi sentencia* ("by unanimous resolution").[158] Last but not least, the federative character of the Christian league is manifest in its emergence as a legal entity that literally 'incorporates' its members (art. 5, 12, 16).

After the turn of the century, the idea of a Europe united in the face of the Ottoman advance was still perpetuated. However, it seems that the tone slightly changed. While sixteenth-century authors still remained affirmative with regard to the continental idea, they also grew a little more pessimistic about whether the European nations were actually capable of settling the intra-continental conflicts. The Turks kept getting closer and closer to the heart of Europe, but no Christian agreement was yet in sight. Among the Neo-Latin authors conveying this partly supportive, partly cynical perspective were the Croatian Marko Marulić (1450–1524) and the Spaniard Juan Luis Vives (1493–1540).

Marulić, to begin with the former, resided in Split, a city under Venetian rule, located at the periphery of the Western World, right on the edge of the Ottoman Empire. The sight of Turkish troops devastating the environs had become customary to Marulić and his fellow citizens, who had felt the Ottoman oppression pretty much since the sultan's conquest of Bosnia in 1463 and his defeat of the Hungarian-Croatian army at the Battle of Krbava in 1493.[159] As a man of letters who firmly believed not only in human reason but also in Christian morals, he deemed the the transition of European Christianity away from selfish national struggles towards unified measures the sole deliverance from the Turkish enemy.[160] His claim that Christians needed to stop fighting Christians – an imbecile paradox – for the purpose of the common good can be found in many of his vernacular and Latin works.

---

158   Cf. art. 4, 15, 16, 18, 21, and 23.
159   Even though Marulić has been widely recognised as an influential Latin author on the one hand and the 'father of Croatian literature' on the other, scholarship still lacks a detailed examination of his life and works, as well as of the political and cultural context informing his writing. For the moment, a general overview of all these aspects is provided in Bratislav Lučin, 'Introduction', in *The Marulić Reader*, ed. by Bratislav Lučin (Split: Književni krug, 2007), pp. 7–31, and Bratislav Lučin, 'Marko Marulić: Kroatischer Dichter und europäischer Humanist', *Colloquia Maruliana*, 18 (2009), 349–55.
160   Lučin, 'Marko Marulić', p. 352.

The text that sums up his thoughts on the matter in a very sharp and almost cynical way is his *Epistola ad Adrianum VI. Pontificem Maximum* (Letter to Pope Adrian VI, 1522).[161]

In this letter, composed in the wake of the fall of Belgrade on 29 August 1521 (to which Marulić explicitly refers: cf. p. 96), the author hauntingly curses the discord among the Christians in Europe and calls for unity in the West against the Turkish threat. Similar in format to Piccolomini's previously mentioned *Epistola ad Mahumetem*, it was not actually intended to be sent to the pope. Rather it served as an open letter or a pamphlet published in wide circulation to influence public opinion and provoke a certain reaction.[162] The tone and twisting plot of the letter fit this aim perfectly. For what starts off as a condemnation of the Turkish atrocities and the harm inflicted on the poor European Christians quickly turns into a rousing attack on the Christians tearing each other apart.

Already in the accompanying letter to friar Dominik Buca (1480–1560), Marulić takes great care to highlight his goal, namely to "persuade our kings and princes to refrain from armed conflict, lead them to unity and induce them to prepare a war against the infidels" (p. 90: "reges atque principes nostros ab armis ad concordiam reuocatos ad expeditionem aduersum infideles parandam compellat"). In this early passage, he creates the opposition between 'us Christians' ("our kings and princes") and 'them' ("the infidels", the Turks). This evocation of Europe by means of othering is kept up throughout the actual letter to Adrian (e.g. p. 92: "Quotidianis infidelium Turcarum incursionibus infestamur [...]" – "[T]he infidel Turks daily inflict suffering on us with their raids [...]"; p. 94: "Omitto superioribus temporibus ista omnium Antichristorum impiissima natio quot regna Christianis abstulerit [...]" – "I shall not enumerate all the kingdoms that these people, the most godless of all Antichrists, have

---

161   The text has been edited by Bratislav Lučin in *The Marulić Reader* and supplied with an English translation by Vera Andrassy (pp. 90–108). An in-depth study of the style and impact of the text is available in Ruggero Cattaneo, 'Sullo stile e la rilevanza culturale dell'*Epistola* a Papa Adriano VI di Marco Marulić', *Colloquia Maruliana*, 17 (2008), 91–124.

162   In the case of Marulić' *Epistola* this is evident even from the fact that it had been written at a time when Adrian's predecessor Leo X (1475–1521) was still in office. The stylised address to Adrian was a mere PR-trick to attract people's attention. If anything, the pope served as a symbol of spiritual leadership. In addition, the address to the pope can be understood as an analogy to Luther's famous *Epistola ad Leonem X* (Letter to Leo X, 1520), in which the German reformer had pushed – and indeed with success – his own reforming ideas. For more information on the question of the timing and address of Marulić' *Epistola*, see Franz Posset, 'Open Letter of a Croatian Lay Theologian to a "German" Pope: Marko Marulić to Adrian VI', *Colloquia Maruliana*, 18 (2009), 135–57 (pp. 137–39).

already seized from us Christians [...]"). This represents a strategy to make the European nations constantly aware of their common Christian traits on the one hand, and the fact that they constitute a community of destiny on the other.

Slowly but surely Marulić develops his argument. First, he reminds all westerners that Hungary (or rather, the Kingdom of Pannonia) marks the gateway to Europe. If it was seized by the Ottomans, Europe would be doomed (p. 96): "Quo ipso amisso quid, quaeso, reliquum spei Christianis erit se suaque tuendi [...]?" – "If that kingdom should fall, what hope will Christians have of protecting themselves and their property [...]?" Therefore, a joint initiative would be needed to fight back the Ottomans, a joint initiative born from upright sentiments of unison and solidarity (p. 96):

> Actum est, mihi crede, de Re publica Christiana nisi omnes pari animo, equali fide, concordi proposito, opes uiresque coniungant et sociis agminibus Christique nomine inuocato simul ad bellum procedant morique magis optent quam barbaricae perfidiae unquam seruire.

> Believe me, the Christian community will be lost, unless they all, with the same intention, the same faith and in unity, join forces and, having combined their armies and called on the name of Christ, go forth to war and choose death rather than slavery to a barbaric heresy.

While words and phrases of insinuative unification abound in this passage – for instance, *omnes pari animo, equali fide, concordi proposito, uiresque coniungant, socii, simul* – Europe is even explicitly called a *res publica Christiana*, a political entity held together by the Christian religion. And as any good Christian ought to feel solidarity with other Christians, no matter where they live on the continent, "[t]he common threat should be repelled in a combined campaign" (p. 98: "Commune periculum communibus armis propulsandum est"). No nation is safe only because it is situated farther east (p. 98):

> Nemo in eo se tutum arbitretur quod ab impiorum finibus multa distet locorum intercapedine. Incendium quod timemus, nisi mature extinguatur, [...] ad extrema quoque proserpendo penetrabit.

> Let no-one think himself safe because a great expanse of territory separates him from the frontiers of the infidels. If the fire which we fear is not soon extinguished, [...] it will gradually spread and reach the farthest limits.

In other words, everybody is urged to lend a helping hand; there is no room for individual actions, only the collective strife can lead to triumph in the end (p. 98):

> Nemo praeterea propriis uiribus confidant nisi fratri ab inimicis circum-uento opem tulerit: et ipse similiter peribit. Potentissimus omnium est si cum singulis conferas. Ad unum illum debellandum tot regum, tot prin-cipum uiribus opus est quot [...] possidet ac regit.

> Moreover, nobody should rely on his own strength alone; if he does not offer help to his brother who is beset by enemies, he himself will perish in a similar fashion. The enemy is most powerful if matched against each of them individually. In order to defeat him the power of as many kings and princes as he himself possesses and rules over is needed [...].[163]

As clear as this message seems, Marulić stumbles over one big problem (which is the point at which the appeal for unity turns into a prosecution of conti-nental discord): Christians hate each other, Christians are at war with each other, Christians mercilessly slaughter each other on the European battlefields (p. 98). This, in turn, only makes the Ottomans stronger, as they profit from the lack of Christian unanimity. Marulić' invective follows immediately in pointed rhetorical questions reminiscent of Cicero's accusation of Catiline (p. 100):

> Resipiscite tandem, resipiscite insipientes! Quousque ratio uos fugiet, quousque perniciem uestram ignorabitis? Non uobis pugnatis, non uobis uincitis, sed uni illi, qui uos omnes devorare parat, futurae de uobis uictoriae praestatis occasionem! [...] Desinite iam tandem, Christiani, aduersus Christianos bella gerere!

> Come to your senses at long last, come to your senses, you lunatics! How long will you persist in your madness? How long will you close your eyes to the peril that threatens you? You are not fighting for yourselves, you are not winning victories for yourselves, but only giving the chance of future victory over you to him who is preparing to devour all of you. [...] Now finally, Christians, stop fighting your fellow Christians!

---

163   In this passage (as well as in the following citation), the translation differs slightly from that in Lučin's edition.

Instead of giving in to rage (*indignatio*), Marulić recommends Christianity to embrace brotherhood (*fraternitas*), reconciliation (*placabilitas*), harmony (*concordia*), justice (*aequanimitas*), and mutual benevolence (*mutua beniuolentia*; p. 100). As his integration of Aesop's fable of the frog and the mouse shows (p. 102), which, while fighting each other, fall victim to a hawk, Christianity can only be saved from the destructive Ottoman power if they become aware of each other as a continental community and stand together as one against the common enemy.[164]

The Spanish humanist Juan Luis Vives presented a view in line with Marulić' thinking. In his dialogue *De Europae dissidiis et bello turcico* (On the Conflicts in Europe and the Turkish War, 1526), he discusses the state of European politics with respect to the continuous Ottoman advance.[165] In the background to this text stood the recent wars in Italy involving the capture of the French king Francis I (1494–1547) at the Battle of Pavia (1525), the peasants' revolts in Germany (also in 1525), and the Ottoman victory at the Battle of Mohács (1526).[166] Torn between disillusionment and hope, Vives dissects the intra-continental disputes of the European powers and weighs them against the danger coming from the common Turkish enemy. The genre and the setting chosen equally convey a message of urgency and danger on the one hand, and of European integration on the other: the adoption of the Lucianic dialogue set in the underworld implies the hopelessness of the situation as well as the 'dialogic' nature needed in European politics to settle the existing conflicts. Furthermore, the writings of Lucian of Samosata (second century CE) constituted a preferred choice of many early modern reformers due to their instructive and moralistic character.[167]

Vives addresses the worrying current situation in Europe already in the first line of the dialogue, suggesting to the reader that there is not much time left until the continent's demise. In this line, the judge of the dead, Minos, asks the prophet Tiresias for information on why "souls are raining down here thick as hail driven by a strong gale" ("animae huc decidunt tam densae quam vel grando vehementi aliquo turbine excussa"; 1.4–7). Tiresias passes the question

---

164   Cf. Posset, p. 141.

165   The text is part of the Latin-English edition of volume twelve of Vives's selected works: *De Europae dissidiis et republica*, ed. by Edward V. George and Gilbert Tournoy (Leiden: Brill, 2019), pp. 89–159. Comprehensive insights into Vives' work and the ideas he was driven by can be gained from Charles Fantazzi (ed.), *A Companion to Juan Luis Vives*, Brill's Companions to the Christian Tradition, 12 (Leiden: Brill, 2008).

166   Malcolm, p. 61.

167   This is illustrated passim in David Marsh, *Lucian and the Latins: Humor and Humanism in the Early Renaissance* (Ann Arbor, MI: University of Michigan Press, 1998).

on to the two newcomers Basilius Colax ("Royal Flatterer") and Polypragmon ("Busybody"), who then expose the wars that have been taking place in Europe from the 1430s to the present (4–18). Their historical description is best summed up in Busybody's introductory statement (3.32): "[...] bellum ubique, discordiae, odia" – "war, discord, and hate are everywhere". Vives does not restrain his harsh criticism of European disunity. He not only bluntly lays bare the Europeans' self-absorption in their respective passions and power struggles by letting Tiresias employ the metaphor of neighbourhood gone wrong (23.22–23): "Nescio quid sperandum sit [...] in tam aspera et confirmata discordia, ubi quisque improvidus sui vicinum vellet perditum." – "I don't know what hope there is [...] in such bitter and deep-rooted discord, where each one thoughtlessly wishes his neighbor's destruction." He also refuses to depict the Christian Europeans in a better light than the Ottoman enemy. In the end, it is almost ironic to hear Tiresias say with regard to a Europe free from the Turkish threat (27.10–11): "Sic Europae, quamdiu nullum est a Turca periculum, illa est unica consolatio, quod quisquis vincat erit Christianus." – "So for Europe, as long as there is no danger from the Turk, one consolation remains: whoever prevails will be a Christian."

Up to this point in the dialogue, Europe has still been waiting to be constructed as an entity. The protagonists have merely figured out the problems contributing to the continent's fragmentation. Eventually, though, Vives is ready to find a solution to these problems: this comes when he has Minos request a concrete "medicinam adhibendam tantis malis" ("remedy to be applied to such great ills"; 23. 16). In other words, how can Europe come together peacefully united? A first answer is provided by the Roman commander Scipio, who suddenly shows up, expressing an "imperialist and chauvinist Eurocentrism *avant la lettre*":[168] he suggests that the discordant princes of Europe only needed to join their forces against the Turks and thus find reward in the systematic expansion of the continent, instead of having to argue over their domestic lands (34.1–4):

> Si Europae principes odio inter se caeci, discordia furentes, arma a Christianis vellent in Turcam convertere, omnia quae expetunt prolixius assequerentur et copiosius.

> If the princes of Europe, blinded by mutual hatred, frenzied with quarrelling, were to choose to turn their weapons away from Christians and

---

168   Detering, p. 70.

against the Turk, they would attain everything they desire more amply and abundantly.

A joint European offence directed at the common enemy coming from outside would make the Europeans forget about their intra-continental disputes. Scipio's advice receives only partial approval. Yet while the imperialist goal is rejected by all protagonists alike, the idea of standing together in the name of the Christian religion catches on. Tiresias eventually gets to pass judgement on the affair. Although he does not bring forward any concrete idea on what actions ought to be taken to enforce an official peace among the Europeans, he creates the fundamental vision of a Europe united by the Christian religion (46.21): "Non suis fidant viribus aut armis, sed Christo." – "Let them put their trust not in the force of arms but in Christ." After all, it makes much more sense to wage war on "the foe of [...] religion, rather than their neighbor with whom they share bloodlines and baptism into the faith" ("potius et pietatis hostem bello impeterent quam vicinum, sanguine et mysteriorum initiatione coniunctum"; 46.26–27). A leading role in this respect Tiresias ascribes to the German Empire (47.7–8): "Habent adhuc Christiani firmissimam Europae partem Germaniam." – "Christians still control Germany, the most stable part of Europe." If only, Tiresias finally concludes the dialogue, "it is not too late" ("utinam non sero"; 49.19–20).

From this perception of Europe, in which the Christian religion takes a prime position and peace has been established by special support of the German imperial power located at the heart of Europe, it is only a small step to the concept of Europe as a universal monarchy.[169]

4.2   *Imperial Authority: Europe as a* Monarchia Universalis

The early modern concept of Europe as a universal monarchy envisioned the unification of the different national and dynastic powers and their international relations under the direction of one single dynastic power. This power would then take on the role of an *arbiter* (arbitrator) in all political affairs of

---

169   An exemplary Latin text combining both aspects to form a comprehensive notion of Europe as a universal monarchy that is, in essence, a Christian empire, is Juan Ginés de Sepúlveda's *Ad Carolum V ut bellum suscipiat in Turcas cohortatio* (1529). In it, the Spanish historiographer encourages Charles V to go on a campaign of conquest against the Turks and consequently set up a European empire, to which the newly subdued Turkish lands are added. A modern edition of the text is available in *Obras Completas: Vol. VII*, ed. by J.M. Rodríguez Peregrina (Pozoblanco: Ayuntamiento de Pozoblanco, 2003), pp. 328–45.

the continent and preserve peace and prosperity in all nations.[170] The idea of the universal monarchy had inspired continual theoretical curiosity since the Middle Ages. One of the most influential texts in this respect was Dante's treatise *De Monarchia* (On Monarchy; conceived around 1310). Discussing the controversial relationship between secular and religious authority, Dante suggested the establishment of a federation of states in Europe, dictated by a court of arbitration with the emperor as its chairman.[171] The theoretical approaches were to continue until the end of the seventeenth century. The dissertation entitled *De monarchia universali* (On the Universal Monarchy) by the German Saxon nobleman Gottlob Christian von Dölau (life data unknown), published in Leipzig in 1681, ranks among the later examples of theoretical analysis.[172] It contains an outline of the history of the universal monarchy from its ancient roots down to the present, as well as of its characteristics and distinctions from tyranny.

Yet by the time Dölau was writing, the idea of establishing a universal monarchy in Europe was already obsolete. This concept had flourished particularly in the sixteenth century, when the universal monarchy had actually seemed enforceable in a reasonable way, due to the rising power of the Habsburg dynasty. After all, Charles v (1500–1558) and his brother Ferdinand I (1503–1564) ruled over a multiethnic territory spanning from Spain, north-eastern Italy, and Istria in the south to the Netherlands, Germany, Austria, Bohemia, Poland, Ukraine, and Hungary in the north and east of Europe. Given this large sphere of influence, the dynasty expressed its hegemonic claim over the continent in various ways and turned into the "major player in Europe's international affairs".[173] There was hardly any conflict in which the Habsburgs were

---

170   The most relevant study of the early modern universal monarchy is still Franz Bosbach, *Monarchia universalis: Ein politischer Leitbegriff der frühen Neuzeit*, Schriftenreihe der Historischen Kommission bei der Bayerischen Akademie der Wissenschaften, 32 (Göttingen: Vandenhoeck & Ruprecht, 1988). On the definition and aim of the term 'universal monarchy', see also Malettke, p. 76.

171   For Dante, see the edition of Maurizio Pizzica quoted earlier, and Lützeler, p. 199; on the mediaeval discourse in general, see Bosbach, pp. 23–40, and Alexander Lee, *Humanism and Empire: The Imperial Ideal in Fourteenth-Century Italy* (Oxford: Oxford University Press, 2018).

172   Gottlob Christian von Dölau, *De monarchia universali, quae Europae imminere dicitur* (Leipzig: Coler, 1681).

173   Paula Sutter Fichtner, *The Habsburg Monarchy, 1490–1848: Attributes of Empire* (New York: Palgrave, 2003), p. xviii. Cf. also Malcolm, p. 68: "[...] the territories of the Habsburgs and the Holy Roman Empire, as united under the rule of Charles v and his brother, were themselves the closest thing that anyone had seen to a pan-European empire since the Roman period. And this empire was hugely augmented by Spanish possessions in the New World." For further information and references on the universal principles of Habsburg

not involved in some way or another; there was hardly any political decision taken on the continent without their consent. In this atmosphere, tendencies of pluralisation and territorialisation naturally had little chance of surviving, which is why we are confronted today with a large number of contemporary texts expressing universal views of Europe.

By the first half of the seventeenth century, the idea of the universal monarchy was more or less deemed a failure. The conflicts leading to and nurturing the Thirty Years' War had proved all too clearly that neither a political nor a religious unity could be a feasible solution to Europe's confessional and territorial struggles. Many contemporaries even insisted that the outbreak of the Thirty Years' War was precisely the result of the Habsburg struggle for universal power.[174] However, as the second biggest Christian power after the German Empire, the French Kingdom, which had occasionally tried to counteract the Habsburgs' universal policies, accurately observed the slow disintegration of German-Austrian authority on the continent after the Westphalian Peace and tried to install the idea of a universal monarchy again despite the universal notion having been doomed.[175] Its success would be confined to the establishment of the French *monarchie absolue*, and it seems to have had little impact on Neo-Latin literature. One of the few examples encountered so far is Johann Caspar Khun's oration *Panegyricus Ludovico XIV. Galliarum et Navarrae regi ob restitutam in Europa pacem* (Praise of Louis xiv, King of France and Navarre, Concerning the Restitution of Peace in Europe), held on 6 February 1698 at the University of Strasbourg.[176] The oration consists almost entirely of an encomium on the French monarchy and an encomiastic explanation of why Louis xiv is destined to become the leader of a European kingdom.

With regard to the discourse of Europe, early modern Latin notions of the universal monarchy most frequently presented themselves in the form of personification. The reasons for personifying the continent were twofold: First of all, during the Renaissance "the figuring of imagined reality was overwhelmingly visual"[177] compared to later centuries. Media such as art, architecture,

---

rule, see Christoph Kampmann, 'Universalismus und Staatenvielfalt: Zur europäischen Identität in der Frühen Neuzeit', in *Europa – aber was ist es? Aspekte seiner Identität in interdisziplinärer Sicht*, ed. by Jörg A. Schlumberger and Peter Segl, Bayreuther historische Kolloquien, 8 (Cologne: Böhlau), pp. 45–76.

174   Malettke, p. 74; Asbach, pp. 120–21; Malcolm, p. 70.

175   Malettke, 68.

176   Johann Caspar Khun, *Panegyricus Ludovico XIV. Galliarum et Navarrae regi ob restitutam in Europa pacem* (Strasbourg: Staedel, 1698).

177   Anderson, p. 23. Interesting insights into how allegorical images of Europe influenced the early modern continental understanding from the sixteenth century onwards can be gained from Sabine Poeschel, *Studien zur Ikonographie der Erdteile in der Kunst des*

cartography, and literature clearly profited from this tendency. Secondly, the connection between the personification of Europe and the political construct of the universal monarchy was quite obvious considering that the universal monarchy – in a stronger way than other, more pluralised concepts of Europe – envisaged a 'corporate' structure of the continent as one entity (which etymologically even hints at the Latin word *corpus* for 'body'). The body metaphor implied the cooperation of all its parts to a degree that the imperial politics of unity must have found appealing.

The metaphorical equation of an entire community with a symbolic body, however, is not something uniquely early modern. While in the Christian tradition the *ecclesia*, the community of believers, was compared to the body of Christ with all its limbs working together in functional inseparability (I Corinthians 12. 12–31), a political interpretation had been submitted already in Roman literature:[178] In the second book of Livy's monumental *Ab urbe condita* (History of Rome; first century BCE), the former consul of the Roman Republic, Agrippa Menenius Lanatus (fifth century BCE), appears and tells the story of the revolt of the limbs against the stomach in the face of the plebs protesting against the patricians (2.32.8–12). The tale is meant to signify the indispensable collaboration of all parts of the body to ensure its smooth operation and, indeed, its survival. With the limbs standing for the rebellious plebs and the stomach for the patricians, Menenius prompts all members of the Republic (the body) to stand together and act according to their respective functions.

The early modern application of the body metaphor in the context of the Latin Europe discourse usually involved female personifications. The reasons for this choice of gender have been outlined sufficiently in previous studies.[179]

16.–18. *Jahrhunderts* (Munich: Scaneg, 1985); Wintle, *Image of Europe*; Marion Romberg, *Die Welt im Dienst des Glaubens: Erdteilallegorien in Dorfkirchen auf dem Gebiet des Fürstbistums Augsburg im 18. Jahrhundert* (Stuttgart: Steiner, 2017).

178   On the Christian metaphor, see Detering, p. 2016; Livy's tale is expounded as a precursor of early modern ideas of Europe in Elke A. Werner, 'Anthropomorphic Maps: On the Aesthetic Form and Political Function of Body Metaphors in the Early Modern Europe Discourse', in *The Anthropomorphic Lens: Anthropomorphism, Microcosmism and Analogy in Early Modern Thought and Visual Arts*, ed. by Walter S. Melion, Bret Rothstein, and Michel Weemans, Intersections, 34 (Leiden: Brill, 2015), pp. 251–72 (p. 263). For a comprehensive view of the political body metaphor, see Albrecht Koschorke and others, *Der fiktive Staat: Konstruktionen des politischen Körpers in der Geschichte Europas* (Frankfurt a.M.: Fischer, 2007), pp. 15–55. For an edition of Livy, see *Ab urbe condita: Libri I–V*, ed. by Robert Maxwell Ogilvie (Oxford: Oxford University Press, 1974).

179   See particularly Wolfgang Schmale, 'Europa – die weibliche Form', *L'Homme: Zeitschrift für feministische Geschichtswissenschaft*, 11 (2000), 211–33; Claudia Bruns, 'Geschlecht – Körper – Karte: Anthropomorphe Europakarten im Übergang zur Frühen Neuzeit', *Zeitsprünge*, 21 (2017), 9–44.

One main incentive certainly was the fact that already in Antiquity, cities and political entities had been represented by female figures (e.g. Roma as a personification of the city of Rome). In addition to this, the 'female' symbolised purity, mercy, and protection. Especially in the patriarchal society of the early modern centuries, during which continents were discovered by male conquerors and written about by male intellectuals, it denoted an 'object' desired and seized by male force. Intertwined with the concept of Europe as a universal monarchy, two iconographic types of Europe personified developed in the sixteenth century, which had a lasting general influence on the allegorical depiction of the four known continents until around 1700.[180] They were set in direct opposition to each other: the one being the so-called *Europa regina* or *Europa triumphans* ("Queen Europe" / "Europe triumphant"), the other one the so-called *Europa lamentans* or *Europa deplorans* ("Europe lamenting" / "Europe deploring").[181] While the former expressed notions of political authority and conformity, the latter made the suffering of Europe, originating from its many intra-continental wars and conflicts, physically tangible.

The personification of Europe was not an original creation by Neo-Latin poets and writers. They only appropriated it and eventually spread it to the vernaculars after the Tyrolean cartographer Johannes Putsch (1516–1542) had invented the prototype of a *Europa regina* on a map dedicated to the later emperor Ferdinand I of Austria in 1534.[182] It depicts Europe in the shape of a woman, whose head covers the Iberian Peninsula, whose chest and heart centre on the Habsburg realms of Austria, Hungary, Bohemia, and the German Empire, whose right arm, holding the imperial orb, stretches along Italy, whose left arm runs along Denmark, touching Britain with the royal scepter, and whose body and dress pour out over central and eastern Europe down to Greece, Bulgaria, the Baltic region, and Russia. Along with the dedication to Ferdinand, the scepter and orb reflect Putsch's idea of Europe very well: a continent pacified and ruled by the House of Habsburg.

---

180   After 1700, allegorical renderings of Europe disappeared. They would only emerge again in caricature in the nineteenth and twentieth centuries, as is shown by Priska Jones, *Europa in der Karikatur: Deutsche und britische Darstellungen im 20. Jahrhundert* (Frankfurt a.M.: Campus, 2009).

181   Werner, p. 251; Detering, p. 209.

182   For a long time, the exemplar preserved in the archive of the *Tiroler Landesmuseum Ferdinandeum* in Innsbruck (sign.: K v/84), dating back to 1537, was believed to be the only extant specimen. It was only in 2019 that a woodcut from 1534 (printed in Augsburg by Jost Denecker) was sensationally rediscovered in the Lower Austrian city museum of Retz. Cf. Detering and Pulina, pp. 17–18.

Putsch's map attracted great attention among Europe's learned community and soon became widely known. The Swiss bibliographer Conrad Gessner (1516–1565), for instance, cited it as "the noble representation of all of Europe in the form of a woman" ("Europae totius luculentam descriptionem effinxit ad formam virginis"; p. 393v).[183] The French polymath Guillaume Postel, whose *De cosmographia disciplina* was mentioned earlier, described it in greater detail in chapter four and added as a concluding remark that the form of depiction Putsch had chosen was "by no means a meaningless invention" ("non omnino inepta inventione"; p. 29). Putsch's map was even reprinted and refined by various cartographers until the end of the sixteenth century, most influentially in the 1588 edition of Sebastian Münster's *Cosmographia* (Cosmography) and in the 1592 edition of Heinrich Bünting's *Itinerarium sacrae scripturae* (Travel Itinerary following the Holy Bible).[184] Also seemingly inspired by Putsch and his followers were the personifications designed by Neo-Latin authors.

Before we take a concrete look at some of them, the piercing ideological symbolism of *Europa* personified must be highlighted. Even though it was common until the seventeenth and eighteenth centuries to dismiss the integration of national borders into maps, the idea of oneness implied by the depiction of a single body was far greater than in any of the 'scientific' European maps of the time – simply due to the fact that the body would become unsightly if dismembered. In contrast to maps, texts inevitably had to forego the visual element. However, the symbolic degree to which inclusion and imperialist expansion were played out by Neo-Latin authors in impersonating the greatest universal empire imaginable was even higher. Waiving exact indications as to which borders Europe was confined to needs to be taken as a sign of absolute inclusivity. It might not have made sense on a political level to ignore the geographical and territorial details of an empire, yet on a symbolic level it was certainly meaningful to imagine an empire so vast, consistent, and uniform that it almost seemed to expand to infinity.[185] The fact that expansion represented a core criterion of European monarchism only adds to this symbolic leaning. Furthermore, in the

---

183 Conrad Gessner, *Bibliotheca universalis sive catalogus omnium scriptorum locupletissimus* (Zurich: Froschauer, 1545).

184 Usually, the political context of universal Habsburg imperialism remained the same. For more information on the maps mentioned and for an overview of further cartographic examples of the *Europa regina*, see Michael Wintle, 'Renaissance Maps and the Construction of the Idea of Europe', *Journal of Historical Geography*, 25 (1999), 137–65 (pp. 151–56); Peter Meurer, '*Europa Regina*: 16th Century Maps of Europe in the Form of a Queen', *Belgeo*, 3–4 (2008), 355–70 <https://doi.org/10.4000/belgeo.7711>; Wintle, *Image of Europe*, pp. 247–52.

185 Walser-Bürgler, '*Europa exultans*', p. 25.

case of both cartographic and literary personifications of Europe, the goal was never to render a 'correct' image of Europe, but to convince the audience of a certain idea of Europe by providing interpretations of the facts.[186]

The first Latin persona of Europe was likewise brought to life by Putsch. Attached to his woodcut from 1534 is a poem consisting of forty-one hexameter verses, presenting a lamenting monologue uttered by Queen Europa. Before the rediscovery of the woodcut, the poem had been thought to be a part of Putsch's lost epic poem *Danubius* (The Danube), especially since the lamenting poem was arbitrarily included in a Swiss poetry collection of contemporary authors in 1544 under the title *Europa lamentans: Lamentatio Europae ad Carolum V. Caesarem et Ferdinandum Romanorum regem fratres* (Europe Lamenting: The Lament of Europe Addressed to the Brothers Charles v, Roman Emperor, and Ferdinand, Roman King).[187] The 'plot' of Putsch's poem is quickly recounted: queen Europa complains about the wars that have shaken her since ancient times. The intra-European conflicts are referred to with utmost disgust by her, as they not only endanger her wellbeing, but also facilitate invasion by external enemies such as the Ottomans. In her distress, Europa turns to Charles and his brother Ferdinand for help.

Putsch's universal idea of Europe is particularly evident in the role he attributes to the German Empire, ruled by Charles v, as the most powerful among the European forces (v. 24–25): "Sola potens armis, medio Germania constans / corpore, firmatas posuit sibi fortius arces." – "Only Germany, strong in arms and steadfast in the middle of my body, has bravely built strong fortresses." Moreover, Europa holds on to the House of Habsburg as her greatest guardian by denoting her relationship to Charles v and Ferdinand i as that of a "faithful marriage" ("fidi thalami"; v. 26), despite being "permanently pursued and sold to unrighteous suitors" ("semper iniquis / poscor venundorque procis"; v. 27–28).[188] Charles and Ferdinand, those "brightest stars in the world" ("clar-

---

186 Cf. Poeschel, p. 70, and Wintle, 'Renaissance Maps', p. 199, on the realities of cartographic and allegorical content in early modern representations of Europe.

187 Johannes Putsch, *Europa lamentans*, in *Poematia aliquot insignia illustrium poetarum recentiorum*, ed. by Anon. (Basel: Winter, 1544), p. 5v–6r. Speculations about the fragmentary epic nature of Putsch's poem are expressed in Wolfgang Kofler and Martin Korenjak, 'Dichtung', in *Tyrolis Latina: Geschichte der lateinischen Literatur in Tirol. Bd. 1: Von den Anfängen bis zur Gründung der Universität Innsbruck*, ed. by Martin Korenjak and others (Vienna: Böhlau, 2012), pp. 225–65 (pp. 250 and 252). The poem was edited and translated into German by Karl Jax, 'Johannes Putschius: Ein Tiroler Heimatdichter (1516–1542)', *Veröffentlichungen des Museums Ferdinandeum*, 18 (1938), 334–47. The Latin text was reprinted together with an English translation in Meurer, pp. 365–66, and Detering and Pulina, pp. 33–34 (which will be used in the following quotations).

188 In this quotation, the translation of Detering and Pulina has been slightly changed.

issima mundi / sydera"; v. 30–31) will bring, Europa is convinced, an "eternal peace" to her "shattered inhabitants" (v. 39–40). The implied marriage between the Habsburgs and Europa as well as Europa's uninterrupted belief in Charles' and Ferdinand's power to save her from internal and external strife serve as clear indications of Putsch propagating Europe as a universal monarchy under Habsburg rule.

As previously mentioned, the Habsburg dynasty represented by Charles v and Ferdinand I remained the predominant category of reference when it came to advertising Europe as a universal monarchy in the sixteenth century.[189] In an emphatic attempt to both imitate and surpass Putsch's lament of a disunited and thus endangered Europe, the Spanish doctor Andrés Laguna (1499–1559) stepped up in 1543 and published what would become probably the most forceful literary plea for European unification of all times: his oration *Europa heautentimorumene* (Europe, the Self-Tormentor).[190] This text is as dark as the description of Europe's demise could be. And although there is some ray of hope shimmering through the last pages, Laguna's lament of Europa could easily be ranked among the apocalyptic-prophetic writings emerging in the sixteenth century as a reaction to the Ottoman threat, as well as it shows support of the universal monarchy.[191]

The oration features two protagonists interacting with each other – one being Laguna himself, who takes the role of the doctor, the other being the personification of Europe (Europa), who appears as a sick, wounded, and old hag close to death. Nothing about her appearance reflects the fact that she has once been a queen beautiful and young. The personification of Europe in that respect turns into the projection of the state of the continent. Similar to

---

189   I do not share the opinion expressed by Nicolas Detering and Dennis Pulina that the Frenchman Hubert de Suzanne devised a reworking of Putsch's poem by means of his own *Lamentatio Europae* (1538) addressed to the French King Francis I (see Detering and Pulina, 'Rivalry of Lament'; the text is edited and translated on pp. 34–36). In my opinion, Suzanne only edited Putsch's poem so that the Dominican Lambert Campester could incorporate it in his *Oratio laudatoria* dedicated to Francis I (1538), which is why Suzanne merely refers to himself as the 'editor' at the end of the poem ("Hubertus Sussaneus / recognoscebat" – "edited by Hubert de Suzanne"; v. 44–45).

190   The text is available in a Latin-Spanish edition: Andrés Laguna, *Europa heautentimorumene, es decir, que míseramente a sí misma se atormenta y lamenta su propia desgracia*, ed. by Miguel Ángel González Manjarrés (Valladolid: Junta de Castilla y León, 2001). Concise overviews of the text and context can be obtained from the substantial introduction in Manjarrés' edition (pp. 27–115); D. José García, 'La *Europa* de Andrés Laguna', *Anales de la Real Academia de Doctores de España*, 16 (2012) 145–53; and Ronny Kaiser, '*Tota caduca et dehiscens*'.

191   Cf. Malcolm, p. 71.

Putsch's version, yet in a more graphic way, Europa as a female personification is not eroticised. On the contrary, she makes an appalling feverish sight. For Laguna personally it must indeed have been an obvious decision to depict Europe like this: not only was he a doctor by profession, constantly exposed to disease, but he also liked to compare the human body to political communities in his medical writings, following the tradition of Livy.[192]

Laguna was a true cosmopolitan who travelled the continent widely and even lived and worked in different European nations. As a result of this lifestyle, he inevitably came into contact with the confessional and political conflicts sweeping Europe.[193] The immediate European background to Laguna's oration was defined by the following political events: the various clashes between Charles v and Francis i of France, particularly in the question of the rule over the duchy of Burgundy and the Italian city-states; the foundation of the Holy League and the truce between Charles and Francis in 1538 (which was dissolved already in 1542 by the French king); Charles' failed intervention at the Diet of Ratisbon in 1541, leaving the German Protestants and Catholics in utter discord; and the incessant Ottoman conquests in the east and southeastern parts of Europe.[194] However, Laguna was even personally affected, in a way, by the increasingly hostile atmosphere across the continent. After having worked as a surgeon at the imperial court in Toledo between 1536 and 1539 and settling in Ghent (where the emperor often resided) and Metz, he came to appreciate the international policies of Charles v. In order to escape the confessional confrontations in Metz – which largely rejected Charles' Catholic stance – Laguna took leave of his profession in Metz in the autumn of 1542 and went to Cologne, accepting the invitation from his friend Adolf Eichholtz

---

192   For references on the political metaphors in Laguna's medical writings, see Antonis A. Kousoulis, Marianna Karamanou, and George Androutsos, 'Andrés Laguna: A Great Medical Humanist (1499–1559)', *História da Medicina*, 24 (2011), 671–74 (pp. 672–73). The association of bodily diseases and politics in early modern literature is more generally expounded in Margaret Healy, *Fictions of Disease in Early Modern England: Bodies, Plagues and Politics* (Basingstoke: Palgrave, 2001).

193   Laguna's biography is among the best-transmitted biographies of Spanish humanism. There are many works elucidating his life. The most comprehensive study – containing references for further reading – is Miguel Ángel González Manjarrés, *Andrés Laguna y el humanismo medico: Estudio filológico* (Salamanca: Junta de Castilla y León, 2000), pp. 37–73.

194   See collectively Francisco Calero, 'Dos grandes europeístas españoles del siglo XVI: Luis Vives y Andrés Laguna', *Revista de la Asociación Española de Semiótica*, 8 (1999), 19–36 (pp. 23–25); José María Pérez Fernández, 'Translation and the Early Modern Idea of Europe', *Translation and Literature*, 21 (2012), 299–318 (pp. 303–304); García, p. 148; Werner, p. 264.

(*c.* 1490–1563), at the time rector of the University of Cologne. During the couple of months spent in Cologne, Laguna's declared aim was to find himself a new position within the Catholic and imperial circles. By means of writing and using every opportunity for networking, he tried to recommend himself to Charles v and his brother Ferdinand I.[195]

It is in the light of these circumstances that Laguna's oration must be understood. Supported by his friend Eichholtz, he devised *Europa heautentimorumene* to be delivered on 22 January 1543 in the main hall of the University of Cologne in front of a scholarly and politically influential audience.[196] Cologne was indeed the ideal place for conveying a pan-European peace mission statement. The city was "a microcosm of the European public sphere",[197] though with strong irenic tendencies, while the university constituted "a bastion of imperial policy and one of its ideological powerhouses". Laguna's political programme of unification and cohesion lay open to everyone at the latest when he addressed his audience with the words "uiri citra controuersiam doctissimi" ("learned men devoid of all controversy"; p. 184). As the oration shows, he was passionately driven by the vision of a continent united by religious and political measures coming from Charles v.

The scenery of the oration is harrowing. This pertains to both the 'stage' setting and the plot setting. As the frontispiece of the printed oration explains, the university hall "was decorated with black torches and other items typical of funeral ceremonies" ("adhibitis tum nigris facibus tum aliis caeremoniis funebribus"; p. 120). Accordingly, the oration itself is advertised as a "declamatio lugubris" (p. 120), a "funerary oration". Potentially, this staging could be explained by the current carnival season in Cologne, which usually involved the entire city and all its institutions. The fact that Laguna's deliberative speech on a serious political issue turns into an acting performance set in a funerary situation in which both 'protagonists', the doctor and Europa, appear in disguise and react alternately as if interacting in a dialogue, matches the carnivalesque

---

195   González Manjarrés, p. 55.

196   Neither the emperor nor his brother seems to have been present (at least, there is no indication of it), yet we know from various sources that members of the Habsburg court, German princes and noblemen, as well as some leading members of the imperial city of Cologne, attended Laguna's lecture (e.g. Hermann of Wied, Eberhard Billick, Henry of Stolberg, and George of Brunswick). For more information on the audience, see Marcel Bataillon, 'Sur l'humanisme du Docteur Laguna: deux petits livres latins de 1543', *Romance Philology*, 17 (1963), 207–34; Calero, p. 32; and González Manjarrés (ed.), *Europa heautentimorumene*, p. 35.

197   Pérez Fernández, p. 308.

approach as well.[198] In terms of the plot setting, a depressing atmosphere is created at the beginning of the speech. Laguna in his role as a doctor recounts how one day he happened to bump into an old repugnant woman (p. 134):

> [...] occurrit mihi mulier quaedam (iudicio meo) multo omnium miser-
> rima, [...] tota lachrymabunda, tristis, pallens, trunca et mutila membris,
> oculis concauis ac ueluti in foueas reconditis, admodumque macilenta
> et squalida qualis uetulae saepe solent ad me uenire laborantes hectica
> febri.

> [...] I ran into a certain woman who (in my opinion) was by far the most
> miserable of all humans, [...] fully reduced to tears, embittered, pale,
> maimed and with mutilated limbs, with eyes empty and sunken, severely
> emaciated, and filthy in the manner of the hags who often come to me
> when suffering from attacks of fever.

Leaning her weak body on a walking stick, the hag addressed the doctor in a "rough voice" ("uoce difficili et rauca"; p. 136). The doctor, however, did not recognise this "uiuum cadauer" ("living corpse"; p. 136–38), until she revealed her identity to him: "Ego sum [...] Europa, quam ipse, meo dum in uigore florescerem, es persaepe admiratus" ("It is me, [...] Europa, whom you have admired so often when I still was full of life and in bloom"; p. 136). As if Europa's suffering was not already shocking enough, she suddenly fainted, and the doctor took great pains over revitalising her (p. 138). In the following doctor-patient-consultation, Europa gave an account of her suffering and its causes. In a distressing parable, she admitted that it was her own 'children', the European princes fighting each other for trivial reasons, who had put her into the state she found herself in (p. 144):

> O me matrem infelicissimam [...] quae prolem plus quam uiperinam
> ediderim [...]. Concepi qui mea laniarent uiscera, genui qui me conter-
> erent, lactaui qui me diriperent, foui qui meum haurirent sanguinem,
> promoui qui me deiicerent, accenderent, labefactarent.

> Oh, what an utterly unfortunate mother I am, [...] having given birth to
> more than just serpent offspring [...]. I have borne those who ripped out
> my intestines; I have delivered those who trampled me underfoot; I have

---

198   The carnivalesque context of Laguna's oration, along with its performative features, is
      outlined in Walser-Bürgler, 'Staging Oratory', pp. 103–106.

breastfed those who tore me apart; I have cared for those who sucked my blood; I have raised those who threw me to the ground, set me on fire, wrecked me.

In a spirited plea, Europa eventually leaves the narrative frame from the past and in the present turns to her audience, begging the European princes to commiserate with her and have mercy on her. For only if they settled their disputes and came together in harmony would her former vigour be regained (pp. 186–88). The vocabulary employed by Laguna in this respect resembles many of the expressions encountered already in the early modern peace discourse: the European leaders of all continental territories, kingdoms, islands, and provinces "should come together in eternal friendship and union and fight only for mutual benefits" ("in perennem amicitiam atque unionem coeuntes solumque mutuis beneficiis certantes"; p. 188).[199] Similar to Vives' exploitation of the dialogue as a genre, Laguna's implementation of the pseudo-dialogic interaction between the two protagonists provides an indication of how European-wide consensus is to be gained, namely by political dialogue.[200] Europa's appeal culminates in her invocation of Charles as the ultimate saviour of the continent. Under his guidance, Europa is sure to be pacified and become whole again. His coordination of the different European powers will guarantee peace and prosperity (p. 156):

> Cuius implorabo suppetias? Cuius fidei me commendabo? Cui me tandem supplex concredam? An diuo Carolo Caesari? [...] ille quippe animo infracto me prae imbecillitate corruentem sustinet; ille meis semper malis medetur; ille mihi semper opitulatur; ille meas curas sibi facit communes; ille oculos gerens in occipicio sedulo mea membra circumspicit, nullum non mouens lapidem, ut sit mihi prospectum optime. Qui quidem ni intercessisset, actum fuisset iampridem de rebus meis.

> Whose help am I going to seek? Whose support am I going to confide in? To whom am I going to address myself in seeking shelter? Perhaps the divine emperor Charles? [...] For he sustains me tirelessly when I collapse due to weakness; he always remedies my suffering; he always assists me in times of need; he turns my sorrows into our common ones; he, whose

---

199   The advantages of collaboration are also illustrated at the end of the oration, where Laguna inserts the parable of the two brothers caught up in a lawsuit, "only to realize [...] that family ties are the best means to bring individual and collective success" (Walser-Bürgler, 'Staging Oratory', p. 100).

200   Walser-Bürgler, 'Staging Oratory', p. 109.

back of the head is endowed with eyes, takes care of all my limbs and leaves no stone unturned to give me a competitive edge. Surely, if he had not intervened, I would have been done for long ago.

Europa's reference to "all her limbs" is of course an obvious hint at the members of the European community in the proper sense of the political body metaphor. A list of the past supporters of Charles in his struggle for continental peace (including, for instance, his brother Ferdinand of Austria, Pope Paul III, King John III of Portugal; King Henry VIII of England; the Archbishops of Cologne and Trier; various foreign diplomats and ministers from Protestant and Catholic territories such as Thomas Wyatt, Nicolas Perrenot de Granvelle, and Louis of Praet; pp. 166–74) leaves the audience with a hopeful feeling that under Charles the European integration will finally succeed.

History tells us that Laguna's hope remained a mere illusion. The unresolved disputes among the European community therefore obliged an anonymous Englishman to devise the two-volume *Querimonia Europae* (Europe's Complaint) in 1625, addressed to the "invincible emperor, the most powerful kings, and the major princes [...] of the Christian world" ("inuictissime Caesar, potentissimi Reges, clarissimique Principes [...] orbis Christiani"; p. 1).[201] It draws heavily on Laguna's personification of Europe, as the 'English' Europa stresses innumerable times the terror and frustration she feels as the victim of the continental power struggles tearing her apart. Furthermore, she appears as a mother figure as well, only this time she particularly fears being ripped apart from the inside by her two unborn sons, one representing the German Protestants, the other the German Catholics (p. 5):

> Sed nihil me grauius angit, quam quod duo populi ambo Europaei, ambo Christiani, bis vterini, semel ortu, iterum spiritu, in opprobrium deitatis Christi sui in meo rursum vtero colluctentur [...].

> Yet nothing frightens me more than the fact that the two European people, both Christian, both coming from the same mother in terms of origins as well as in spirit, wrestle with each other, abusing Christ himself within my womb [...].

The anonymous text's originality resides in two features: First, it constitutes a relatively late example of a Latin personification of Europe. After the reign of the Emperor Ferdinand I, Latin personifications of Europe slowly lost their

---

201   Anon., *Querimonia Europae, divisa in libros duos* (London: Stansby, 1625).

popularity as the trust in the Habsburgs' pacifying abilities diminished in the face of the inner-dynastic conflicts between Ferdinand and his sons on the one hand, and the unresolved confessional issues in the Empire and the Turkish advance on the other. Second, the anonymous author deviates from the trodden sixteenth-century paths by concentrating neither on the unifying power of the House of Habsburg nor on that of the French Kingdom as the second most powerful authority on the continent. Instead, his focus is on the newly enthroned King Charles I of England (1600–1649), to whom he assigns the task of intervening in the German confessional struggles and repelling the Ottoman danger in order to prevent a European civil war (e.g. pp. 17–18; 138).[202]

As innovative as the lamenting versions of Putsch, Laguna, and the anonymous English author might have been in terms of the format of personifying an entire continent, they all had one common literary ancestor: Erasmus' *Querela pacis* (The Complaint of Peace, 1516).[203] As suggested by the title, this text is a single declamatory monologue delivered by the personification of Peace, bemoaning the confessional and military conflicts going on in Europe. Like the personified Europa, Peace is deeply frustrated, desperate, and angry with the European princes and tells them off for having let her down. Even though lady Peace does not stand for Europe itself wishing to become a universal monarchy headed by Charles V, she does at least advertise continental solidarity with reference to Charles' irenic powers (the text is dedicated to the emperor). As is typical of the early modern discourse on European peace, it "has hardly ever tried to promote European identity as a totalizing concept",[204] yet it reminded Europeans of their shared responsibility in "protecting [the continent] against destructive forces from within and without". Many humanists – among them Erasmus – were driven by high hopes that Emperor Charles V would be the one to settle all disputes and turn Europe into a peaceful, coherent community.[205]

Erasmus' *Querela pacis* does not constitute a major political blueprint, but it involves strong criticism of human behaviour in Europe; the people accused in the monologue are clearly the Europeans (p. 398):[206]

---

202 Cf. Detering, pp. 211–12.

203 Erasmus of Rotterdam, *Querela pacis undique gentium ejectae profligataque*, in *Ausgewählte Schriften, lateinisch und deutsch: Bd. 5*, ed. by Gertraud Christian, 2nd edn (Darmstadt: Wissenschaftliche Buchgesellschaft, 1995), pp. 359–451.

204 Lützeler, p. 198.

205 Detering and Pulina, p. 16. Erasmus' complaint had a realistic context, as he devised the text as a preparation for an international peace congress to be held in Cambrai in 1517 (which ultimately never took place).

206 Erasmus even concretely cites some of the warring parties in Europe, such as France, Italy, Spain, Hungary, Germany, Bohemia, and England (cf. pp. 403 and 409).

Repetamus decem ab hinc annis acta, ubi non gentium crudelissime pug-
natum est terra marique? Quae regio non Christiano sanguine comma-
duit? Quod flumen, quod mare, non humano cruore tinctum est?

Let us picture in our mind the past ten years. Where among the nations
was there not fighting with utmost cruelty by sea and land? What region
was not dripping with Christian blood? What river, what sea was not
stained with human bloodshed?

Despairingly, lady Peace expounds that peace is not to be found anywhere in
Europe, neither at court, nor in the cities, nor at the universities, nor in monastic communities and the church, nor in families, nor even in individual souls
(pp. 371–79). People fight people all the time, everywhere, and for multiple
reasons, despite the fact that nature has taught mankind concord. Lions do
not fight lions, boars do not turn against their fellow boars, lynxes spare other
lynxes, and snakes remain peaceful towards other snakes (p. 365). Alliance is in
the nature of all beings – also of human beings. Humans would have to perish
if they could not rely on alliances, that is, help from other states in times of
political crisis, help from one's own parents in growing up, help from midwives
in being born, and so on (p. 368). In a pointed manner, lady Peace closes her
speech with praise of concord as the highest virtue, whose value would even
be increased when enjoyed in company, and a concluding appeal to all princes
and authorities to stand together as one (pp. 443–451).

A less despairing – and in fact quite cheerful – personification of Europe
is encountered in the pastoral poem *Europa Eidyllion* (Europe, an Idyll).
This poem of 111 verses was devised by the German-Bohemian writer Johann
Lauterbach (1531–1593) in 1558 on the occasion of Ferdinand I's accession
to the imperial throne, succeeding his brother Charles V two years after his
abdication.[207] The poem's scene is set in Ingelfingen, a small town in the north-
east of today's Baden-Württemberg, Germany. The narrator-persona recalls a
beautiful day out in the fields, herding his sheep, when suddenly a crowd of
goddesses and nymphs entered the scene. Among them the narrator recognised Europa, who started to sing a song to which the narrator and Europa's

---

207   Despite the title and the genre, the poem has nothing to do with the pastoral poem *Europa*
       by the Greek poet Moschus (second century BCE), recounting the myth of Europa and
       the bull. A substantial investigation into the context and content of Lauterbach's poem
       (pp. 1–35), along with a critical edition and an English translation (pp. 36–43), is provided
       in Walser-Bürgler, '*Europa exultans*'. The following details concerning the poem and its
       processing of the Europe discourse are entirely taken from this article.

companions listened joyfully. The way that Europa showed up in the beautiful countryside, itself described as a typically bucolic *locus amoenus* (v. 32–41), she constituted a *locus amoenus* herself, outdoing her entire surroundings in terms of beauty and even instilling awe in her fellow goddesses (v. 13–14): "ex auro gemmisque Europa coruscans / Fulgebat, stellas inter ceu fulget Apollo" ("Europa, shimmering in gold and gems, was shining like Apollo among the stars"). Europa's physical integrity and loveliness might have been deliberately created by Lauterbach as an antitype to Putsch's, and especially Laguna's, miserable and sick personifications.

Lauterbach was a humanist par excellence. As a student of Philip Melanchthon in Wittenberg, he was trained in the art of writing elegantly, had been introduced into the erudite circle of contemporary German poets and scholars (among them Petrus Lotichius, Nicodemus Frischlin, and Martin Crusius), and received the privilege of serving the German nobility.[208] In an act of imperial and public recognition, Lauterbach was crowned poet laureate by the newly enthroned emperor Ferdinand I, probably due to his encomiastic efforts in *Europa Eidyllion*. After all, it was not only dedicated to Ferdinand, but the emperor also played a central role in the poem. Consisting largely of Europa's song, it is but a praise of the Habsburg dynasty and its power. Ferdinand clearly was the one on whose shoulders Lauterbach's hope for the eventual enforcement of the European universal monarchy rested after Charles' failure. Ferdinand now ruled over an empire so vast as to be called a 'world empire' according to contemporary standards, having combined dynastic with imperial policies. In addition, he had already supported his brother Charles in many aspects of his imperial reign during the preceding decades (especially in relation to the Ottoman threat and the confessional split, of which Ferdinand seemed to have a more balanced assessment) and was thus sufficiently acquainted with his imperial duties. Last but not least, Ferdinand could not have been considered any less a European than Erasmus or any other contemporary humanist. He had been brought up internationally in Spain, Belgium, and Austria, he spoke at least six languages (including Latin), preached tolerance towards other nations, and was known for his extraordinary amounts of travel across the continent.[209]

---

208   Lauterbach's biography is not very well known due to the lack of relevant sources. The most comprehensive overview of his life can be found in Walser-Bürgler, 'Europa exultans', pp. 5–7.

209   All these aspects making Ferdinand a proper 'European citizen' are expounded in great detail in Alfred Kohler, *Ferdinand I., 1503–1564: Fürst, König und Kaiser* (Munich: Beck, 2003), pp. 17–18; 91–92; 118–122; 130–142; 157; and 211–12.

These marked characteristics all formed the background to Lauterbach's poem. The idea that Europe rejoices at Ferdinand's imperial power finds expression in the poem's 'unofficial' second title, interposed right before the first verse of the poem: *Europa exultans* ("Europa rejoicing"). The song that the personified Europa performs in the bucolic scenery is, in fact, a proper wedding song. Disguised by the name *Eubulus*, which translates as "a good advisor" or "a reliable guardian", Ferdinand is at the centre of Europa's thoughts. Full of hope and joy she speaks of the planned marriage between Ferdinand and her (v. 61: "Ille mihi sponsus" – "He is destined to be my bridegroom"), which would eventually lead her into the *Saturnia regna*, the "Golden Age", in which peace, piety, equality, and prosperity reign (v. 56–101). The symbolic meaning of having Europa and Ferdinand bound by marriage is, of course, unmistakable: the continent needs to coalesce with the emperor in order to turn into paradise; Ferdinand needs to put his sheltering hands around the continent and embrace it. The notion of universal monarchy contained in this image fitted the political procedures of the time. In the Early Modern Period, empires were often "expanded not only by warfare but by sexual politics [...]."[210] The House of Habsburg proved particularly successful over the centuries in enhancing its territorial power by means of marriage. The proverbial motto "Bella gerant alii, tu, felix Austria, nube!" ("Others may wage wars, thou, happy Austria, marry!") was indicative of this dynastic policy.[211]

Lauterbach's claim for the Habsburg universal power pervades the entire poem. The text is practically laden with allusions to Ferdinand's continental mission. This begins with the author's copious use of the adjective *omnis* in all cases and declensions (e.g. v. 62, 77, and 108–109), carried to the extreme in v. 91 where the consequences of the Golden Age are described: "Omnibus ex votis omnis feret omnia tellus." – "The earth will fully supply each and every one with everything as required." Then there is the typographical highlighting of the two 'lovers', Europa and Eubulus, in small capitals throughout the text (v. 13; 22–24; 31; 54; 57; 75; 97; 102; 107). This measure immediately draws attention to the political concept conveyed in the poem and supports it. Given that the personification of Europe together with the concept of Europe as a universal monarchy originally derived from the visual medium of cartography, it is certainly intriguing to find the main message of the poem imparted through visual components. Of special significance regarding Ferdinand's claim to Europe are the many passages in which Europa expresses her political mind.

---

210   Anderson, p. 20.
211   Cf. Schmale and others, pp. 253–54; Anderson, p. 20.

In v. 54 to 59, for example, she styles Ferdinand the ultimate saviour of the continent, who has the reputation, the divine nature, and the power to protect the continent from all evil (internal and external):

> Sed EUBULUS solatia sparget,
> Hic solus rigidos inter caput exeret Austros,
> Hic reddet vires, dabit hic Saturnia regna!
> Inclitus EUBULUS, qui caelo semina ducit,
> Hic nunc immensi decus est memorabile mundi,
> Hic defensor adest, nostras hic protegit arces!

> But EUBULUS will offer comfort, he alone will raise his head among the austere south winds [= the Turkish threat], he will retrieve his power, he will usher in the Saturnian reign! As of now, famous EUBULUS, bearing traces of heavenly origin, is the praised adornment of our vast world, he defends us, he protects our fortresses!

And even if other suitors – i.e. all the other princes trying to make Europe a universal monarchy, particularly France – might try to seduce Europa, she would manage to remain steadfast and loyal to Ferdinand due to his virtue and strength (v. 61–65):

> [...] Ille mihi sponsus, taedas servare iugales
> Intactas poterit Christo ductore per omnes
> Insidias, turpis quas ponit turba procorum,
> Quos iuvat illicitis flagrare furoribus, intra
> Pollutam caeca suadente libidine mentem.

> [...] he is destined to be my bridegroom; with the help of Christ he will manage to preserve our wedding flares unaffected by all traps set in bad faith and on the advice of blind caprice by the disgraceful crowd of suitors, who take pleasure in flaring up with dishonourable rage.

Ferdinand's rightful entitlement to Europe is juxtaposed in this passage with the unrightful and violent attempts coming from the 'suitors' to seize Europa. Yet in her final address to her treasured Eubulus, Europa makes it clear once and for all that she belongs to Ferdinand and Ferdinand alone (v. 100–101): "Ne, quaeso, ne linque tuam ne desere vitam! / Sola tibi servit solique placere laborat!" – "I beg you neither to leave nor to let down your beloved Europa! She is the only one to serve you, and she aims to please you as the only one!"

4.3   *United in Diversity: Europe between Plurality and Balance of Power*

Visions of Europe united under the association of a universal monarchy were shattered in the course of a long series of wars which gripped the continent in its entirety. During the first half of the seventeenth century, the number of state breakdowns and clashes surpassed almost every other period before or after in European history, which is why historians also have come to speak of this period as 'the general crisis'.[212] According to historical records, every year between 1611 and 1669 saw at least one war raging on the continent. Among the bigger ones we particularly remember today the Dutch War of Independence (1568–1648) and the Thirty Years' War (1618–1648), as well as the civil wars in France, Russia, Sweden, Denmark, Scotland, Ireland, Portugal, Naples, Germany, and Austria. And throughout the time these were going on, the joint fight against the Ottomans was not yet over. However, in some ways all these conflicts provided an opportunity for Europe and its leaders, an opportunity to change the old ways of interacting and negotiating with each other.

In the middle of these upheavals on the continent, a new concept of Europe developed, emphasising the continent's pluralistic tendencies and federalist order. Instead of supporting greedy monarchs trying to constantly expand their territory and dominate Europe (and thus destroying it), a balance of power based on cooperative principles was postulated to regulate the international relationships.[213] Reconciliation and harmony among all parts seemed the perfect answer to the loss of authorities which the confessional split and the humanist understanding of the world had brought about. The ultimate goal was to mitigate any hegemonic efforts on the part of any of the big dynastic powers and to render political behaviour on the continent more predictable. Peace, stability, mutual tolerance, and political equilibrium should govern Europe, guaranteeing smaller states also a right to existence.[214] As a discipline of law concerned with the recording and analysis of governmental systems, the *Ius publicum Europaeum* (European public law) played a crucial role in

---

212   For an overview of the numerous disputes, see Geoffrey Parker, 'Crisis and Catastrophe: The Global Crisis of the Seventeenth Century Reconsidered', *American Historical Review*, 113 (2008), 1053–79. In the German Empire alone, the Thirty Years' War led to a demographic loss ranging between 20 and 45 percent (p. 1058).

213   Burke, 'Did Europe Exist', p. 25; Detering, p. 77.

214   Michael Sheehan also put forward the thesis that the concept of the balance of power thrived in the seventeenth century as this century was "dominated by an intellectual fascination with the mechanics of the universe [...]. The laws of planetary motion were published by Kepler in 1619 and by 1687 Newton had developed the laws of gravity. The material for analogy was thus increasingly steady." Michael Sheehan, *The Balance of Power: History and Theory* (London: Routledge, 1996), p. 43. This certainly is an interesting idea that would deserve further examination.

contriving and consolidating the idea of a European balance of power. Its comparative approach established guidelines for international legal relations, on the one hand, and revealed similar patterns of conduct, on the other, as if referring to a bond keeping Europe together.[215]

The concept of a Europe characterised by pluralistic attitudes has continued to have an effect up to the very present. It lingers on in the official motto of the European Union: *in varietate concordia* ("United in Diversity").[216] As a concept of Europe it makes proper sense, since Europe has at no point in time existed as a homogeneous space. The concept's roots, however, can be traced to fifteenth-century Italy. The emergence of the Italian city-states gave rise to equalising policies in inter-state relations, because each city-state took great pains to prevent the other states from gaining predominance over Italy (especially the five great powers Milan, Venice, Naples, Florence, and the Papal States). The practice of balancing powers hence predated its theoretical discussion in the seventeenth century.[217] Probably the first author ever to mention the concept of the balance of power was the Italian jurist Alberico Gentili (1552–1608) in his *De jure libri tres* (Three Books on Law, 1598).[218] Employing a scientific metaphor when describing the power relations between the Italian city-states, he writes (book one, p. 104): "Etiam perseverantia concordia inter elementa sic ab aequa partitione est. Et dum in nullo aliud ab alio vincitur." – "The preservation of unity among the atoms depends on their equal distribution as well as on the fact that in no respect is one outperformed by another." Regarding the discourse of Europe, it is particularly noteworthy that Gentili invokes the idea of a 'union' prevailing between the single city-states despite their political singularity.

---

215   Malettke, p. 79.
216   Dirk Ansorge rightly points out that the motto of the United States of America, *e pluribus unum* ("One from many"), carries a completely different, if not to say a reverse, stress. It goes back to the declaration of independence in 1776, when single states of North America joined together. Dirk Ansorge, 'Europas pluralistische Identität: Eine historische und begriffsgeschichtliche Einführung', in *Pluralistische Identität: Beobachtungen zu Herkunft und Zukunft Europas*, ed. by Dirk Ansorge (Darmstadt: Wissenschaftliche Buchgesellschaft, 2016), pp. 7–23 (p. 7 n. 2).
217   A useful introduction into the history of European balance of power is offered in Heinz Duchhardt, *Balance of Power und Pentarchie, 1700–1785* (Paderborn: Schöningh, 1997), pp. 5–94. According to more recent but controversial opinions, a complex understanding of the balance of power must have already existed in ancient Greece among the individual *poleis* (for more on this, see Sheehan, pp. 25–29). Early modern contemporaries, however, do not seem to have known about this. Sheehan himself calls the balance of power system "a child of the Renaissance" (p. 29).
218   Alberico Gentili, *De jure belli libri tres, nunc primum in lucem editi* (Hanau: Antonius, 1598).

Yet there was one big problem with the concept of the balance of power: even though peace constituted the envisaged goal, it might not necessarily be achieved permanently. For whenever the balance would tip, the European powers would need to intervene to reinstate an equilibrium. As Ludwig Martin Kahle (1712–1775), professor of philosophy at the University of Göttingen, argues in his *Commentatio juris publici de trutina Europae* (Public-law Deliberations on a Balanced Europe, 1744), every state and every power on the continent has the natural right to defend its political position. Hence, if the pendulum swung too far to one side, any war that serves to maintain the balance of power would have to be considered a just war, simply because it is fought for the common good. Whoever infringes the system and wrecks Europe's political balance must inevitably be forced to surrender by force of arms.[219] Yet, paradoxically, this was exactly where the principle of European unity was somehow undermined. Once arms were to be raised, national interests would automatically come into play, even though a war might be fought in the name of continental unity. For the unity of Europe was always in danger when national interests entered the continental political agenda, which is why so many texts propagating a European unity denounced 'nationalism' as damaging. Already Erasmus condemns the emerging nationalist tendencies of his time in his *Querela pacis* by dismissing them as ridiculous (p. 428):

> Et saepe Principum privatum quiddam est, quod orbem ad arma compellit. [...] Anglus hostis est Gallo, ne ob aliud, nisi quod Gallus est. Scoto Britannus infensus est, nec aliam ob rem, nisi quod Scotus est. Germanus cum Franco dissident, Hispanus cum utroque. O pravitatem [...]!

> And often it is a personal affair of the princes that compels the world to take up their arms. [...] The Englishman is the enemy of the Frenchman for no other reason than his being French. The Briton is despised by the Irishman for the simple reason that he is Irish. The German hates the Frenchman, the Spaniard both. O perversity [...]![220]

Following Erasmus' criticism of nationalism, the German diplomat Johann Joachim von Rusdorf (1589–1640) published an elegiac-dramatic poem entitled *Scena Europaea* (The European Stage) in 1628 under the pseudonym

---

219   Ludwig Martin Kahle, *Commentatio juris publici de trutina Europae quae vulgo adpellatur Die Balance von Europa praecipua belli et pacis norma* (Göttingen: Schmid, 1744).
220   The translation slightly deviates in this passage from that in Christian's edition.

Anastasius de Valle, which was republished in extended form in 1631.[221] In the five acts of the piece, five groups of persons successively enter the stage in hierarchical order: first come the emperor and several European kings; second, other princes, electors, cardinals, and personified nations; third, minor princes and influential nobility, city representatives, and confessional groups like the Calvinists and the Jesuits; fourth, the generals; and fifth, powerful diplomats and envoys. Each individual delivers a short speech of five to ten distichs, revealing intriguing insights into the reality of European foreign affairs. The reality conveyed offers a disturbing picture to the reader by showing that Europe's discord is very much based on the individual interests of the nations, empires, and states. All of them seek to preserve their level of power or even enhance their spheres of influence in utter disregard of their neighbours, but no one is ready to take the blame for the disintegration of the continent.[222] The French king Louis XIII (1601–1643), for example, evasively justifies his letting down of Europe by citing domestic matters that need to be cleared up (p. 10):

> Quod patiar veteres perdi, reprehendor, amicos,
>   quod non suppetias auxiliumque feram:
> Europae video, fateor, commune periclum
>   [...].
> At me divertit retinetque domestica cura,
>   et mala transversum me propiora trahunt.

I am being reprimanded for tolerating the loss of old friends and for not providing assistance and support. I admit that I see the common danger to Europe [...]. But the concern for internal conflicts distracts me and keeps me from intervening while closer evils pull me away.

Philip IV of Spain (1605–1665), on the other hand, aims at exploiting the ongoing international and national strifes for his own benefit. In his opinion, the state in which the continent finds itself poses the ideal opportunity to take over the world (pp. 9–10):

---

221 Johann Joachim von Rusdorf, *Scena Europaea, personis suis instructa, praecipuas regum, principum, rempublicarum, virtutes, consilia et actiones, ac totius Europae praesentem et futurum statum repraesentans* (Stralsund: Saxo, 1631). The text has received some attention from Detering, pp. 231–39, and Ulrich Heinen, 'Rubens' Europe and the *Pax Hispanica*', in *Contesting Europe: Comparative Perspectives on Early Modern Discourses on Europe, 1400–1800*, ed. by Nicolas Detering, Clementina Marsico, and Isabella Walser-Bürgler, Intersections, 67 (Leiden: Brill, 2019), pp. 104–45 (pp. 104–106).

222 Detering, p. 231.

Omnia regna ruunt et sunt matura ruinae.
    Quis mihi nunc Regum se opposuisse potest?
[...]
Hic status Europae vires animumque ministrat.
    Quid moror ergo? Potest impedijsse nihil.
Aut nunc aut nunquam dominatum consequar Orbis.
    Audendum est, fortes forsque Deusque iuvant.

All empires collapse and are ready for their ruin. Who among the kings is now able to resist my force? [...] This state of Europe supplies strength and spirit. So why do I hesitate? Nothing can stop me. Either now or never I will seize world domination. I must dare it, for fortune and God favour the brave.

The appearance of personified Europe among other national and state personifications like Venice, Germany, and Bohemia eventually testifies to the continent's bad state. Her desperate concluding verse illustrates the damage done by national missions and the continuous self-interest of the European powers (p. 20): "Sed me [...] solvere nemo potest." – "Yet no one can deliver [...] me." Europa clearly has abandoned any dreams of a united Europe since the different political entities within the continent have started poaching in foreign terrain.

Similar sentiments from around the same time are expressed in the anonymous pamphlet *De praesenti Europae statu oratio* (Oration on the Present State of Europe, 1640).[223] In response to what is now known as the Thirty Years' War, the text is dedicated "to the leaders and people of Europe" ("ad principes populosque Europaeos"), as its subtitle indicates. In a sweeping blow of thirty pages, the author mercilessly confronts his audience with everything that "has happened politically everywhere in each European nation and that is still happening at present" ("ubique apud Europae nationes in publico acta sunt, ac in praesens etiamnunc tempus aguntur"; p. A2r). Concretely, this involves "the abominable alliances, the ensuing wars, and the civil wars" ("horrenda foedera, mox bella, bella civilia"; p. A2r) that only came into being because "everybody was insisting on their own respective advantage" ("omnibus tamen cujusque suis in proprium destinatis emolumentum"; p. A2v). At the end of

---

223 Anon., *De praesenti Europae statu oratio ad principes populosque Europaeos* (n. p.: n. pub., 1640). Cf. also Detering, p. 184, and Walser-Bürgler, 'Continuities of Historical Crises', p. 556.

the pamphlet, rounding off the condemnation of harmful pursuit of national interest, the author urges the princes and people of Europe to make friends with their continental enemies in order to preserve Europe for the benefit of the public good (p. D4v).

A theoretical solution to the problem of Europeans fighting Europeans in just wars to preserve the balance of power on the continent is outlined in a 200-verse poem entitled *Lusus in Europae nationes* (Gimmick concerning the European Nations; composed *c.* 1600) by the Dutch lexicographer Cornelis Kiliaan (1528–1607).[224] Reacting to the circumstances of the Dutch War of Independence, which he closely observed as an ardent, though irenic, supporter of the seven Dutch provinces (today: Belgium, the Netherlands, and Luxembourg) against the Spanish hegemony, Kiliaan's 'Europe' centres on the northern and western parts of Europe. It includes Germany, the Netherlands, France, Spain, Italy, Britain, Denmark, Norway, and Sweden, that is, the nations surrounding the Netherlands on the one hand, and the nations involved in the War of Independence on the other. The political and cultural Renaissance that the Netherlands went through during the sixteenth century are well expressed in this 'provincialised' vision of Europe, at the heart of which stand the Netherlands themselves.

The poem features a dialogue between two characters, a *laudator* ("eulogist") and a *calumniator* ("slanderer"), alternately listing Europe's virtues and vices in elegiac distichs. In a striking manner, though, their descriptions of the various nations' military characteristics boil down to similar attributes: all nations appear to be unanimously warlike and belligerent despite their differences in most other aspects of life. The German, for instance, is called "insignis bello ac armis" ("excellent in war and arms"; p. 38); the Frenchman is "militia egregius" ("great at waging war"; p. 39); the Italian stands out as "bellator valida strenuitate potens" ("a quick and able fighter"; p. 41), and the Englishman proves "bellica ad arma citus" ("quick to take up arms"; p. 42). A potential conclusion drawn from this emphatic sameness in military matters could be Kiliaan's irenic perception of a European balance of power. Given that no nation seems to be able to defeat another due to their equivalent military competence, making war, Kiliaan suggests, would not pay off. The winner could ultimately only be Europe as an entity based on the interplay of balanced nations. The idea

---

224   The poem was published in Jan Gruter's anthology *Delitiae poetarum Belgicorum, huius superiorisque aevi illustrium, tertia pars* (Frankfurt: Hoffmann, 1614), pp. 37–44. First presented in Detering, pp. 77–79, amendments regarding Kiliaan's understanding of Europe are provided in Walser-Bürgler, 'Geopolitical Instruction', pp. 326 and 330–31.

of collective self-preservation hence outclasses any international imbalance caused by national strife, eliminating wars before they can erupt.

Apart from such implicit hints at non-nationalist policies, the concept of Europe as a pluralistic place governed by balanced power also found concrete expression in Neo-Latin texts. Although it generally tended to be a phenomenon of the seventeenth (and partly eighteenth) century, the prototype for this kind of writing emerged in the fifteenth century with Piccolomini's treatise *De Europa*, mentioned earlier in the context of the coinage of the adjective *Europaei* (part 4). The way that Piccolomini had organised his geographical-historical-ethnographic overview of Europe enduringly influenced all later pluralistic descriptions of the continent. Chapter by chapter he makes his way across Europe, with each of the sixty chapters dedicated exclusively to one European nation. Paying great attention to the details, Piccolomini describes each nation first in geographical and territorial terms, before turning to its history, political form, and customs. All in all, the reader is confronted with an astounding panorama of beauty and diversity shaping the continent.

One thing noticeable in Piccolomini's approach, as well as in that of many of his later followers, is the tendency to ethnographic stereotyping.[225] However, this is not to be taken as a bad trait leading to the distortion of reality. On the contrary, stereotypisation was a crucial part of early modern nation-building, on the one hand, and of the creation of a European awareness, on the other.[226] In both cases it was essential to understand which people lived in which territories of the continent and which characteristics either set them apart or rendered them similar. Thereby, Europe gained contours and significance by means of pluralistic qualities. Within the pan-European framework, national stereotypes also served as useful tools to reduce contrasts and overcome feelings of national superiority.

---

225   Testimonies to early modern national stereotyping are the so-called 'tables of nations' (*Völkertafeln*). The most popular table is a Styrian example from the early eighteenth century bearing the title *Kurtze Beschreibung der in Europa Befintlichen Völckern und Ihren Aigenschaften* (A Short Description of the People Living in Europe and Their Characters). Unfortunately, there is not much information on the origin and background of this *Völkertafel*. Wolfgang Brückner, 'Die Wiener Völkertafel in Berlin', *Bayerische Blätter für Volkskunde*, 21 (1994), 202–16.

226   Cf. also Walser-Bürgler, 'Geopolitical Instruction', pp. 326–27. The unfolding of national stereotypes in the context of Europeanisation is further discussed in Winfried Schulze, 'Die Entstehung des nationalen Vorurteils: Zur Kultur der Wahrnehmung fremder Nationen in der europäischen Frühen Neuzeit', in *Menschen und Grenzen in der Frühen Neuzeit*, ed. by Wolfgang Schmale and Reinhard Stauber (Berlin: Spitz, 1998), pp. 23–49, and Joep Leerssen, *National Thought in Europe: A Cultural History* (Amsterdam: Amsterdam University Press, 2006).

An illustrative example of this is the treatise *Icon animorum* (A Mirror of the Minds; 1614) by the French-Scottish writer John Barclay (1582–1621), which promotes a pluralistic and balanced concept of Europe.[227] After the Anglo-Spanish War raging from 1585 to 1604, and amid growing French suspicion regarding the emperor's pacifying role on the continent towards the end of the sixteenth century, notions of balanced continental policies were particularly pronounced at the the the beginning of the seventeenth century in Britain and France.[228] Against this background it might not have been a coincidence that Barclay encountered the concept. After all, he spent most of his short life in England at the court of King James I (1566–1625) and in France among the courtly circles of King Louis XIII.[229] Seeking patronage from the latter was what eventually inspired Barclay to devise the *Icon animorum*. At the time of its publication, Louis was only thirteen years old, having taken the throne after the assassination of his father Henry IV (1553–1610) in 1610. In his dedication to the young French king, Barclay does not fail to exhibit his admiration for Louis, whose official reign on his arrival at adulthood "all the world awaits" ("orbis expectat"; Dedicatio, 3.11). Until that moment, the author offers to familiarise him with the agents and societies dwelling in Europe, in order for the king to recognise their value and later preserve their variegation in the service of the common good (Dedicatio, 1.6–10):

> Sed privatum bonum est ad suae unius mentis notitiam pervenire. Plurimorum autem varios genios impetusque animorum curiosa diligentia posse distinguere, res adeo publicae utilitatis ut nec indignum duxerim munus, quod Tuae Maiestatis adolescentiae traderetur, hanc mentium morumque picturam.

---

227 The text was edited by Mark Riley, who added the English translation produced by the English poet Thomas May (1595–1650) in 1631: John Barclay, *Icon animorum or The Mirror of Minds*, ed. by Mark Riley, Bibliotheca Latinitatis Novae, 8 (Leuven: Leuven University Press, 2013). In-depth studies of the text in terms of its European dimension are available in Fumaroli, pp. 50–64, and Walser, '*Unitas multiplex*', on which the following presentation relies.

228 See Klaus Müller, 'Die Idee des europäischen Gleichgewichts in der Frühen Neuzeit', in *Europa – Begriff und Idee: Historische Streiflichter*, ed. by Hans Hecker, Kultur und Erkenntnis, 8 (Bonn: Bouvier, 1991), pp. 61–74; Sheehan, pp. 35–36.

229 Biographical sketches of Barclay's international life can be found in David Baird Smith, 'John Barclay', *The Scottish Historical Review*, 12 (1914), 37–59; David A. Fleming, 'John Barclay: Neo-Latinist at the Jacobean Court', *Renaissance News*, 19 (1966), 228–36; Walser, '*Unitas multiplex*', pp. 535–38.

Knowledge of one's own mind is a benefit to individuals, but to attain by close investigation knowledge of the natures and impulses of all kind of men is a thing of such public usefulness that I consider this portrait of minds and manners to be a very worthy gift for the benefit of Your Majesty's education.

After all, as Barclay adds at the beginning of the description of Europe, it is only in knowing those with whom one is in permanent political, economic, cultural, or social exchange that it is possible to behave appropriately towards them and anticipate their intentions. Barclay's repeated reference to 'proper conduct' at this point could, in fact, be well understood on a metaphorical level as 'not stirring up any conflicts' or 'keeping peace' (2.12.1–4):

> Et quoniam nihil utilius quam ex genio variorum gentium sic animum instruere, ut diversus sit cum diversis cognoscatque quid a quaque expectandum aut timendum, operae pretium erit aliquot populorum praecipuos mores in conspectum [...] dare [...].

> And seeing that nothing is more beneficial than from the genius of divers nations to be so informed as to know how to behave ourselves in different countries and what to expect or fear from every place, it will be worth our labour to define here the especial manners of some nations [...].

The actual description of the European nations is contained in chapters 2–9, which are framed by general observations on individual characters affected by age (chapter 1) as well as by people's profession and innate idiosyncrasies (chapters 10–16). In sum, therefore, the text constitutes a broad reflection on individual and collective self-perception, on the one hand, and on the European nations' position in space and time, on the other. As such it perfectly matches the discourse of Europe, which often has been defined by its reflective nature.[230]

Barclay's pluralistic attitude is manifest, first of all, in the impressive scope of continental coverage. From the Iberian Peninsula to the Balkan region and Turkey, and from Britain to Scandinavia and Russia, Europe – compared to both

---

230   Cf. Blanks, pp. 37–38: "Indeed, it has been put forth time and again that one of the fundamental drives/urges that makes Europe what it is, that makes European culture European – along with artefacts such as man as a political animal, the rule of law and custom, mixed government and self-governance – is this need to know, this drive toward self-realization, self-reflection."

contemporary and modern standards – is practically grasped in its entirety. This bespeaks Barclay's affirmation of pluralism as much as did his inclusion of Russia (8.13–18), Turkey (9.1–24), and the Jews, to whom Barclay refers as a people scattered all over the continent (9.25–26). Apparently, Barclay considers variety enriching, because when it comes to seventeenth-century descriptions of Europe the focus was usually on European civilisation and its achievements, excluding the 'barbarian' periphery like the Russian or Turkish Empires.[231] Furthermore, Barclay shows that for him Europe is dominated not merely by Christianity but by other religions as well. In terms of the actual description of the European nations themselves, Barclay follows Piccolomini's approach: in a comprehensive manner and by proceeding from nation to nation, he unfolds a European panorama of varying topography, climate, history, customs, and – most extensively – national characters.

The pluralistic picture drawn fully complies with notions of a balance of power among the different nations described. This pertains, in the first instance, to the fact that no nation is depicted as superior. In each description virtues and vices are evenly distributed. The Dutch people, for example, are said to be accustomed to alcohol from an early age, but at the same time Barclay praises them for their outstanding industry (5.23.10–25); Italians, to cite another example, indulge in humanity and erudition in an unparalleled manner due to their outstanding achievements in architecture, literature, and arts (6.17.7–18), yet their passions also drive them to display the utmost brutality when dealing with enemies (6.9.21–26). Barclay's aim to present a balanced picture of Europe is further manifest in the fact that in the course of his investigation he mentions not only Louis XIII as the treatise's dedicatee, but also a series of European princes contemporary and past who were particularly known for their peace policies in Barclay's times. Among them we find Frederick II of Denmark, who – according to Barclay – brought growth and affluence to Denmark after the Northern and Livonian Wars (8.23.13–15); Isabella I of Castile and her husband Ferdinand II of Aragon, who were the first to unite the Spanish principalities, who expelled the Moors, and who bound the Netherlands to Spain (7.4.16–24); and James I, who has just recently joined England and Scotland together in a promising political vision (4.22.21–29).

Barclay rounds off his pluralistic but balanced picture of Europe by foregoing isolated depictions of the individual European nations, instead establishing

---

231   Michael Maurer, '"Nationalcharakter" in der frühen Neuzeit: Ein mentalitätsgeschichtlicher Versuch', in *Transformationen des Wir-Gefühls: Studien zum nationalen Habitus*, ed. by Reinhard Blomert, Helmut Kuzmics, and Annette Treibel (Frankfurt a.M.: Suhrkamp, 1993), pp. 45–81 (pp. 67–68).

mutual links between them. The European nations are presented as dependent on each other as they all have characteristics at their disposal which others lack and from which the rest of the continent can benefit. In this way, Europe turns into a 'superstate' whose system compensates all strengths and weaknesses in their combination. "Europe constitutes the frame, the individual nations its content."[232] France, in Barclay's vision, for instance, provides the standard guidelines for comportment, style, and fashion (3.6.1–3.7.22); England stands for remarkable success in the most obscure fields of philosophy and science (4.13.24–4); Norwegian people excell at shipbuilding and navigation (8.22.7–10); Spain is the most knowledgeable of all nations when it comes to administration (7.12.21–25); Poland thrives on grain and honey, exporting both goods to barren nations (8.7.19–22 and 8.7.28–5); Hungarians are proficient in political negotiations to enforce their political goals (8.3.9–15); and the Turks present themselves as forerunners in terms of the instatement of a welfare system to take care of the sick and poor (9.12.24–28).

This method of highlighting elements of national separation without neglecting elements of association was typical of seventeenth-century concepts of continental organisation, analysing and propagating cross-border linkage in Europe.[233] In order for the reader not to misunderstand his plea for a Europe united in diversity, Barclay puts an illustrative anecdote right in front of his description of the European nations, which constitutes, in essence, a praise of variegation (2.1.5–2.2.4). Barclay recounts how one day he was hiking up a hill in Greenwich whose top offered a splendid view of the surroundings. The red roofs down in the city of London, the colourful ships on the glittering river Thames, the green hills and blossoming fields crowded with sheep and cattle of all sorts, as well as the blue sky, literally took his breath away. Uncertain about which of the sights he liked most, it suddenly hit him that it was not one single aspect that filled his heart with joy and admiration but the combination of all of them. The individual components only received their beauty from the beauty of the entire landscape. Barclay understood that diversity must be the key to anything beautiful in the world, as is taught by mother Nature (2.3.5–17):

> Cum his ego nec provisa voluptate diducerer, tandem revocare animum coepi et sic mecum reputare: quid esset quod incogitantem rapuisset; unde ille aspectus sic placeret; quae occulta vis, quae ratio meam mentem tetigisset? [...] Subiit inde cogitatio: nihil esse in mortalium rebus ad

---

232   Walser, 'Unitas multiplex', pp. 541–42.
233   Notions of alliance and interdependence were central to contemporary balance-of-power policies. Cf. Malettke, pp. 64–65; Sheehan, pp. 53–59.

suam pulchritudinem sic exactum quod tandem non fatiget contemplantem, nisi ad hunc quem intuebar modum diversarum dotium beneficio in aliam aliamque venustatem mutetur, semperque lassatos improvisa novitate reficiat. Et quoniam ad omnis decoris fastigium perducendus orbis erat, nequaquam tantae artis oblita natura est.

Whilst I was carried away with this sudden delight, I began to recall my mind and thus to consider with myself what should it be that thus unawares had ravished me? Why should this prospect so wonderfully please? What hidden force, or reason, had thus wrought upon my mind? [...] I began then to think with myself that there was nothing in the world so exactly beautiful, but at last would glut and weary the beholder, unless after that manner (as this place was) it were beautified with diversities and change of endowments to refresh continually the wearied beholder with unexpected novelties. And because the world was to be framed in perfection of beauty, Nature was not forgetful of so great an art.

The analogy to his ensuing description of the diversity of the European nations in terms of geography, religion, mentality, history, language, and customs is evident – especially given the insistent admonition added: "Let us sincerely acknowledge our own vices and be truly delighted in the contemplation of virtue in others." ("Et nostra vitia fideliter agnoscamus et virtutes in aliis nos delectent"; 2.12.11–12). In this respect, Barclay was far ahead of his times. Today we define pluralism normatively as a desirable value offering alternatives to our fixed view of the world (which is why these alternatives are sometimes even enshrined in constitutions).[234] And even though Barclay shies away from offering a clear political directive on how to organise Europe beyond the mere appreciation of ethnographic and social diversity, he does not act in a utopian-idealistic way. The Europe that he depicts essentially constitutes a Europe that really existed. In this sense, and in contrast to most of the other concepts of Europe we have seen so far, the *Icon animorum* is rather descriptive than prescriptive, which makes it a highly valuable contribution to the early modern discourse of Europe.

A more practically orientated example of European pluralism and balance of power is the didactic poem *Europa* (1650) by the German professor of politics, Cyriacus Lentulus (1609–1678).[235] It consists of 6000 hexameter verses

234 Ansorge, p. 8.
235 Cyriacus Lentulus, *Europa: regionum cultissimae terrarum orbis partis situm, urbium ac fluviorum junctam et separatam descriptionem, terrarum fertilitatem et inopiam,*

profoundly analysing Europe's nations from a geopolitical point of view. Addressed to the German emperor Ferdinand III (1608–1657), the political analysis of geostrategic interests marks a preform of what since the beginning of the twentieth century has been understood by the term 'geopolitics' according to the French tradition:[236] an account of regional planning, coupled with outlines of social, demographic, religious, cultural, economic, and historical factors that, taken all together, are supposed to enable a comprehensive political assessment of the respective area of interest (in Lentulus' case: Europe).

With his substantial description of Europe, Lentulus aimed at promoting the continent as an entity of balanced powers under the supervision of Ferdinand. His attribution of the role of the continental chair to the emperor was based on Ferdinand's decisive role in the preparation and execution of the peace negotiations leading to the Westphalian peace treaties and the eventual execution of their stipulations in the peace of Nuremberg (1649–1650).[237] This is expressed in the dedicatory preface to the *Europa*-poem where Lentulus, among others, addresses the emperor as "supremo Europae arbitro, et pacis in ea bellorumque moderator" ("Europe's highest arbitrator and its mediator of peace and war"; p. 2r) with reference to the peace of Nuremberg ("decreto

---

nationum mores et instituta, statuum origines, incrementa, vires: brevi quasi tabella exprimens (Herborn: Corvinus, 1650). The poem has been studied as a piece of geographical didactic poetry in Beate Czapla, 'Neulateinische Lehrdichtung zwischen der literarischen Tradition von Hesiod bis Manilius und der neuzeitlichen *Ars apodemica* am Beispiel von Bernardus Mollerus' *Rhenus* und Cyriacus Lentulus' *Europa*', *Neulateinisches Jahrbuch*, 1 (1999), 21–48. However, Czapla completely misses the discursive European aspect, which is treated in Walser-Bürgler, 'Geopolitical Instruction', (esp. pp. 331–43). All aspects outlined in the following have originally been put down in the latter.

236   The French approach remained largely unaffected by the ambiguities of the German tradition and the impact the Nazi ideology had on it. The history of modern geopolitics in relation to early modern approaches is outlined in Walser-Bürgler, 'Geopolitical Instruction', pp. 319–31 (including further references to geopolitical studies). The definition of modern French geopolitics is derived from Yves Lacoste, *Geographie und politisches Handeln: Perspektiven einer neuen Geopolitik*, Kleine kulturwissenschaftliche Bibliothek, 26 (Berlin: Wagenbach, 1990), p. 29.

237   Ferdinand had become German emperor in 1637 and from the beginning of his reign was driven by the urge to put an end to the confessional and hegemonic war raging on the continent since 1618. His commitment to the organisation of the peace negotiations was of crucial importance and has often been understated by historians. The concrete actions taken by the emperor and his influence on other European princes to settle their military conflicts are specified in Peter H. Wilson, *Europe's Tragedy: A New History of the Thirty Years' War* (London: Penguin, 2010), pp. 588 and 671–747. The Westphalian Peace Treaties (*Acta Pacis Westphalica*) themselves contain elements of a marked balance-of-power philosophy – which is not surprising given the international circumstances in which they were developed. An examination of the Treaties from the pan-European perspective is offered in Walser-Bürgler, 'Reflections of "Europe"'.

Norimbergensi"; p. 2r). The terms *arbiter* and *mediator* certainly are not used accidentally in this respect by the author. They carry the political message he sets out to convey, as they constitute terms belonging to the realms of international peace covenants originally introduced by the Dutch lawyer Hugo Grotius (1583–1645) and popularised by German jurists like Samuel Pufendorf (1632–1694).[238] An independent *arbiter* was usually employed to pronounce judgement when political parties were unable to reach an agreement regarding a controversial issue. A *mediator*, on the other hand, was appointed to offer mediation between parties at war. Convinced of Ferdinand's conciliating authority, Lentulus thus both metaphorically and literally puts Europe at Ferdinand's feet (p. 2r: 'Europam [...] submittere debui' – 'I need to consign Europe [to you]'), meaning the continent as well as his eponymous poem.

Taking on the role of an imperial advisor who comprehensively instructs the emperor in the geopolitical affairs of Europe so as to familiarise him with the diverse area to be monitored, Lentulus might have recommended himself for imperial service. Some sources mention him in a consultative capacity on the side of Emperor Leopold I (1640–1705), Ferdinand's successor, during the negotiation of the Peace Treaties of Nijmegen (1678–1679).[239] In addition, as a professor of politics at the *Academia Nassauensis* in Herborn, who had travelled the continent for study purposes and published widely on political matters, and as the official historiographer of the House of Nassau-Katzenelnbogen, he was well-versed in many issues faced by the European nations after the Thirty Years' War.

Geopolitical lines of thought had emerged in international politics already before the outbreak of the war in 1618, yet it was only after the end of the war and the growing territorialism brought about by the Westphalian Peace Treaties that those lines of thought gained a previously unknown prevalence in Europe.[240] Lentulus' approach shows a tendency to structure the space called Europe on various topical levels and to render the information usable

---

238 The concepts of *arbiter* and *mediator* are discussed from a pragmatic and historical point of view in Heinz Duchhardt, *Studien zur Friedensvermittlung in der frühen Neuzeit*, Schriften der Mainzer Philosophischen Fakultätsgesellschaft, 6 (Wiesbaden: Steiner, 1979), pp. 94–115.

239 For biographical information on Lentulus, see Friedrich Wilhelm Strieder, *Grundlage zu einer Hessischen Gelehrten und Schriftsteller Geschichte: Seit der Reformation bis auf gegenwärtige Zeiten, Bd. 7* (Kassel: Cramer, 1787), pp. 484–90; Christian Daniel Vogel, 'Nachrichten über das Leben und die Schriften des ehemaligen Professors und Nassauischen Historiographen Cyriacus Lentulus', *Annalen des Vereins für Nassauische Alterthumskunde und Geschichtsforschung*, 3 (1839), 111–16; Walser-Bürgler, 'Geopolitical Instruction', pp. 331–32.

240 Jan Helmig, 'Geopolitik – Annäherung an ein schwieriges Konzept', *Aus Politik und Zeitgeschichte*, 20/21 (2007), 31–37 (p. 31).

for political purposes. In contrast to Barclay's depiction of Europe from almost forty years earlier, Lentulus' description is a lot more detailed and differentiated. The impressive taxonomic range of eighteen nations in total – each of them constituting a chapter or book of the poem – combine profound knowledge of their geographical, historical, political, economic, legal, and ethnographic conditions in an almost encyclopaedic fashion. This encyclopaedic character of the poem is not only visible in its ambitious length, but it is somehow even indicated in the poem's full title: *Europa: regionum cultissimae terrarum orbis partis situm, urbium ac fluviorum junctam et separatam descriptionem, terrarum fertilitatem et inopiam, nationum mores et instituta, statuum origines, incrementa, vires: brevi quasi tabella exprimens* ("Europe: Enclosing, in the Form of a List, the Geographical Position of the Territories of the Most Civilised Part of the World, both an Interrelated and a Distinct Description of Towns and Rivers, the Fertility and Shortage of the Earth, the Customs and Characters of the Nations, the Origins, the Development, and the Power of the States").

Furthermore, it is precisely in this dense encyclopaedic approach that Lentulus' geopolitical vision of Europe as a pluralistic entity monitored by Ferdinand crystallises. Each national portrait (in the order Spain, France, Britain, Italy, Sicily, Switzerland, Prussia, Belgium, the Holy Roman Empire, Denmark, Norway, Sweden, Poland, Russia, Hungary, Illyricum, Thrace, and Greece) follow the exact same pattern of description with only little variation, necessitated by the seeming diversity of the nations in order not to get lost. In combination with the marginal headings marking the text for the reader, the continuous uppercase writing of city names and the concise, unagitated style of the text lend it the appearance of a reference book, endowed with 'hooks' to help the reader (the emperor) look things up, rather than the appearance of an entertaining and aesthetically pleasing poem. And while Lentulus' assertion that his description of Europe is "nothing but the naked truth about the world as received by me on perpetual travels" ("mihi [...] ex diuturna peregrinatione nihil praeter nudam rerum contemplationem referenti"; p. 2v) holds the poem accountable and credible for pragmatic use, the intuitive rhythm of the hexameter supports the content's memorisation.[241]

The information conveyed to the emperor by Lentulus is fully in the service of his geopolitical mission. Ferdinand's role as Europe's arbitrator and

---

241   In a similar way, the German humanist Conrad Celtis has 150 years earlier employed elegiac couplets in his collection of love poems *Quatuor Libri Amorum secundum quatuor latera Germaniae* (Four Books of Love Stories Pursuant to the Four Sides of Germany, 1502) to express geographical details. Piechocki, p. 63.

mediator, holding together the range of nations by a stable peace, is implied by the position the German Empire takes in the panorama of European nations: it is located right in the middle of the poem (pp. 83–127). The other nations gather round it. This matches Lentulus' initial declaration to introduce his addressee to Europe as a whole (v. 1): "Europae populos, urbes et flumina dicam" – "I am going to talk about the peoples, cities, and rivers of Europe". With this goal in mind he – deliberately or unconsciously – unfolds a continent full of geographical, historical, political, and cultural diversity. Bound by the demands of his mission, he naturally pays great attention to anything that could be of potential importance for a foreign administrator to know, but that at the same time only demonstrates the continent's variegation.

With regard to the geographical portraits, for example, Lentulus lingers over the exact description of Switzerland's mountains, rivers, and division into four parts (v. 1561–1570), while the delineation of Poland warns of the nation's swamps, forests, and vast fields (vv. 5110–5123). The cities are described according to whether they mark politically or economically crucial centres, such as Copenhagen as the Danish city of royal residence (v. 4647) or Bergen as the Norwegian commercial trading centre (vv. 4665–4666). The ethnographic portraits are usually set in conjunction with religious or political deliberations (the Britons, for instance, are referred to as pious [v. 817–25], the Swedes as belligerent [v. 4823–26]). In historical terms, the individual accounts of the nations' respective past and present conflicts points to their acquired rights in the face of potential future clashes in order to understand and anticipate better the driving forces behind certain political decisions (Italy's loss of the imperial crown, for example, serves as a justification of the Italians' competitive struggle for international recognition [v. 1280–431], while the French alliance with the Ottoman enemy serves as a warning sign against French attempts at supremacy [v. 643–44]).

What is generally striking about Lentulus' European panorama is that – similar to Barclay's description – all nations receive the same treatment; none is preferred or depicted in a better or worse light than the others. The picture drawn is as neutral as it could be against the background of a continental peace vision. According to Lentulus' perception of Europe and how the single nations are aligned within its borders, Europe forms a peaceful entity of different yet balanced nations, whose peaceful equalised state is to be maintained by the efforts of Ferdinand as the executive of the continent.

4.4   One Culture, One Europe: Continentality and Civilisation

Early modern contemporaries often defined culture and civilisational achievements as one of the key characteristics of Europeanness, rendering the continent distinct from the rest of the world and linking the European nations by a common bond. Notions of cultural communality, by which Europeans understood themselves as a homogeneous group in terms of a collectively shared lifestyle, constituted an essential part of the early modern Europe discourse.[242] However, these notions usually were not discussed at length in texts exclusively dedicated to the topic but rather tended to pop up in the context of any given idea of Europe. The reason for this was that defining Europe by a common continental culture supported any arguments advanced in favour of pan-European tendencies. After all, similar to respective notions of 'nationness', cultural notions of Europeanness work like "cultural artefacts"[243] and thus dispose of an enormous emotional power.

Even though Johann Gottfried Herder was the first to define the concept of culture as a holistic denominator of communities in the late eighteeinth century, and even though many knowledgeable studies still hold that the European concept of culture only emerged after 1700,[244] this does not mean that the concept had not existed *avant la lettre*. As so often in the field of early modern studies, this is once again proven by samples from Neo-Latin literature, whose authors seem to have understood Europe in a common cultural sense since the beginning of the Europe discourse in the fifteenth century. This hardly comes as a surprise given that Europe basically 'found' itself by means of confronting itself with the world. The overseas discoveries, along with the ensuing imperial and religious missions to the Americas and Asia in the sixteenth and seventeenth centuries, on the one hand, and the experiences of alterity acquired in the course of the Ottoman advance, on the other, challenged the hitherto unquestioned Eurocentric view of the world and revealed to the Europeans a number of diverging cultural practices. As Peter Burke puts it:

> Europe was defined by contrast not only to the Ottoman Empire but also to India, China, Peru and Brazil. Whether they liked or disliked the lands

---

242   Cf. Detering, p. 364. The understanding of culture as a holistic concept related to a social group and in demarcation to other groups has been discussed in the context of cultural theories: Andreas Reckwitz, *Die Transformation der Kulturtheorien: Zur Entwicklung eines Theorienprogramms* (Weilerswist: Velbrück, 2000), pp. 64–91. Asbach, p. 138, also speaks of Europe as a "community of memory" ("Erinnerungsgemeinschaft") in this respect, since much of Europe's cultural understanding was rooted in the ancient or Christian past.

243   Anderson, p. 4.

244   On Herder's concept of culture, cf. above, note 47. Among the proponents of a late cultural concept of Europe are Detering (pp. 365–66); Wolfgang Schmale, 'Europa, Braut der Fürsten: Die politische Relevanz des Europamythos im 17. Jahrhundert', in *Europa im 17. Jahrhundert: Ein politischerMythos und seine Bilder*, ed. by Klaus Bußmann and Elke A. Werner (Wiesbaden: Steiner, 2004), pp. 241–67; and Wintle, *Image of Europe*.

they visited, [European] travellers in other continents were forced into awareness of what it meant to be European, and printing spread this awareness to others.[245]

In other words, European identity was created by conquering other parts of the world and by fear of being conquered by them. These dramatic events gave Europeans the opportunity to realise what rendered them distinct from other 'worlds' and what they shared with other European nations. Borne by an overwhelming feeling of civilisational superiority compared to what they saw, as well as a generalised terror of potentially losing their common European values to external threats, they set out to either 'Europeanise' the foreign worlds by imposing their culture on them (which was the case with the American and Asian worlds discovered) or to fight them to preserve their culture (which happened in the European-Ottoman conflict). The Bohemian Johan Amos Comenius enunciates this thought in the preface to his encyclopedic work *De rerum humanarum emendatione consultatio catholica* (General Consultation on an Improvement of All Things Human, 1657), addressed to "Europe's adornment, learned, pious, and great men" ("Europae lumina, viri docti, pii, eminentes"; p. 12):[246]

Nos nimirum Europaei vna quasi communi vehimur naui: contemplamurque *Asianos, Africanos, Americanos, caeterosque* vt suis naviculis in eodem communi mundi et mundanarum calamitatum (ignorantiae, superstitionum, seruitutisque miserrimae) Oceano fluctuantes. Iam itaque si nobis noster Christus, nostra nobiscum naui vectus, abunde benedixit, [...] ecquid melius cogitare possumus, quam vt innuamus sociis, qui sunt in aliis nauibus, vt veniant et iuuent nos? (p. 18)

We Europeans sail, in a sense, on a common ship, whence we contemplate the Asians, Africans, Americans, and all the others swaying in their boats in this joint sea of the world and the mundane calamities like ignorance, superstition, and outright miserable servitude. So since our Christ, sailing with us on our ship, has already abundantly blessed us, [...] can we

---

245 Burke, 'Did Europe Exist', p. 25. See also Asbach, pp. 148–61 on European cultural demarcation.

246 Johan Amos Comenius, *De rerum humanarum emendatione consultatio catholica, ad genus humanum ante alios vero ad eruditos, religiosos, potentes, Europae*, 3rd edn (Halle: Orphanotrophius, 1702).

think of anything better than making those, who dwell in the other boats, our allies so that they come and support us?

Given that the ship was the main vehicle of European conquering missions, the metaphor equating Europe with a ship is fitting. In addition, Comenius expresses the European sense of cultural superiority in three ways: firstly, while Europe is compared to a proper ship (*nauis*), the other continents and people are diminutively seated in boats (*nauiculae*). Then there is the juxtaposition of "we Europeans", standing in a prime position right at the beginning of the passage, while the motley assortment of the rest of the world only follows after the colon and the first-person verb, again referring to the Europeans. Finally, Comenius picks one central aspect of Europeanness, namely the Christian faith, to illustrate how European feelings of superiority are transmitted to foreign places, in order to turn Europe's potential foes into subordinate supporters, thus keeping them at bay and in dependence on the Europeans.

The exceptional role played by Christianity as an element empowering notions of European cultural superiority was based on the early modern belief that God had chosen the Europeans to rule the world due to their civilised descent. For while all barbarians inhabiting the non-European realms of the world had always led savage lives without any order at all or dictated by tyrannical order, Europeans from all over the continent had dwelled in law-governed and free communities. Therefore, the arts and sciences had only been able to reach their full potential and push society towards progress in Europe, so the argument went.[247] Hence, when the Jesuits, for example, left for China for the first time in the sixteenth century, they took clocks, astrolabes, telescopes, clavichords, Venetian prisms, suction pumps, and other devices with them. They were meant to verify the European exceptionalism by divine sign: if God had instructed the Europeans in how to develop such ingenious things, the European God, the Christian God, must be the only true God.[248] It was also in this very sense of European cultural and scientific superiority given by God that Juan Luis Vives had the Roman general Scipio exclaim in his dialogue *De Europae dissidiis et bello turcico* that "the bravest and most energetic people on earth are those who inhabit Europe" ("fortissimam mundi gentem et animosissimam esse eam quae Europam incolit"; 41.21–23), while the seer Tiresias has remarked earlier that due to their Christian religion, the Europeans were

---

247   Pagden, pp. 10 and 49.
248   Pagden, p. 50.

the happiest and most prolific people on earth, knowing how to rule themselves and foreign lands (20.17–28).[249]

Early modern European cultural and civilisational superiority was also closely linked to Europe's ancient heritage. Yet *Europa culta*, a 'cultivated Europe', included not only those nations which had once been part of or in close political contact with the Roman Empire. It pertained to any European nation ready to engage with classical sources and derive their understanding of humanity and the sciences from the ancient tradition. The rediscovery and appropriation of the Latin language, Roman law, Greek philosophy, imperial administration, and other achievements of the Greek and Roman past brought new stimuli to the continental self-perception.[250] The French philosopher Paul Valéry (1871–1945) once formulated Europe's practical and theoretical exchange with Antiquity as follows:

> Partout où les noms de César, de Gaius, de Trajan et de Virgile, partout où les noms de Moïse et de saint Paul, partout où les noms d'Aristote, de Platon et d'Euclide ont eu une signification et une autorité simultanées, là est l'Europe.[251]

One of the first testaments to Europe as a cultural entity is traceable in Lorenzo Valla's *Oratio in principio studii* (Oration Held at the Beginning of the Semester), which he delivered on the occasion of inaugurating the new academic year

---

249 Christian-European superiority is also displayed in Nicholas of Cusa's (1401–1464) attempt at conceiving a religious peace plan right after the fall of Constantinople in 1453: *De pace fidei* (On the Peace of Faith). A critical edition is available: Nicholas of Cusa, *Opera omnia: Vol. 7: De pace fidei, cum epistula ad Ioannem de Segobia*, ed. by Raymond Klibansky and Hildebrand Bascour (Hamburg: Meiner, 1970). This Latin treatise recounted the vision of a conference held in heaven whose participants were representatives of seventeen different religions. In the end, it was decided to hold a council of all religions on earth with the declared aim "to take up one joint belief in the name of everyone and to settle an eternal peace by relying on this belief" ("omnium nominibus unam fidem acceptent et super ipsa perpetuam pacem firment"; p. 3). From now on there should only be "one religion, merely differing in the form of their rites" ("religio una in rituum varietate"; pp. 10–11). However, since this religion was endowed with Christian principles, the Christian world view, and a Christian 'leader', it was easy to see Nicholas of Cusa's propagation of Christianity as the most powerful, the truest of all religions. Cf. Reinhold F. Glei, 'Die Polemik des "Christlichen Abendlandes" gegen Judentum und Islam', in *Pluralistische Identität: Beobachtungen zu Herkunft und Zukunft Europas*, ed. by Dirk Ansorge (Darmstadt: Wissenschaftliche Buchgesellschaft, 2016), pp. 68–83 (p. 83).
250 Schulze, p. 31; Asbach, pp. 132–33.
251 Paul Valéry, 'Note (ou L'Européen)', in *Oeuvres: Vol. 1*, ed. by Jean Hytier (Paris: Gallimard, 1957), pp. 1000–14 (p. 1013).

1455/56.[252] At one point in his speech he comes to address the value of the
Latin language. He explains how Latin once united the entire Roman Empire
as its common language. Yet while after the demise of the Roman Empire Asia
and Africa have slid back into barbary, Europe has continued to flourish from
century to century due to the continent's maintenance of the Latin language,
under the protection of the Holy See (p. 198):

> [...] ex Asia atque Africa, ex quibus quia lingua Latina cum imperio eiecta
> est, ideo omnes bonae artes pariter eiectae sunt et pristina barbaries
> rediit in possessionem. Quod cur in Europa non contingit? Nempe [...]
> quia id fieri sedes apostolica prohibuit.

> [...] When the Latin language was banned from Asia and Africa in the
> course of the downfall of the Roman Empire, all liberal arts were equally
> ejected and the former barbarity returned to these regions. Why did this
> not happen to Europe? Indeed [...] because the Apostolic See forbade
> this to happen.

In Barclay's *Icon animorum* Europe's common ancient heritage is conjured as
a means to set the scene for the ensuing description of Europe.[253] For Barclay,
the Greek and Roman past serve as a form of collective memory encompassing all the nations delineated. While he generally praises the Romans for their
refinement of the Latin language and the demonstration of how peace can
be lastingly enforced (2.6.19–3), Barclay particularly focuses on Greece as the
cradle of European culture (2.5.11–15):

> Florentibus Graeciae rebus quid ad humanitatem aut astum illis gentibus
> defuisse existimes? Artificiorum tanta vis ut in auro vel saxis sive homi-
> num sive pecudum formas paene etiam animarent. Ea eloquentia ac in
> poetis suavitas, ut illam sibi sumeret Romana ambitio quam imitaretur,
> non vinceret.

---

252   Carlo Ginzburg found Valla to be the first to have used the term 'Europe' in a cultural sense
       (*Rapporti di forza: storia, retorica, prova* [Milan: Feltrinelli, 2000], pp. 84–85). However, as
       will be shown in the following pages, Piccolomini, in fact, predated his cultural concept of
       Europe. For an edition of Valla's oration, see Lorenzo Valla, *Orazione per l'inaugurazione
       dell'anno accademico 1455–1456: Atti di un seminario di filologia umanistica*, ed. by Silvia
       Rizzo (Roma: Roma nel Rinascimento, 1994).
253   This idea is argued in greater detail in Walser, *'Unitas multiplex'*, pp. 538–40.

When the affairs of Greece did flourish, what civility, what wit or subtlety was wanting to that nation, do you think? So great was the skill of their craftsmen, that their carved statues of men and beasts in gold or in stone did seem almost to live; so fluent their oratory, so sweet their poetry, that even the ambition of Rome appropriated them only to imitate, not to outdo.[254]

Links to Barclay's own present are eventually established when the aspect of continuity comes in, lending the idea of ancient culture a certain authority not to be messed with. In the Middle Ages, Barclay argues, the Greek and Latin culture and languages deteriorated due to different political and social upheavals (2.7.4–2.9.3). Yet when the age of humanity set in on the continent, that is, in the present times, the arts and sciences have been revived according to the ancient spirit. Education and learning are attributed a new value unseen in the previous centuries, penetrating all spheres of contemporary life. To emphasise the recent blossoming of ancient culture all over the continent, Barclay even employs the humanistic topos of the 'dark Middle Ages', contrasting them with the light of the present (2.10.4–5): "Isto denique saeculo haec ex hominum animis caligo evanuit iam ad omnis generis astum lucemque compositis." – "Last of all, in this age, that dark mist is vanished away from the minds of men, which are now composed to all kind of light and subtlety." At this point, Barclay launches into the ensuing description of the European nations.

References to the Greek and Roman heritage as the roots of early modern European culture constituted a particularly crucial theme when it came to the question of whether to rank the Ottoman Empire (sometimes also Russia) among the constituent parts of Europe.[255] More often than not, the Ottoman enemy was emphatically denounced as non-European. Apart from religion, this had to do with the tragic circumstances accompanying the fall of Constantinople in 1453. The wealth of ancient knowledge and literature – both Greek and Latin – stored in the city's libraries had fallen victim to the

---

254 The English translation by Thomas May, as offered in Riley's edition of Barclay's *Icon animorum*, has been slightly changed here.

255 General ideas on the inclusion and exclusion of the Russian and Ottoman Empires are outlined in Piirimäe, 'Russia, the Turks and Europe'. The Russian case, in particular, which will not form part of the following investigation, is investigated in George Gale, 'Leibniz, Peter the Great, and the Modernization of Russia: Or Adventures of a Philosopher-King in the East', *Divinatio*, 22 (2005), 7–36, and Ovanes Akopyan, 'Europe or Not? Sixteenth-Century European Descriptions of Muscovy and the Russian Responses', in *Contesting Europe: Comparative Perspectives on Early Modern Discourses on Europe, 1400–1800*, ed. by Nicolas Detering, Clementina Marsico, and Isabella Walser-Bürgler, Intersections, 67 (Leiden: Brill, 2019), pp. 248–71.

Ottoman pillage. Eyewitnesses escaping to Venice and other places on the continent spoke of the loss and destruction of more than 120,000 manuscripts.[256] With respect to this occurrence, Piccolomini opens his speech at the Diet of Frankfurt in 1454 with the sentence: "Constantinopolitana clades, [...] Thurcorum grandis victoria, Grecorum extrema ruina, Latinorum summa infamia fuit [...]" ("The fall of Constantinople, [...] a great victory for the Turks, meant the greatest disaster for the Greeks and the greatest ignominy for the Latins [...]"; p. 494). Although the words *Greci* and *Latini* relate to both the Eastern and Western Church, their application sets up a certain frame of reference within Piccolomini perceives European culture. After all, Piccolomini derives the cultural origin of all European people from ancient Greece. This is why he repeatedly mourns the fall of Constantinople as the "domicilium litterarum" ("home of literature"; p. 514) and laments the cultural damage done to Europe with the devastation of Greece: "o nobilis Grecia! ecce nunc tuum finem, nunc demum mortua es!" ("O noble Greece! Now lo thy end, now thou finally hast died!"; p. 512). The argument eventually culminates in Piccolomini's desperate exclamation (p. 520):

> Ac contrita nunc deletaque Grecia, quanta sit facta litterarum iactura, cuncti cognoscitis, qui Latinorum omnem doctrinam ex Grecorum fontibus derivatam non ignoratis!

> How big the loss of literature will prove to be now that Greece is devastated and destroyed you all know, who are very well aware that the entire education of the Latin world is taken from Greek roots!

Although Constantinople did not form part of the *translatio imperii*, Piccolomini thus makes it a part of a *translatio artium*. According to his understanding of European culture, Constantinople is ranked among the cultural tradition beginning in Antiquity, deserving to be placed on the same footing as Athens and Rome.[257] Hence, when Constantinople collapsed through the force of the Ottomans, Europe lost an essential part of its culture, and with it an essential part of its identity. In this respect, Europe is depicted as a cultural community opposed to the Ottoman world.

To underline his promotion of a European community sharing the same culture based on the achievement of the ancients, Piccolomini employs some additional arguments. First of all, he believes the Turks to descend from the

---

256   Malcolm, p. 18 (including illustrative quotations from eyewitness accounts).
257   Cf. Kaiser, 'Antiketransformationen', pp. 96–97.

Scythians, a nomadic people from the Pontic steppe and thus not privy to the European cultural space.[258] As "Scytharum genus [...] ex media barbaria profectum" ("a Scythian tribe [...] originating right from the heart of barbarity"; p. 516), he deems them "gens immunda et ignominiosa" ("an unclean and ignominious people"; p. 516), who "litteras odit, humanitatis studia persequitur" ("hate literature and persecute education and erudition"; pp. 517–18). The contrast between these barbarians and the civilised Europeans nurturing the fine arts and letters is evident. Therefore, Piccolomini's observation that Mehmed II prefers to compare himself with Caesar and Alexander the Great, two of the greatest commanders of Antiquity (pp. 554–555), is supposed to aim at two things: to demonstrate the arrogance of the barbars and to infuriate the Europeans, who are proud of their ancient legacy, inciting them to defend their rightful inheritance with all their might. Piccolomini's cultural programme is further supported by the dense intertextual network consisting of allusions, citations, and adaptations from various Latin authors, such as Cicero, Caesar, Sallust, Livy, Suetonius, Ovid, Vergil, Horace, and Juvenal.[259] Finally, when reminding the Germans and the other European nations to fight together and to recall the international military collaboration of their ancestors (quoted above on pp. 53–54), Piccolomini postulates virtues inspired by the Roman *virtutes imperatoriae* (e.g. courage, strength, and military resources).[260]

While many authors followed Piccolomini's conception of Europe as a cultural unity, as opposed to the uncultured Ottoman enemy,[261] the Turks were often also perceived as a part of Europe. This corresponds with the inclusion

---

258   Bisaha, p. 46. Declaring the Turks descendants of the Scythians was only one line of thought in the Early Modern Period. On the other side, they were often said to have descended from the Trojans (*Teucri*) due to their regional settlement and the similarity in name. As Anna Akasoy shows, the opponents of the Ottomans usually rejected the Trojan theory: Anna A. Akasoy, 'Die Selbstdefinition Europas während der Renaissance im Kontext der Auseinandersetzung mit dem Osmanischen Reich', in *Pluralistische Identität: Beobachtungen zu Herkunft und Zukunft Europas*, ed. by Dirk Ansorge (Darmstadt: Wissenschaftliche Buchgesellschaft, 2016), pp. 84–102.

259   The oration represents a perfect humanist text, full of appreciation of the power of ancient literature, on the one hand, while being driven by an innovative force to create a rhetorically efficient text, on the other. Piccolomini's intertextual play is examined more closely in Kaiser, 'Antiketransformationen', pp. 92–94.

260   Kaiser, 'Antiketransformationen', pp. 98–99.

261   Marko Marulić, for example, emphasises the difference between Europeans and Ottomans in his *Epistola ad Adrianum VI* by pointing out their distinct cultural characteristics (p. 94): "Quomodo enim ullius Christiani amicus esse potest qui Christo aduersatur, qui neque religione neque legibus neque moribus nobiscum conuenit? Profecto ubi tanta rerum dissimilitudo est, ibi nulla unquam intercedere amicitia potest nisi simulata." – "But how can one who opposes Christ be a friend to any Christian? One who differs from

of Turkey in various catalogues of nations from the sixteenth and seventeenth centuries, or the appearance of the sultan among the European princes in early seventeenth-century ballet performances.[262] However, since this inclusion was never free from controversy, it must be taken as a serious statement whenever it turned up. When, for example, Piccolomini a few years after his speech at the Diet of Frankfurt hints at least implicitly at the European and Ottoman common knowledge of Greek and Roman natural philosophy and mediaeval theology in developing his rational arguments in the *Epistola ad Mahumetem*,[263] which is ostensibly trying to convert Mehmed to Christianity, there is a specific purpose behind his argument. For Piccolomini, reason and philosophy play a mediating role as a common base for discussion and dialogue, facilitating a European peace.[264] A similar thought might have convinced Johann Joachim von Rusdorf to allow Sultan Ahmed (1590–1617) to enter his *Scena Europaea* in third place, right after the Pope and the Holy Roman Emperor (pp. 8–9).[265]

Convinced that they belonged to the most advanced civilisation with the greatest cultural achievements, early modern Europeans self-confidently set out to 'Europeanise' the new worlds after their discovery. This process of 'Europeanising' the world owed a lot to the missionary efforts of monastic orders such as the Benedictines, the Franciscans, and – most importantly – the Jesuits. Members of these orders most frequently expressed the exploration of the 'other', in which the image of the 'self' was reflected paradigmatically, either in official reports sent to the orders' headquarters in Europe or in travel reports. The latter constituted a flourishing genre during the sixteenth and especially the seventeenth centuries, satisfying the growing interest in the exotic and the culture of foreign places. A unique sample of Eurocentric perspectives projected onto external cultures may be seen in the travel report *De missione legatorum Iaponensium ad Romanam curiam dialogus* (A Dialogue Concerning the Mission of the Japanese Ambassadors to the Roman Curia, 1590). Instead of describing Japanese culture from the European perspective, thus rendering Europe in comparison the peak of civilisation, this text depicts Europe, in an inversion of the typical travel account, from the Japanese perspective (even if

---

us in faith, in laws and in customs? Indeed, where there is such a difference in everything, no friendship can be established other than feigned friendship."

262 Detering, pp. 64–65.

263 Piccolomini quotes extensively from these sources, yet not from a superior instructive position but rather in the manner of an erudite conversation between two equally knowledgeable men of letters (cf., for instance, the way he discusses Epicurus', Pythagoras', and Aristotle's doctrines in §29–30, or Pliny the Elder's calculations in §138).

264 Cf. Akasoy, p. 89–90.

265 Detering, p. 233. Strikingly, the first edition of 1628 still lacked Ahmed's speech.

this involves a 'Europeanised' Japanese perspective behind which stood the European Jesuits in the Japanese mission): In February 1582, the Jesuit missions in Japan chose four young Japanese pupils to send to Europe. The aim of sending them was to improve the reputation of Japan among the Europeans, but especially to

> impress upon the four youths the glory and grandeur of the Christian religion, the majesty of the European rulers who had embraced it, the richness and splendour of Europe's kingdoms and cities, and the honour and authority that the Christian religion enjoyed throughout Europe.[266]

The supposedly superior features of European culture should impregnate the Japanese pupils' minds as examples to follow upon their return to Japan. When they finally did so, in August 1590, the text was published in Macau in the form of thirty-four travel dialogues (*colloquia*) conducted by the four Japanese boys Michael, Mancio, Martin, and Julian. Its authorship is not entirely clear; it was probably composed by one of the higher-ranking Asian Jesuit missionaries, Duarte de Sande (who is recorded on the title page of the original printing) or Alessandro Valignano SJ, who supervised the Latin edition. In their Latin form, the dialogues served to teach students at the Jesuit colleges in Japan. Even though their publication was monitored by European missionaries, they display an image of a highly cultured Europe from an intriguing external perspective by recounting meetings between the boys and some of the most powerful men on the continent, such as Pope Gregory XIII (1502–1585), Pope Sixtus V (1521–1590), and King Philip II of Spain (1527–1598). Furthermore, they provide ample admiring accounts of the continent's geography, religion, political systems (especially monarchies and republics), economic interests, customs,

---

266   This quotation is taken from the introduction to the English translation of the original Latin text (pp. 1–31 [p. 7]): Duarte de Sande, *Japanese Travellers in Sixteenth-Century Europe: A Dialogue Concerning the Mission of the Japanese Ambassadors to the Roman Curia* (1590), ed. by Derek Massarella and Joseph F. Moran (London: Ashgate, 2012). The Latin text has recently been edited, along with a Portuguese translation: Duarte de Sande, *Diálogo sobre a missão dos embaixadores japoneses à Cúria romana: 2 vols*, ed. by Américo da Costa Ramalho and Sebastião Tavares de Pinho, Portugaliae monumenta neolatina, 1 (Coimbra: Imprensa da Universidade de Coimbra, 2009). As this edition was not available, the Latin quotations page are taken from the early modern print: Duarte de Sande, *De missione legatorum Iaponensium ad Romanam curiam rebusque in Europa ac toto itinere animadversis dialogus* (Macau: n. pub., 1590). The text has briefly been discussed in Walser-Bürgler, 'Continuities of Historical Crises', pp. 558–59. The following details on the text's origins are collectively taken from Massarella's and Moran's introduction.

education, scholarship and science, art, literature, architecture, and history. In
the last dialogue, *colloquium* 34, all European values are cumulatively summa-
rised and acknowledged as unsurpassed (Latin print: pp. 400–12; English translation: pp. 438–49): Europe may be small as a territorial entity in comparison to
the other continents, yet it is not the other continents that are the most powerful and cultivated in the world. Power and worth, the boys thus conclude, are
not determined by size. Michael has the final say on it, declaring (Latin print:
p. 407; English translation: p. 446):

> [...] iudico, ingenueque assero, Europam omnium orbis terrarum partium
> excellentissimam esse, qua Deus plenissima manu plurimis, praestant-
> issimisque bonis cumulavit. Quo fit, vt caeli natura, nationum ingenijs,
> industria, et nobilitate, viuendi, gubernandique ratione, multitudine
> bonarum artium, inter omnes alias regiones praestet [...].

> [...] I judge and frankly declare that Europe is the most excellent of all the
> parts of the world, the part on which God with most generous hand has
> conferred the most and the best good things. Accordingly, it stands out
> among all other regions for its climate, for the abilities, the industry, and
> the nobility of its nations, for its organization of life and of government,
> and for the multiplicity of its arts [...].

The exclusivity of European culture and civilisation usually went only one
way. As in the case of the European-Japanese exchange, Europe represented
the paragon bringing progress to the rest of the world, which the Europeans
considered mere barbarian places. The reverse perspective, according to which
foreign places also had something to offer to Europe other than just natural
resources to exploit, was relatively rare. Too strong was the Eurocentric vision,
too unidirectional the Europeans' patronising view of the world. Only a few
European intellectuals believed in the equality of all human beings regardless of their race or origin and attributed cultural or scientific values also to
non-European communities.

One of those individuals was the German polyhistor Gottfried Wilhelm
Leibniz (1646–1716). As an ardent supporter of Enlightenment thinking, he was
greatly interested in the progress of humanity in general and far removed from
the typical romanticising affirmation of Europe, despite displaying a strong
sense of Europeanness in most of his letters and writings. For the purpose
of leading mankind in its entirety to the peak of its existence, he also looked
beyond Europe and towards nations he could not visit himself (like Russia

and China).[267] Above all, he idealised China and projected onto the Empire everything he missed or could not find in Europe. In the face of the thriving Christian mission to China at the end of the seventeenth century, Leibniz encouraged the Protestant lands not to entrust the Chinese mission entirely to the Catholics.[268] However, this plea was driven not by petty confessional arguments but by Leibniz' sincere scientific interest. He had realised that the Catholic missionaries were highly acknowledged as astronomers or engineers among the Chinese officials and even at the Chinese court. This clearly signalled to him that the Chinese deemed science and technology the greatest achievements of European civilisation, which made them want to learn more and more about it. So far, there is nothing exceptional about the Chinese admiration of European civilisation. Leibniz' thinking only turned in an uncommon direction when he derived from the Chinese interest in Europe's scientific achievements the necessity for Europeans to learn from Chinese culture as well. He expresses this thought in a letter addressed to the missionary, engineer, and director of the astronomical office in Bejing, Claudio Filippo Grimaldi (1638–1712), dated 21 March 1692 (pp. 34–36):[269]

Summa desiderii nostri huc redit, ut pro sapientia tua cogites, commissam Tibi a providentia rem magnam in generis humani beneficium, commercium scilicet novum lucis introducendum inter dissitas gentes. [...] Fers illis [= Sinensibus] nostras artes, nam in Te ac tot viris praeclaris, quos tecum ducis, velut compendium quoddam intueor sapientiae Europae: aequum est, ut vicissim ad nos perveniant physica imprimis Sinensium arcana, traditione florentis per tot saecula gentis et imperii servata, et aucta. Haec una commutandi ratio iusta est; illi observatis,

---

267 On the relationship between Leibniz and Russia, see Gale, 'Leibniz, Peter the Great, and the Modernization of Russia'; on Leibniz and China, see Wenchao Li, 'Un commerce de lumière – Leibniz' Vorstellungen von kulturellem Wissensaustausch', in *Umwelt und Weltgestaltung: Leibniz' politisches Denken in seiner Zeit*, ed. by Friedrich Beiderbeck, Irene Dingel, and Wenchao Li (Göttingen: Vandenhoeck & Ruprecht, 2015), pp. 293–306.

268 On the circumstances and results of the European mission to China and Leibniz' opinion on it, see Wenchao Li, *Die christliche China-Mission im 17. Jahrhundert: Verständnis, Unverständnis, Missverständnis. Eine geistesgeschichtliche Studie zum Christentum, Buddhismus und Konfuzianismus*, Supplementa Studia Leibnitiana, 32 (Stuttgart: Steiner, 2000).

269 Gottfried Wilhelm Leibniz, *Der Briefwechsel mit den Jesuiten in China (1689–1714)*, ed. by Rita Widmaier and Malte-Ludolf Babin, Philosophische Bibliothek, 548 (Hamburg: Meiner, 2006), pp. 34–47.

nostri excogitatis praevalent; misceamus beneficia et lumen de lumine accendamus.

> Our greatest wish relates to this one thing: that you, by virtue of your prudence, consider the important task assigned to you by providence for the benefit of humankind, namely to initiate a new exchange of knowledge between two people living at a great distance from one another. [...] You bring our sciences to the Chinese, for in you and so many of your accompanying men I recognise, as it were, a compendium of European knowledge. Hence it is only fair that in return we attain insights into the hidden scientific knowledge of the Chinese, which has been preserved and augmented thanks to the transmission of a people and empire prospering for so many hundred years. This sort of exchange is just, because the Chinese outclass us in their observations, while we outclass the Chinese by our inventions. Let us throw our findings together and ignite light with light.

With this rather singular idea to join continental forces, Leibniz already paved the way for our modern understanding of a global community. The promotion of Europe as the leading cultural community, however, was upheld until the nineteenth century when nationalism drew people's attention away from the merits of the continent competing with other continents and had them focus on the merits of the individual European nations competing against each other instead.

4.5 *Intellectual Unity: Europe as a* Res Publica Literaria

The international community of learned men, known also as the *res publica literaria* (republic of letters), was not just a random cluster of intellectuals loosely tied to the contemporary idea of European peace, as is often claimed in literature.[270] In fact, as a community they represented a proper concept of Europe – or rather lived it. Therefore, the *res publica literaria* seems to have been the only early modern project of European integration that came to fruition. Surprisingly, though, the republic of letters has not yet received much attention in scholarship as an early modern example of European integration.

Scholars following the studies of Françoise Waquet have approached the republic of letters from a much more critical angle, insisting that it remained a mere notion, a phantom chased.[271] Waquet's view is based on two failed

---

270   Cf. Kläger and Bayer, p. 3.
271   In one of her latest publications dedicated to the republic of letters, Waquet expands on her opinion ('The Republic of Letters', in *A Guide to Neo-Latin Literature*, ed. by Victoria

attempts at institutionalising the continental intellectual exchange in the first half of the eighteenth century: first, the miscarriage regarding the establishment of an official *societas literaria* ('literary society') in 1712 and 1721, intended to facilitate the publication and dissemination of scholarly discussions and scientific findings; second, the abortive implementation of a federal bureau of international studies in the late 1740s.[272] However, just because an officially institutionalised union of European intellectuals never came into being, this does not mean that the union did not exist with an unofficial status. The only difference pertained to the fact that the *res publica literaria*, in the way in which it existed, had evolved naturally and thrived precisely due to the lack of statutes, regulations, and administrative officials. In addition, we can see in it a concept of European integration fulfilled when understanding that the European public represented by the members of the *res publica literaria* had not been there a priori but was created deliberately by them.[273]

The republic of letters encompassed by definition the entirety of educated men and women all over Europe – scholars, poets, scientists, clerics, noblemen – irrespective of their geographical, confessional, or political separations.[274] Despite its socially heterogeneous composition, the members' common denominator consisted in their high esteem of education, based on classical knowledge and literature, as well as the Christian tradition. If there existed any hierarchy at all, it remained unspoken, merely traceable through the awe and respect with which outstanding figures like Erasmus were met. In short, the republic's main feature was its egalitarianism. It not only stood in stark contrast to the sentiments of the time but also found expression in the

---

Moul [Cambridge: Cambridge University Press], pp. 66–80 [p. 68]): "It [= the Republic of letters] was, and remained, a grand dream, never realized but always potentially realizable, which conferred upon the intellectual world a force, a cohesion and a unity previously unknown."

272   Waquet discusses the failed attempts in greater detail in 'Republic of Letters', p. 68.

273   The reference work on Erasmus and his contemporaries contains a list of 1900 fellows who were part of Erasmus' network. The establishment of this network resulted from conscious acts of intellectual exchange and dialogue. The second and third volume succeed particularly in showing the slow but steady growth of the republic of letters in the sixteenth century and how, step by step, it seized Europe like a wave. Peter G. Bietenholz and Thomas B. Deutscher (eds.), *Contemporaries of Erasmus: A Biographical Register of the Renaissance and Reformation*, 3 vols. (Toronto: University of Toronto Press, 1985).

274   On the characteristics of the *res publica literaria*, see Korenjak, p. 17; Waquet, 'Republic of Letters', p. 70. A comprehensive overview of the members' communality is provided in Françoise Waquet, 'Qu'est-ce que la République des Lettres? Essai de sémantique historique', *Bibliothèque de l'école des chartes*, 147 (1989), 473–502; Hans Bots and Françoise Waquet, *La République des Lettres* (Paris: Belin, 1997).

democratic denomination *res publica*. As Anthony Grafton pointedly states, the republic of letters

> had no borders, no government, and no capital. In a world of sharp and well-defined social hierarchies [...] its citizens insisted that they were all equal [...]. The Republic of Letters imagined itself as Europe's first egalitarian society.[275]

Against this background, the *res publica literaria* has often been considered an early modern reproduction of Plato's Academy.[276] It was a utopian state, an ideal of international intellectual cooperation become real. The only guidelines the members had to follow were to speak and write in Latin as the commonly comprehensible language, on the one hand, and to act in good faith and with loyalty when conversing with fellow members, on the other. By respecting these rules, any member could reach out to another one, no matter where they lived or to what confession they belonged. Everybody was heard and welcome as long as both the sciences and the *belles lettres* were maintained with dignity.

It is no coincidence that many representatives of the *res publica literaria* were involved in the foundation of academies (Leibniz, for instance, was among the founding fathers of the Academy of Sciences set up in Berlin in 1700), or taught at early modern universities. What distinguished them from intellectuals of earlier times was their strong belief in the "universality of knowledge"[277] and "fundamental codes of civility". Therefore, as well, stories told of mutual solidarity in the name of scholarship, literature, and science despite international conflicts were anything but rare. The first half of the seventeenth century, for instance, saw an intensified blossoming of intellectual exchange on the continent, as if the international community of scholars had deliberately decided to set an example against the Europe-wide conflicts fought out in the course of the Thirty Years' War.[278] More than a century later, the French astronomer Jérôme de Lalande (1732–1807) paid a visit to the Royal Society of London in 1763 and was warmly welcomed there, while French and English soldiers were slaughtering each other on the European battlefields in the Seven Years War (1756–1763).[279]

---

275 Grafton, p. 9.
276 Waquet, 'Qu'est-ce que la République des Lettres', p. 474.
277 Aspaas, p. 283.
278 Grafton, p. 17.
279 Lalande's warm welcome and the fruitful collaboration in London is outlined in Danielle M.A. Fauque, 'La correspondance Jérôme Lalande et Nevil Maskelyne: Un exemple de collaboration internationale au XVIIIᵉ siècle', in *Jérôme Lalande (1732–1807): Une*

Similarly to the term 'Europe', the phrase *res publica literaria* had been pretty much non-existent before the Renaissance. It was mentioned for the first time in a letter by the Venetian humanist Francesco Barbaro (1390–1454), addressed to his fellow humanist Poggio Bracciolini (1380–1459), when talking about newly discovered manuscripts.[280] In the course of the following decades and centuries, the phrase ultimately gained traction along with the expansion of the intellectual network all over the continent. Yet since the *res publica literaria* was in fact a *Europe vécue* rather than a *Europe voulue* or *pensée*,[281] it was acted out day by day so that not much theoretical discussion of it was provided as a specific form of European integration. Every member was well aware that the community constituted such a paradigm of European integration, but its value as a European concept remained a mere unspoken truth. As late as 1681, Leibniz – himself one of the key contemporary figures of the republic of letters – complained about the lack of treatises on the *res publica literaria* and its international achievements for the benefit of the European public in the first draft of his ideas on universal knowledge (p. 428):[282] "De Republica literaria nemo adhuc satis ex usu publico aut pro argumenti dignitate scripsit." – "No one has yet sufficiently written about the republic of letters to the public advantage or for the recognition of its concept."

However, several contemporary definitions of the *res publica literaria* at least referred to the idea of a Europe united by the forces of education and love of knowledge. Attributing a prime position to the principle of *humanitas*,

---

trajectoire scientifique, ed. by Guy Boistel, Jérôme Lamy, and Colette Le Lay (Rennes: Presses universitaires de Rennes, 2010), pp. 109–28.

280   Elizabeth L. Eisenstein, *The Printing Press as an Agent of Change: Communications and Cultural Transformations in Early Modern Europe, Vol. 1* (Cambridge: Cambridge University Press, 1979), p. 137 n. 287.

281   In order to better understand nuances in the conceptualisation of Europe, the historians Hartmut Kaelble and René Girault have introduced analytical categories to decipher the meaning of Europe in linguistic usage: they distinguish between *Europe vécue* (the real Europe, as it exists and is experienced), *Europe pensée* (a merely imagined, fictitious sort of Europe), and *Europe voulue* (a Europe meant to be manifested by means of an urging appeal). Hartmut Kaelble, 'L'Europe vécue et l'Europe pensée au XXᵉ siècle: Les spécificités sociales de l'Europe', in *Identité et conscience européennes au XXᵉ siècle*, ed. by René Girault (Paris: Hachette Littératures, 1994), pp. 27–45; René Girault, 'Das Europa der Historiker', in *Europa im Blick der Historiker: Europäische Integration im 20. Jahrhundert. Bewusstsein und Institutionen*, Historische Zeitschrift. Beihefte, 21, ed. by Rainer Hudemann, Hartmut Kaelble, and Klaus Schwabe (Munich: Oldenbourg, 1995), pp. 55–90.

282   Gottfried Wilhelm Leibniz, *De republica literaria*, in *Philosophische Schriften: Bd. 4: 1677– Juni 1690, Teil A*, ed. by Leibniz-Forschungsstelle Münster (Berlin: Akademie Verlag, 1999), pp. 428–38.

the republic of letters thus represented a plan for continental peace and harmonious cooperation as much as any other concept of Europe that was part of the Europe discourse. In his dialogue *Antibarbarorum liber unus* (One Book of Erudite Thoughts; composed in 1494), for example, Erasmus uses the phrase *res publica literaria* as an opposing draft to anybody shutting themselves off from *humanitas* and education (p. 68).[283] A few decades later, the French scholar Isaac Casaubon (1559–1614) went a few steps further, markedly emphasising the peaceful transnational coherence of the republic of letters, when highlighting its principles of universality, equality, freedom, truth, and reason in a letter (epistle no. 36, p. 23) to the German-Dutch lawyer Fridericus Lindenbrogius (1573–1648):[284] "Habet hoc communio studiorum, ut et animos iungat, et ignotos atque in diversissimis oris positos conciliet invicem atque devinciat." – "The community of those who study the same topics links minds and conciliates and unites men who do not know one another and who live in far removed parts of the world."

The student Carl Friedrich Romanus (1679–1745) gives a similar definition of the *res publica literaria* in his eponymous dissertation *De republica litteraria*, disputed in 1698 at the University of Leipzig.[285] In twenty-six chapters he investigates the notion of the republic of letters, its origins, members, principles, goals, and methods of communication. At one point he arrives at its international European alignment, held together by reason like a queen ruling over a vast empire of equal and free subjects (pp. 28–29):

> Pervadit illa [= res publica literaria] regiones omnes [...]. Sedet in throno ipsa ratio, veluti regina [...]; pares omnes, nisi quod excellentiores animi dotes inter aequales discrimen aliquod faciant; utuntur interim universi eius cives libertate plane eximia atque incomparabili [...].

> This republic of letters sprawls out across all regions [...]. At their head presides, like a queen, reason [...]; all its members are equal with the sole exception that some gifted minds stand out among the equal

---

283   Waquet, 'République des Lettres', p. 474. For an edition of the text, see *Antibarbarorum Liber*, in *Opera omnia Desiderii Erasmi Roterodami: Recognita et adnotatione critica instructa notisque illustrata, vol. I.1*, ed. by Kazimierz Kumaniecki (Amsterdam: North Holland, 1969), pp. 35–138.

284   Isaac Casaubon, *Epistolae, insertis ad easdem responsionibus*, ed. by Theodor Jansonius van Almeloveen, 3rd edn (Rotterdam: Fritsch & Böhm, 1709). The translation is taken from Waquet, 'Republic of Letters', p. 73.

285   Carl Friedrich Romanus, *Dissertatio academica de republica litteraria* [...] (Leipzig: Götz, 1698).

partners; all its universal citizens make use of their great and incomparable liberty [...].

References to a community transcending the boundaries of nationality and human strife, following egalitarian policies of a proper 'republic' which accommodates free citizens working for the common good, are also found in eighteenth-century promotions of the *res publica literaria*. In 1708, the later general superintendent Christian Löber (1683–1747) held a politically underpinned disputation on the *res publica literaria* at the University of Jena, entitled *Dissertatio politica de forma regiminis reipublicae literariae* (Political Dissertation on the Form of Rule of the Republic of Letters).[286] Even though his examination constitutes a straightforward political search for democratic and republican elements in the *res publica literaria* rather than an educational praise of it, his concluding thesis proves unambiguous and in accordance with the existing definitions (pp. 4–5):

> De generali illa societate loquimur, cujus membra dispersa in orbe, hoc communi salutis humanae studio copulantur, ut sapientiam veram, veramque eruditionem servent, doceant, defendant et ad posteros quoque transmittant.

> I am speaking of this universal society, whose members are dispersed over the globe and linked by the joint desire for human salvation. This is why they put themselves in the service of true wisdom and true erudition, this why they teach it, defend it, and pass it on to posterity.

In this passage, Löber also refers to the maintenance and future of the *res publica literaria*. This look away from the current state towards a continuity reaching into the future makes his investigation a perfect contribution to the discourse of Europe, as it unfolds a lasting (and yet unfulfilled) vision of the republic of letters.

An intriguing analogy defining the *res publica literaria* provides Christoph August Heumann (1681–1764) in his handbook of early modern literary history, the *Conspectus republicae literariae* (Overview of the Republic of Letters, 1718).[287] Despite its title suggesting otherwise, it does not contain a specific

---

286   Christian Löber, *Dissertatio politica de forma regiminis reipublicae literariae* [...] (Jena: Werther, 1708).

287   Christoph August Heumann, *Conspectus reipublicae literariae sive via ad historiam literariam iuventuti stud. aperta*, 2nd edn (Hannover: Förster, 1726).

treatment of the republic of letters as an international community, but rather assembles highlights of various literary genres and authors from Antiquity to Heumann's present. It is only in a footnote at the end of his chapter on the most noteworthy authors of literary history that Heumann mentions the existence of a community of learned men, whose shared identity, camaraderie, and unity he compares to that of the theological concept of 'the Church invisible' (p. 198 n. 1):

> Resp. literaria ratione formae simillima est Ecclesiae invisibili. Vti hic nullus monarcha, nullum ciuile imperium, sed summa libertas, sola regnante S. Scriptura; sic illic sola regnant (sic) Ratio, nec quisquam in alterum quicquam habet iuris ciuilis. Ac libertas ista adeo est reip. literariae anima [...].

> The republic of letters in the organisation of its structure is very similar to the invisible Church: just as the latter comprises no monarch, no political empire, but there is the greatest liberty and the only guidelines are provided by Holy Scripture, so in the former reason alone rules and no one is in need of civil law against another. This freedom of living constitutes the soul of the republic of letters [...].

Here again we encounter the notion of peaceful collaboration inherent in the *res publica literaria*, whose members believe in the 'word' only and, in this belief, dwell as totally free and equal citizens. The comparison with the 'invisible Church' points to the reality of the 'learned state' superimposed on Europe without any concrete political manifestations.

As all the examples cited have shown, the *res publica literaria* was, in essence, a world of authors and texts. Its impact spanned their scholarly production in the name of the preservation and advancement of knowledge. As a result, its contribution to the discourse of Europe was of a very specific kind and cannot be demonstrated by its members' theoretical approach to Europe (as has been the case with all the concepts of Europe outlined previously) but by their practical approach to it. If one wants to know more about the continental understanding shared by the members of the republic of letters, one needs to look at the works they produced and disseminated among the European public. Their letters especially – usually written in the supranational Latin language – offer valuable insights into their world, as they served as the main means of communication among the members scattered all over the continent before the introduction of scholarly journals after 1700.[288] Collaboration was most feasible via letters, which is why many correspondences confront us today with literally thousands of letters by early modern contemporaries.[289] Those letters impart an image of the European dimension of the scholarly networks as well as their authors' common sense of belonging.

The advantages of correspondence by letter are even outlined in contemporary studies such as Daniel Georg Morhof's encyclopaedic *Polyhistor* (Polymath; 1688).[290] His deliberations reveal once more the transnational affiliation of European individuals, on the one hand, and the harmonius collaboration towards a common goal, on the other. Firstly, letters bridge spatial separation (§57, p. 168: "Cum absentis conversamur per epistolas" – "We converse by means of epistles with those who are absent") and strengthen the bond of common passions (ibid.: "Illa homines conversatio sola ingenii similitudine conjungit, cum se nunquam viderint, quo affectus saepe plus, quam praesentium conversatione incendi solet." – "This sort of conversation links people solely on the basis of their like-mindedness. Since they never meet in person, their passion is often incited more than it generally is in a personal conversation."). Secondly, letters conceal the bad habits and vices of people that tend to emerge in face-to-face conversations – which only goes to show the conciliatory nature of epistolary correspondence (ibid.):

> Tegit epistola et celat omnes illos defectus, qui forte in moribus aut forma colloquentis apparent; solus hic animus loquitur, seque nudum exhibet.

---

288   For a broader overview of the international communication between the members of the republic of letters, see Paul Dibon, 'Communication in the *Respublica Litteraria* in the 17th Century', *Res publica litterarum*, 1 (1978), 43–56. The importance of letter exchange is emphasised in Grafton, p. 21.

289   Joseph Scaliger (1540–1609) wrote about 1700 letters; Francesco Filelfo (1398–1481) more than 2000; Erasmus some 3000; Justus Lipsius (1547–1606) more than 4000; and Leibniz an incredible number of 20,000 letters. The scope and significance of letter-writing in the Early Modern Period as a means to exchange scholarly opinions and foster scientific insights can also be observed from contemporary descriptions of the epistolary culture. In chapter XXIII ('De epistolarum scriptoribus' – On Writers of Letters) of Daniel Georg Morhof's *Polyhistor* (cf. note 51) humanists from Petrarca to his own times are listed as exemplars.

290   On Morhof and selected aspects of his *Polyhistor*, see Françoise Waquet (ed.), *Mapping the World of Learning: The* Polyhistor *of Daniel Georg Morhof*, Wolfenbütteler Forschungen, 91 (Wiesbaden: Harrassowitz, 2000).

A letter covers and hides all those deficiencies that might come out in the behaviour or character of an interlocutor; in the case of letter-writing, it is only the mind that speaks and presents itself as naked.

In the introductory preface to his treatise *De conscribendis epistolis* (On the Art of Writing Letters, 1522), Erasmus, decades before Morhof, equally evoked the pacifying force of international correspondence when decrying the military conflicts between Emperor Charles V and the French king Francis I, which had been taking a toll on all of Christianity. Despite these military conflicts, Erasmus states in an attempt to link his complaint with the actual topic of his treatise that the war would not be able to put an end to international epistolary exchange.[291] In this statement the opposition between war and peace, conflict and conciliation, national strife and international openness pointedly culminates, displaying the position attributed to epistolary exchange in times of continental upheaval. Writing letters to each other for the sake of a common goal, regardless of the ongoing political splits ripping the continent apart, was an important tool for staying on top of all the information available since the introduction of printing; it constituted the fount of the European scholars' knowledge, an expression of mutual respect (for reciprocity in writing letters was crucial) and recognition of international citizenship within the *res publica literaria*.[292]

The principles of internationality, equality, freedom, reason, and *humanitas* characterising the European *res publica literaria* were complemented by a genuine sense of cosmopolitanism. Countless members of the republic of letters travelled the continent throughout their lifetime without exhibiting any national preference whatsoever. Erasmus, for example, was born in the Netherlands and took up residence in England, Switzerland, France, and Germany. Juan Luis Vives, originally from Valencia, studied in Paris and worked in England and Belgium. John Barclay, the son of a Scottish father and a French mother, left his home in France already as a child, and from this moment on settled in England and Italy, among other places, after extensive travels to various European nations. Gottfried Wilhelm Leibniz' scholarly and diplomatic missions not only led him from England and France to Germany, Austria, and Italy, but his geopolitical interests even extended from his own home to China,

---

291   Erasmus of Rotterdam, *Ausgewählte Schriften, lateinisch und deutsch: Bd. 8: De conscribendis epistolis*, ed. by Kurt Smolak, 2nd edn (Darmstadt: Wissenschaftliche Buchgesellschaft, 1995), pp. 4–7.

292   Dena Goodman, *The Republic of Letters: A Cultural History of the French Enlightenment* (Ithaca, NY: Cornell University Press, 1996), pp. 16–18; Waquet, 'Republic of Letters', pp. 75–76.

Russia, and Egypt.[293] Needless to say, all of them wrote largely or exclusively in Latin. The universal citizenship that they claimed for themselves coincided with their membership of the *res publica literaria* and ultimately turned them into exemplary bearers of a pan-European identity.[294]

Erasmus, among all the members of the republic of letters from the fifteenth to the eighteenth centuries, was its undisputed prince and the pinnacle of European citizenship.[295] National sentiments were but a nuisance to him, unnecessary and pointless. This is evident from an incident in which he was involved as a mediator: In 1520 two of his friends and fellow members of the *res publica literaria*, the Frenchman Germain de Brie (1490–1538) and the Englishman Thomas More (1478–1535), had fallen out with each other over respectively hurt national feelings. As any proper citizen of the republic of letters would do, they waged their personal war by means of letters and pamphlets. And what was deemed by them a decent medium to use was equally appropriate for the prince and mediator, Erasmus, himself: he calmed the excited minds of de Brie and More and led them back to the path of supranational solidarity beyond any petty national resentments by reminding them of their common values which would know no nationality nor border.[296]

This approach was typical of Erasmus, whose supranational, pacifist, and uniform affirmation of Europeanism found expression in many ways: by dedicating the majority of his humanist works to the most influential European princes and leaders of his time, such as the emperor Charles V, his brother Ferdinand I, King of the Romans, Francis I of France, and Henry VIII of England; by sending letters to humanists of all European nations as well as to their inimical scholastics, to representatives of various European courts, the papal court, members of different religious orders, and Protestants and Catholics alike. Moreover, he chose the provocative path of praising one nation in one letter and celebrating another nation as the most accomplished in another.[297] In this way, he not only made it quite clear how little the emerging national disputes

---

293   On Erasmus, see Wilhelm Ribhegge, 'Erasmus und Europa: Studien zur Korrespondenz des Erasmus von Rotterdam', *Zeitschrift für Historische Forschung*, 25 (1998), 549–80; on Barclay and Vives, see Schulze, p. 30, and Walser, '*Unitas multiplex*', p. 543; on Leibniz, see Gale, p. 7.

294   Cf. Bots and Waquet, pp. 31–34; Aspaas, p. 282.

295   On Erasmus' biography, see Léon-E. Halkin, *Erasmus: A Critical Biography*. Transl. by John Tonkin (Cambridge, MA: Blackwell, 1994).

296   The quarrel and Erasmus' conciliating Latin letters are discussed in Ribhegge, pp. 572–73.

297   This explicit pan-European view of the world is remarked upon by Erasmus himself in a letter to the French nobleman Louis Ruzé (*c.* 1455–*c.* 1534) from 19(?) March 1519. The letter is edited in the third volume of Percy S. Allen's monumental collection of Erasmus' letters: Erasmus of Rotterdam, *Epistle no. 928 to Louis Ruzé*, in *Opus epistolarum Des.*

meant to him and how insignificant he deemed any form of national rivalry, but he also reduced such squabbles *ad absurdum*.[298]

Erasmus even voiced his affirmation of supranationality in a series of illustrative dictums decorating his letters. These enunciations help us to reconstruct the underlying notion of the *res publica literaria* and to understand its mission within a clearly defined European framework. In a letter addressed to the Swiss reformer Ulrich Zwingli (1484–1531) and presumably dated 3 September 1522 from his temporary home in Basel, Erasmus exclaims in the context of an unrelenting disease confining him to his bed (p. 129):[299] "Ego mundi ciuis esse cupio, communis omnium vel peregrinus magis." – "I wish to be a citizen of the world, or even better, a common foreigner to everyone." In similar fashion he informs the Dutch scholar Marcus Laurinus (1488–1540) a few months later, on 1 February 1523, about his stay in Basel and his occasional trips to Konstanz and Sélestat (p. 217):[300] "Ego [...] respondi me velle ciuem esse totius mundi, non vnius oppidi." – "To this I [...] answered that I desire to be a citizen of the entire world, not merely one city."

This cosmopolitan view of the world as expressed by Erasmus was, in fact, strongly tied to notions of Europeanness. For even though Erasmus hardly ever used the word 'Europe' in any of his works other than to denote the continent's geographical space, his view naturally derived from a Eurocentric conception of the world.[301] His 'world' was essentially European, and his cosmopolitanism, therefore, was at its core a Europeanism. After all, early modern contemporaries merely knew the world as a European place where European culture and civilisation dominated and foreign cultures and traditions – if they were recognised at all – only played a minor role.[302] Following the ancient meaning of the term 'cosmopolitan', documented for the first time in the writings of the

---

Erasmi Roterodami: Vol. 3: 1517–1519, ed. Percy S. Allen (Oxford: Oxford University Press, 1992 [1913]), pp. 509–12.

298 Erasmus' supranational vision of Europe, along with his strategy for propagating this vision in his letters, is expounded in Jean-Claude Margolin, 'Erasme et la psychologie des peuples', *Revue d'ethno-psychologie*, 25 (1970), 373–424. Cf. also Schulze, p. 28.

299 Erasmus of Rotterdam, *Epistle no. 1314 to Ulrich Zwingli*, in *Opus epistolarum Des. Erasmi Roterodami: Vol. 5: 1522–1524*, ed. Percy S. Allen (Oxford: Oxford University Press, 1992 [1924]), pp. 129–30.

300 Erasmus of Rotterdam, *Epistle no. 1342 to Marcus Laurinus*, in *Opus epistolarum Des. Erasmi Roterodami: Vol. 5: 1522–1524*, ed. Percy S. Allen (Oxford: Oxford University Press, 1992 [1924]), pp. 203–27.

301 Ribhegge, p. 551.

302 The implications of European cultural superiority for the early modern discourse of Europe have been discussed in the previous part.

Greek cynic philosopher Diogenes (fourth century BCE), being a cosmopolitan simply implied locating oneself in the world order beyond one's *polis* or *patria* (homeland).[303] In the early modern centuries, the only world order known was the European world order. This held true for Erasmus as much as for any other member of the *res publica literaria*:

> While the Republic of Letters set forth a universal ideal, its geographical extent appeared, in reality, rather more limited. It was confined to Europe.[304]

In keeping with the Erasmian perception, the Erasmus programme, started in 1987 on a European basis to enable young students to study abroad, was limited to Europe for almost twenty years. It was only in 2003 that the additional programme *Erasmus Mundus* was founded, offering a worldwide student exchange supported by the European Union.

While many intellectuals on the continent picked up Erasmus' famous cosmopolitan saying until the end of the eighteenth century, the cosmopolitanism praised by the *res publica literaria* was also increasingly equated with the term 'Europe' from the end of the seventeenth century onwards. In good Erasmian tradition, the German historian and librarian Peter Lambeck (1628–1680) sticks with the 'citizen-of-the-world' idea in the announcement of his *Oratio de peregrinationum utilitate* (Oration on the Utility of Travelling Abroad), held on 15 July 1652 at the *Gymnasium illustre* in Hamburg.[305] He has been appointed professor of history only one year earlier and he takes the occasion now to make himself heard as a young open-minded academic to address his students by encouraging them to travel and see the continent (p. 84):

---

303   The term's etymology is explained and traced throughout Antiquity in Andrea Albrecht, *Kosmopolitismus: Weltbürgerdiskurse in Literatur, Philosophie und Publizistik um 1800*, spectrum Literaturwissenschaft / spectrum Literature, 1 (Berlin: de Gruyter, 2005), pp. 22–23. While Cicero had translated the Greek word with *mundanus* when attributing cosmopolitanism to Socrates (Tusc. v.8), Erasmus seems to have derived the phrase *civis totius mundi* from Seneca's Latin arrangement *mundus* and *patria*, a literal translation of the Greek nouns *kósmos* and *pólis* (v. beat. 20.5). For editions of Cicero and Seneca, see Cicero, *Tusculanae disputationes*, ed. by Michelangelo Giusta (Turin: Paravia, 1984), and Seneca, *Dialogorum libri duodecim*, ed by Leighton Durham Reynolds (Oxford: Clarendon Press, 1977).

304   Waquet, 'Republic of Letters', p. 73.

305   Waquet, 'République des Lettres', pp. 495–96. Peter Lambeck, *Programma orationis peregrinationum utilitate*, in *Orationes aliquot in illustri Gymnasio Hamburgensi habitae, una cum programmatibus nonnullis publice propositis* (Hamburg: Piper, 1660), pp. 84–85.

> [...] ego [...] iam a teneris annis sic mihi persuaserim, natali quidem solo prae aliis cunctis locis natura nos devinctos esse, sed neque ita tamen superstitiose illud adamandum, ut nos reliqui etiam totius mundi incolas et cives esse obliviscamur.

> [...] I [...] have lived with the persuasion from an early age that although we are bound to our native land by nature above all other places, we should not be so superstitiously in love with it that we forget to be inhabitants and citizens of the entire remaining world.

Lambeck's thoughtful reminder of supranationality not only echoes Erasmus' famous conviction. Even more intriguingly, it contains a message of separate yet not mutually exclusive identities. By explicitly pointing out that one must not give up the love of one's native country in order to feel or be cosmopolitan, Lambeck makes a valuable statement with respect to the early modern discourse of Europe: regionalism, nationalism, and Europeanism can exist alongside each other. This has been confirmed by modern theories surrounding the psychology of identity.[306] In general, everybody can take on several identities at the same time, which leads one's personal and other group identities to coincide at some point. A supporter of Europe might thus be characterised by an equally strong affiliation towards his town and his nation. In terms of European identity this means that nationalist pride and European affiliation need not be opposed to each other. A prime example of how continental attitudes can be amicably matched with local stances was – unsurprisingly – Erasmus himself, who preferred to go by the designation Erasmus 'of Rotterdam'.[307]

In contrast to Lambeck, the Erasmian 'citizen-of-the-world' phrase was of hardly any significance in Leibniz' vast correspondence around and after 1700, despite Leibniz' undisputed role as the contemporary prince of the *res publica literaria* after Erasmus. Leibniz himself never referred either to himself as a cosmopolitan nor to Europe as an intellectual landmark. His Enlightenment philosophy encompassed all of humanity and not only European civilisation (as has been shown in the previous part). However, most of his correspondents evaluated him and his work within a European framework. Therefore, he was usually addressed as the most dignified and versed among the European intellectuals, in the context of which the *res publica literaria* was as much

---

306   Cf. Wolfgang Schmale, *Geschichte Europas* (Vienna: Böhlau, 2000), p. 13, and Edwards, p. 19.

307   Burke, 'Did Europe Exist', p. 27. On the conflicting issue of 'identity', see generally Burke, *Languages and Communities*, p. 6; Edwards, p. 2.

equated with Europe as Leibniz' supposed world view. An illustrative example is provided by a letter from the German historiographer Christian Juncker (1668–1714), dated 1 May 1705, in which he presents his current study projects to Leibniz.[308] Juncker opens his letter with the sentence (p. 575):

> [...] innumera exstent in rem pariter publicam et litterariam merita Tua, et ideo nemo sit Eruditorum per omnes Europae cultioris provincias, qui singulari aut favore aut honore Te non prosequatur.

> [...] your innumerable merits stand out both in the republic of letters and in public. Hence, there is none among the learned men in any of the parts of our cultured Europe who would not approach you with favour and honour.

Here, Leibniz is clearly styled a European – indeed, the greatest European in intellectual terms – whose impact reaches all of Europe and whose frame of reference is the *res publica literaria* as a European institution.

Returning to Erasmus' notion of cosmopolitanism one last time, we can see how intricately linked his understanding of Europe was to contemporary learnedness. In this way, he rendered the *res publica literaria* a proper concept of Europe characterised by supranational efforts in scholarship. In a letter of 5 April 1518 addressed to Marcus Laurinus, this time from Leuven, he describes his ideal home, which he has previously defined as everywhere on the continent, as a place of erudition (p. 266):[309] "Illic opinor habeo sedem, vbi bibliothecam meam habeo." – "I deem home where there is my library." Following this assertion, Erasmus conceives of everyone who consecrates themselves to the cult of the Muses as a fellow citizen in this republic of letters encompassing the continent (p. 511):[310] "quisquis communibus Musarum sacris initiatus est, hunc ego *homopatrida* duco." – "Whoever is committed to the common solemnities

308 Gottfried Wilhelm Leibniz, *Epistle no. 321 from Christian Juncker to Leibniz*, in *Sämtliche Schriften und Briefe: Erste Reihe. Allgemeiner, politischer und historischer Briefwechsel: Bd. 24: Oktober 1704–Juli 1705*, ed. by Leibniz Forschungsstelle Hannover der Akademie der Wissenschaften zu Göttingen (Berlin: Akademie Verlag, 2015), pp. 575–78.

309 Erasmus of Rotterdam, *Epistle no. 809 to Marcus Laurinus*, in *Opus epistolarum Des. Erasmi Roterodami: Vol. 3: 1517–1519*, ed. Percy S. Allen (Oxford: Oxford University Press, 1992 [1913]), pp. 263–70.

310 Erasmus of Rotterdam, *Epistle no. 928 to Louis Ruzé*, in *Opus epistolarum Des. Erasmi Roterodami: Vol. 3: 1517–1519*, ed. Percy S. Allen (Oxford: Oxford University Press, 1992 [1913]), pp. 509–12.

of the Muses I hold as my compatriot." It is in the studies of *bonae litterae* that Erasmus sees the ideal way out of the conflicts prevailing in Europe. This is exactly where he has come full circle, acknowledging the European dimension of the joint undertaking called the *res publica literaria*, on the one hand, and emphasising its potential for unanimity as a sustainable vision of Europe, on the other.

5   Perspectives

Europe is not only a contested topic nowadays but has been one since the beginning of the Early Modern Period. Thanks to its role as the continent's *lingua franca*, Latin played a particularly crucial role in defining and conceptualising notions of continental communality from the fifteenth to the eighteenth centuries. In all kinds of genres, authors from different European nations expressed their visions of a Europe united by different forms of political, religious, cultural, or ethnic measures. While the Neo-Latin research into the history of Europe has produced some remarkable first results in recent years, enabling a better understanding of the centuries-long process of European integration and complementing the historical results based on vernacular texts, there is still a lot more work to be done. In fact, the Neo-Latin making of Europe and its historical reappraisal still lacks fundamental research on multiple levels.

This would begin with the systematic hunt for original manuscripts and printed editions in online catalogues and databases, archives, and libraries. After this quantitative assessment, a profound qualitative classification would have to follow. This qualitative classification and study of the texts found would entail both a synchronic and a diachronic treatment of the discourse of Europe; different ideas of Europe would have to be surveyed from different regional, national, confessional, and mental points of view at different points in time according to different genres (asking, for example: how did a French Jewish author living in Paris in the middle of the seventeenth century conceive of Europe in his letters?); case studies would have to be compared and put in relation to one another, so as to understand on a broader level how Europe was perceived and through what mechanisms European identity was created over the course of the early modern centuries.[311]

---

311   In this respect, Wolfang Schmale speaks of so-called "universally European" and "partially European structural elements" ("universaleuropäische" und "teileuropäische Strukturelemente"; Schmale, *Geschichte Europas*, p. 13). By comparing those elements

It is only once these parameters have been met that we will be able to safely make comprehensive statements about the formation of Europe and about who has deployed the term 'Europe' and/or other signifiers in what part of the continent, for what reasons, with what underlying notions and purpose, and in what contexts. An initial step in the direction of an overview of the Neo-Latin literature of Europe (even if merely in the form of an early interim report) is marked by the present study.

References

Primary Literature

Albericus Trium Fontium. 1874. *Chronica a monacho Novi Monasterii Hoiensis interpolata*, ed. by Paul Scheffer-Boichorst, in *Monumenta Germaniae Historia: Scriptores, Bd. 23*, ed. by Georg Heinrich Pertz (Hannover: Hahn), pp. 631–950.

Anon. 1625. *Querimonia Europae, divisa in libros duos* (London: Stansby).

Anon. 1640. *De praesenti Europae statu oratio ad principes populosque Europaeos* (n. p.: n. pub.).

Anon. 1966. *Karolus magnus et Leo papa: Ein Paderborner Epos vom Jahre 799*, ed. by Helmut Beumann, Franz Brunhölzl, and Wilhelm Winkelmann, Studien und Quellen zur Westfälischen Geschichte, 8 (Paderborn: Bonifatius).

Barclay, John. 2013. *Icon animorum or The Mirror of Minds*, ed. by Mark Riley, Bibliotheca Latinitatis Novae, 8 (Leuven: Leuven University Press).

Boccaccio, Giovanni. 1918. *Il commento alla Divina Commedia e gli altri scritti intorno a Dante, vol. 3*, ed. by Domenico Guerri, Scrittori d'Italia, 12 (Bari: Laterza).

Casaubon, Isaac. 1709. *Epistolae, insertis ad easdem responsionibus*, ed. by Theodor Jansonius van Almeloveen, 3rd edn (Rotterdam: Fritsch & Böhm).

Catwulf. 1895. *Cathwulfus Carolo I Francorum regi prosperitatem gratulatur eumque ad virtutem sequendam admonet*, in *Monumenta Germaniae historica: Epistolae Karolini aevi, Bd. 4*, ed. by Ernst Dümmler (Berlin: Weidmann), pp. 501–505.

Cicero. 1984. *Tusculanae disputationes*, ed. by Michelangelo Giusta (Turin: Paravia).

Comenius, Johan Amos. 1657. *Latium redivivum: Hoc est de forma erigendi Latinissimi Collegii, ceu novae Romae Civitatulae*, in *J.A. Comenii Didacticorum operum pars IV* (Amsterdam: Cunradus and van Rot), coll. 75–80.

Comenius, Johan Amos. 1702. *De rerum humanarum emendatione consultatio catholica, ad genus humanum ante alios vero ad eruditos, religiosos, potentes, Europae*, 3rd edn (Halle: Orphanotrophius).

---

with each other, ideally the common historical identity of European nations can be constructed, even though their joint history seems to be no older than a couple of decades.

Continuatio Hispana anno DCCLIV. 1894. In *Monumenta Germaniae historica: Auctores antiquissimi, Bd. 11*, ed. by Theodor Mommsen (Berlin: Weidmann), pp. 323–69.

Cusa, Nicholas of. 1970. *Opera omnia: Vol. 7: De pace fidei, cum epistula ad Ioannem de Segobia*, ed. by Raymond Klibansky and Hildebrand Bascour (Hamburg: Meiner).

Dante Alighieri. 1988. *De Monarchia*, ed. by Maurizio Pizzica (Milan: Biblioteca universale Rizzoli).

Deutsche Reichstagsakten unter König Albrecht II.: Bd. 13.1: 1438. 1957. Ed. by Gustav Beckmann (Göttingen: Perthes).

Dölau, Gottlob Christian von. 1681. *De monarchia universali, quae Europae imminere dicitur* (Leipzig: Coler).

Erasmus of Rotterdam. 1969. *Antibarbarorum Liber*, in *Opera omnia Desiderii Erasmi Roterodami: Recognita et adnotatione critica instructa notisque illustrata, vol. I.1*, ed. by Kazimierz Kumaniecki (Amsterdam: North Holland), pp. 35–138.

Erasmus of Rotterdam. 1992 [1913]. *Opus epistolarum Des. Erasmi Roterodami: Vol. 3: 1517–1519*, ed. Percy S. Allen (Oxford: Oxford University Press).

Erasmus of Rotterdam. 1992 [1924]. *Opus epistolarum Des. Erasmi Roterodami: Vol. 5: 1522–1524*, ed. Percy S. Allen (Oxford: Oxford University Press).

Erasmus of Rotterdam. 1995. *Ausgewählte Schriften, lateinisch und deutsch: Bd. 8: De conscribendis epistolis*, ed. by Kurt Smolak, 2nd edn (Darmstadt: Wissenschaftliche Buchgesellschaft).

Erasmus of Rotterdam. 1995. *Querela pacis undique gentium ejectae profligataque*, in *Ausgewählte Schriften, lateinisch und deutsch: Bd. 5*, ed. by Gertraud Christian, 2nd edn (Darmstadt: Wissenschaftliche Buchgesellschaft), pp. 359–451.

Erchanbert. 1829. *Breviarium regum Francorum*, in *Monumenta Germaniae historica: Scriptores, Bd. 2*, ed. by Georg Heinrich Pertz (Hannover: Hahn), pp. 327–30.

Ermoldus Nigellus. 1884. *Carmina*, in *Monumenta Germaniae historica: Poetae Latini medii aevi, Bd. 2*, ed. by Ernst Dümmler (Berlin: Weidmann), pp. 5–93.

Gagliuffi, Marco Faustino. 1833. *Specimen de fortuna Latinitatis. Accedunt poemata varia meditata et extemporalia* (Turin: Favale).

Gentili, Alberico. 1598. *De jure belli libri tres, nunc primum in lucem editi* (Hanau: Antonius).

Gessner, Conrad. 1545. *Bibliotheca universalis sive catalogus omnium scriptorum locupletissimus* (Zurich: Froschauer).

Gesta Treverorum: Pars prior usque ad a. 1101. 1848. Ed. by Georg Waitz, in *Monumenta Germaniae historica: Scriptores, Bd. 8*, ed. by Georg Heinrich Pertz (Hannover: Hahn), pp. 111–200.

Herodotus. 2015. *Historiae*, 2 vols., ed. by Nigel G. Wilson (Oxford: Oxford University Press).

Heumann, Christoph August. 1726. *Conspectus reipublicae literariae sive via ad historiam literariam iuventuti stud. aperta*, 2nd edn (Hannover: Förster).

Horace. 2008. *Opera*, ed. by David R. Shackleton Bailey (Berlin: de Gruyter).

Isidore of Seville. 1911. *Etymologiarum sive Originum Libri XX*, ed. by Wallace Lindsay (Oxford: Clarendon Press).

Jordanes. 1882. *Romana et Getica: Monumenta Germania historica, Bd. 5.1*, ed. by Theodor Mommsen (Berlin: Weidmann).

Kahle, Ludwig Martin. 1744. *Commentatio juris publici de trutina Europae quae vulgo adpellatur Die Balance von Europa praecipua belli et pacis norma* (Göttingen: Schmid).

Khun, Johann Caspar. 1698. *Panegyricus Ludovico XIV. Galliarum et Navarrae regi ob restitutam in Europa pacem* (Strasbourg: Staedel).

Kiliaan, Cornelis. 1614. *Lusus in Europae nationes*, in *Delitiae poetarum Belgicorum, huius superiorisque aevi illustrium, tertia pars*, ed. by Jan Gruter (Frankfurt: Hoffmann), pp. 37–44.

Kühlmann, Wilhelm, Robert Seidel, and Hermann Wiegand (eds.). 1997. *Humanistische Lyrik des 16. Jahrhunderts: Lateinisch und deutsch*, Bibliothek der frühen Neuzeit, I.5 (Frankfurt a.M.: Deutscher Klassiker Verlag).

Laguna, Andrés. 2001. *Europa heautentimorumene, es decir, que míseramente a sí misma se atormenta y lamenta su propia desgracia*, ed. by Miguel Ángel González Manjarrés (Valladolid: Junta de Castilla y León).

Lambeck, Peter. 1660. *Programma orationis peregrinationum utilitate*, in *Orationes aliquot in illustri Gymnasio Hamburgensi habitae, una cum programmatibus nonnullis publice propositis* (Hamburg: Piper), pp. 84–85.

Lauterbach, Johann. 2018. *Europa Eidyllion* in Isabella Walser-Bürgler, '*Europa Exultans*: The Personification of Europe as a Representation of the Habsburg Universal Monarchy in Johann Lauterbach's Pastoral Poem *Europa Eidyllion* (1558)', *Lias. Journal of Early Modern Intellectual Culture and its Sources*, 45: 1–43 (pp. 36–43).

Leibniz, Gottfried Wilhelm. 1877. *Kurzes wohl gemeyntes Bedencken vom Abgang der Studien und wie denenselben zu helffen*, in *Die Werke von Leibniz gemäß seinem handschriftlichen Nachlasse in der Königlichen Bibliothek zu Hannover: Bd. 10*, ed. by Onno Klopp (Hannover: Klindworth), pp. 435–42.

Leibniz, Gottfried Wilhelm. 1999. *De republica literaria*, in *Philosophische Schriften: Bd. 4: 1677–Juni 1690, Teil A*, ed. by Leibniz-Forschungsstelle Münster (Berlin: Akademie Verlag), pp. 428–38.

Leibniz, Gottfried Wilhelm. 2006. *Der Briefwechsel mit den Jesuiten in China (1689–1714)*, ed. by Rita Widmaier and Malte-Ludolf Babin, Philosophische Bibliothek, 548 (Hamburg: Meiner).

Leibniz, Gottfried Wilhelm. 2015. *Epistle no. 321 from Christian Juncker to Leibniz*, in *Sämtliche Schriften und Briefe: Erste Reihe. Allgemeiner, politischer und historischer Briefwechsel: Bd. 24: Oktober 1704–Juli 1705*, ed. by Leibniz Forschungsstelle Hannover (Berlin: Akademie Verlag), pp. 575–78.

Lentulus, Cyriacus. 1650. *Europa: regionum cultissimae terrarum orbis partis situm, urbium ac fluviorum junctam et separatam descriptionem, terrarum fertilitatem et inopiam, nationum mores et instituta, statuum origines, incrementa, vires: brevi quasi tabella exprimens* (Herborn: Corvinus).

Livy. 1974. *Ab urbe condita: Libri I–V*, ed. by Robert Maxwell Ogilvie (Oxford: Oxford University Press).

Löber, Christian. 1708. *Dissertatio politica de forma regiminis reipublicae literariae* [...] (Jena: Werther).

Lucan. 1997. *De bello civili libri X*, ed. by David R. Shackleton Bailey, 2nd edn (Stuttgart: Teubner).

Marcus Aurelius. 2011. *Meditations with Selected Correspondence*, ed. by Robin Hard and Christopher Gill (Oxford: Oxford University Press).

Marulić, Marko. 2007. *Epistola domini Marci Maruli Spalatensis ad Adrianum VI. pontificem maximum* in *The Marulić Reader*, ed. by Bratislav Lučin (Split: Književni krug), pp. 90–109.

Miechowita, Maciej. 1517. *Tractatus de duabus Sarmatiis Asiana et Europiana et de contentis in eis* (Krakow: Haller).

Mommsen, Theodor. 1909. *Gesammelte Schriften, Bd. 7: Philologische Schriften* (Berlin: Weidmann).

Morhof, Daniel Georg. 1747. *Polyhistor litterarius, philosophicus et practicus*, 4th edn (Lübeck: Boeckmann).

Olmo, Michael. 1816. *De Lingua latina colenda et civitate latina fundanda liber singularis. Accedit epistola auctoris ad Barberium Vemars, cum responsione Barberii* (Toulouse: Douladoure).

Piccolomini, Enea Silvio. 1984. *Pii commentarii rerum memorabilium que temporibus suis contigerunt, vol. 1*, ed. Adrian van Heck, Studi e testi, 312 (Vatican City: Biblioteca Apostolica Vaticana).

Piccolomini, Enea Silvio. 2001. *De Europa*, ed. by Adrian van Heck, Studi e testi, 398 (Vatican City: Biblioteca Apostolica Vaticana).

Piccolomini, Enea Silvio. 2001. *Pius II. Papa Epistola ad Mahumetem. Einleitung, kritische Edition, Übersetzung*, ed. by Reinhold F. Glei and Markus Köhler, Bochumer Altertumswissenschaftliches Colloquium, 50 (Trier: Wissenschaftlicher Verlag).

Piccolomini, Enea Silvio. 2013. *Constantinopolitana clades*, in *Deutsche Reichtagsakten unter Kaiser Friedrich III.: Bd. 19.2: Reichsversammlung zu Frankfurt 1454*, ed. by Johannes Helmrath (Munich: Oldenbourg), pp. 463–565.

Podiebrad, George of and Martin Mair. 2016. *Tractatus pacis toti christianitati fiendae*, in Magda Schusterová, *Der Friedensvertrag Georgs von Podiebrad von 1464 vor dem Hintergrund der spätmittelalterlichen Vertragspraxis*, Osnabrücker Schriften zur Rechtsgeschichte, 17 (Göttingen: v&r unipress), pp. 195–204.

Polybius. 1882–1904. *Historiae,* 5 vols., ed. by Ludwig Dindorf and Theodorus Büttner-Wobst (Leipzig: Teubner).

Postel, Guillaume. 1636. *De cosmographica disciplina et signorum coelestium vera configuratione libri III,* 3rd edn (Leiden: Maire).

Putsch, Johannes. 1544. *Europa lamentans,* in *Poematia aliquot insignia illustrium poetarum recentiorum,* ed. by Anon. (Basel: Winter), pp. 5v–6r.

Putsch, Johannes. 2019. *Europa lamentans: Lamentatio Europae ad Carolum V. Caesarem et Ferdinandum Romanorum regem fratres,* in Nicolas Detering and Dennis Pulina, 'Rivalry of Lament: Early Personifications of Europe in Neo-Latin Panegyrics for Charles V and Francis I', in *Contesting Europe: Comparative Perspectives on Early Modern Discourses on Europe, 1400–1800,* ed. by Nicolas Detering, Clementina Marsico, and Isabella Walser-Bürgler, Intersections, 67 (Leiden: Brill), pp. 13–38 (pp. 31–34).

Romanus, Carl Friedrich. 1698. *Dissertatio academica de republica litteraria* [...] (Leipzig: Götz).

Rusdorf, Johann Joachim von. 1631. *Scena Europaea, personis suis instructa, praecipuas regum, principum, rempublicarum, virtutes, consilia et actiones, ac totius Europae praesentem et futurum statum repraesentans* (Stralsund: Saxo).

Sallust. 1991. *Catilina, Iugurtha, Historiarum Fragmenta Selecta. Appendix Sallustiana,* ed. by Leighton D. Reynolds (Oxford: Oxford University Press).

Sande, Duarte de. 1590. *De missione legatorum Iaponensium ad Romanam curiam rebusque in Europa ac toto itinere animadversis dialogus* (Macau: n. pub.).

Sande, Duarte de. 2009. *Diálogo sobre a missão dos embaixadores japoneses à Cúria romana,* 2 vols., ed. by Américo da Costa Ramalho and Sebastião Tavares de Pinho, Portugaliae monumenta neolatina, 1 (Coimbra: Imprensa da Universidade de Coimbra).

Sande, Duarte de. 2012. *Japanese Travellers in Sixteenth-Century Europe: A Dialogue Concerning the Mission of the Japanese Ambassadors to the Roman Curia (1590),* ed. by Derek Massarella and Joseph F. Moran (London: Ashgate).

Seneca. 1977. *Dialogorum libri duodecim,* ed by Leighton Durham Reynolds (Oxford: Clarendon Press).

Sepúlveda, Juan Ginés de. 2003. *Ad Carolum V ut bellum suscipiat in Turcas cohortatio* in *Obras Completas: Vol. VII,* ed. by J.M. Rodríguez Peregrina (Pozoblanco: Ayuntamiento de Pozoblanco), pp. 328–45.

Strabo. 2002–2011. *Geographika,* 10 vols., ed. by Stefan Radt (Göttingen: Vandenhoeck & Ruprecht).

Suzanne, Herbert de. 2019. *Ad Christianissimum Francorum regem Franciscum lamentatio Europae,* in Nicolas Detering and Dennis Pulina, 'Rivalry of Lament: Early Personifications of Europe in Neo-Latin Panegyrics for Charles V and Francis I', in

Contesting Europe: Comparative Perspectives on Early Modern Discourses on Europe, 1400–1800, ed. by Nicolas Detering, Clementina Marsico, and Isabella Walser-Bürgler Intersections, 67 (Leiden: Brill), pp. 13–38 (pp. 34–36).

The Homeric Hymns. 1980 [1936]. Ed. by Thomas W. Allen, 2nd edn (London: Oxford University Press).

Valla, Lorenzo. 1994. *Orazione per l'inaugurazione dell'anno accademico 1455–1456: Atti di un seminario di filologia umanistica*, ed. by Silvia Rizzo (Roma: Roma nel Rinascimento).

Vergil. 2009. *Aeneis*, ed. by Gian Biagio Conte (Berlin: de Gruyter).

Vives, Juan Luis. 2019. *De Europae dissidiis et republica*, ed. by Edward V. George and Gilbert Tournoy, Selected Works of J.L. Vives, 12 (Leiden: Brill), pp. 89–159.

Secondary Literature

Agai, Bekim. 2016. 'Europa im Spiegel der Wahrnehmungen von Reisenden aus der islamischen Welt', in *Pluralistische Identität: Beobachtungen zu Herkunft und Zukunft Europas*, ed. by Dirk Ansorge (Darmstadt: Wissenschaftliche Buchgesellschaft), pp. 120–45.

Akasoy, Anna A. 2016. 'Die Selbstdefinition Europas während der Renaissance im Kontext der Auseinandersetzung mit dem Osmanischen Reich', in *Pluralistische Identität: Beobachtungen zu Herkunft und Zukunft Europas*, ed. by Dirk Ansorge (Darmstadt: Wissenschaftliche Buchgesellschaft), pp. 84–102.

Akopyan, Ovanes. 2019. 'Europe or Not? Sixteenth-Century European Descriptions of Muscovy and the Russian Responses', in *Contesting Europe: Comparative Perspectives on Early Modern Discourses on Europe, 1400–1800*, ed. by Nicolas Detering, Clementina Marsico, and Isabella Walser-Bürgler, Intersections, 67 (Leiden: Brill), pp. 248–71.

Albrecht, Andrea. 2005. *Kosmopolitismus: Weltbürgerdiskurse in Literatur, Philosophie und Publizistik um 1800*, spectrum Literaturwissenschaft / spectrum Literature, 1 (Berlin: de Gruyter).

Almási, Gábor and Lav Šubarić. 2015. 'Introduction', in *Latin at the Crossroads of Identity: The Evolution of Linguistic Nationalism in the Kingdom of Hungary*, ed. by Gábor Almási and Lav Šubarić, Central and Eastern Europe, 5 (Leiden: Brill), pp. 1–26.

Anderson, Benedict. 2006. *Imagined Communities: Reflections on the Origin and Spread of Nationalism*, 2nd edn (London: Verso).

Ansorge, Dirk. 2016. 'Europas pluralistische Identität: Eine historische und begriffsgeschichtliche Einführung', in *Pluralistische Identität: Beobachtungen zu Herkunft und Zukunft Europas*, ed. by Dirk Ansorge (Darmstadt: Wissenschaftliche Buchgesellschaft), pp. 7–23.

Arribas-Ayllon, Michael and Valerie Walkerdine. 2008. 'Foucauldian Discourse Analysis', in *The SAGE Handbook of Qualitative Research in Psychology*, ed. Carla Willig and Wendy Stainton-Rogers (Los Angeles, CA: SAGE Publications), pp. 91–108.

Asbach, Olaf. 2011. *Europa – Vom Mythos zur Imagined Community? Zur historischen Semantik 'Europas' von der Antike bis ins 17. Jahrhundert*, Europa und Moderne, 1 (Hannover: Wehrhahn).

Aspaas, Per P. 2014. 'The Use of Latin and the European Republic of Letters: Change and Continuity in the Seventeenth and Eighteenth Centuries', *Nordlit. Tidsskrift i litteratur og kultur*, 33: 281–95.

Barbero, Alessandro. 2004. *Carlo Magno: un padre dell'Europa* (Rome and Bari: Laterza).

Bataillon, Marcel. 1963. 'Sur l'humanisme du Docteur Laguna: deux petits livres latins de 1543', *Romance Philology*, 17: 207–34.

Bauer, Stefan. 2013. 'Enea Silvio Piccolomini', in *Enciclopedia italiana di scienze, lettere ed arti: Appendice 8.5: Il contributo italiano alla storia del pensiero*, ed. by Giuseppe Galasso and others (Rome: Istituto della Enciclopedia Italiana), pp. 137–43.

Baumgärtner, Ingrid and Hartmut Kugler (eds.). 2008. *Europa im Weltbild des Mittelalters: Kartographische Konzepte*, Vorstellungswelten des Mittelalters, 10 (Berlin: Akademie Verlag).

Behringer, Wolfgang. 2011. 'Einführung: Das frühneuzeitliche Europabild als Forschungsaufgabe', in *Departure for Modern Europe: A Handbook of Early Modern Philosophy (1400–1700)*, ed. by Hubertus Busche (Hamburg: Meiner), pp. 781–803.

Bietenholz, Peter G. and Thomas B. Deutscher (eds.). 1985. *Contemporaries of Erasmus: A Biographical Register of the Renaissance and Reformation*, 3 vols. (Toronto: University of Toronto Press).

Bisaha, Nancy. 2004: 'Pope Pius II and the Crusade', in *Crusading in the Fifteenth Century: Message and Impact*, ed. by Norman Housley (Basingstoke: Palgrave Macmillan), pp. 39–52.

Blanks, David. 2016. 'Europeans before Europe: Modernity and the Myth of the Other', in *Early Modern Constructions of Europe: Literature, Culture, History*, ed. by Florian Kläger and Gerd Bayer, Routledge Studies in Renaissance Literature and Culture, 29 (New York: Routledge), pp. 27–40.

Bloemendal, Jan. 2015. 'Introduction: Bilingualism, Multilingualism and the Formation of Europe', in *Bilingual Europe: Latin and Vernacular Cultures. Examples of Bilingualism and Multilingualism c. 1300–1800*, ed. by Jan Bloemendal (Leiden: Brill), pp. 1–14.

Bosbach, Franz. 1988. *Monarchia universalis: Ein politischer Leitbegriff der frühen Neuzeit*, Schriftenreihe der Historischen Kommission bei der Bayerischen Akademie der Wissenschaften, 32 (Göttingen: Vandenhoeck & Ruprecht).

Bots, Hans and Françoise Waquet, *La République des Lettres* (Paris: Belin, 1997).

Böttcher, Winfried (ed.). 2019. *Europas vergessene Visionäre: Rückbesinnung in Zeiten akuter Krisen* (Baden-Baden: Nomos).

Brückner, Wolfgang. 1994. 'Die Wiener Völkertafel in Berlin', *Bayerische Blätter für Volkskunde*, 21: 202–16.

Bruns, Claudia. 2017. 'Geschlecht – Körper – Karte: Anthropomorphe Europakarten im Übergang zur Frühen Neuzeit', *Zeitsprünge*, 21: 9–44.

Buch, Esteban. 2003. 'Parcours et paradoxes de l'hymne européen', in *Figures d'Europe – Images and Myths of Europe*, ed. by Luisa Passerini (Brussels: Lang), pp. 87–98.

Burke, Peter. 1980. 'Did Europe Exist before 1700?', *History of European Ideas*, 1: 21–29.

Burke, Peter. 2004. *Languages and Communities in Early Modern Europe* (Cambridge: Cambridge University Press).

Calero, Francisco. 1999. 'Dos grandes europeístas españoles del siglo XVI: Luis Vives y Andrés Laguna', *Revista de la Asociación Española de Semiótica*, 8: 19–36.

Cattaneo, Carlo. 1944. *Sulle interdizioni israelitiche*, ed. by Giulio A. Belloni (Rome: Sestante).

Cattaneo, Ruggero. 2008. 'Sullo stile e la rilevanza culturale dell'*Epistola* a Papa Adriano VI di Marco Marulić', *Colloquia Maruliana*, 17: 91–124.

Chevallier, Raymond. 1998. 'L'Europe dans les textes géographiques grecs et latins', in *D'Europe à l'Europe. Vol. 1: Le mythe d'Europe dans l'art et la culture de l'antiquité au XVIIIe siècle. Actes du colloque tenu à l'ENS, Paris (24–26) avril 1997*, ed. by Rémy Poignault and Odile Wattel-De Croizant (Tours: Centre Piganiol), pp. 39–54.

Curcio, Carlo. 1958. *Europa: storia di un idea* (Florence: Valecchi).

Czapla, Beate. 1999. 'Neulateinische Lehrdichtung zwischen der literarischen Tradition von Hesiod bis Manilius und der neuzeitlichen *Ars apodemica* am Beispiel von Bernardus Mollerus' *Rhenus* und Cyriacus Lentulus' *Europa*', *Neulateinisches Jahrbuch*, 1: 21–48.

Dawson, Christopher. 1932. *The Making of Europe: An Introduction to the History of European Unity* (New York: Sheed & Ward).

Dejung, Christof and Martin Lengwiler. 2016. 'Einleitung: Ränder der Moderne. Neue Perspektiven auf die Europäische Geschichte', in *Ränder der Moderne: Neue Perspektiven auf die Europäische Geschichte (1800–1930)*, ed. by Christof Dejung and Martin Lengwiler (Cologne: Böhlau), pp. 7–35.

Detering, Nicolas. 2017. *Krise und Kontinent: Die Entstehung der deutschen Europa-Literatur in der Frühen Neuzeit* (Cologne: Böhlau).

Detering, Nicolas, Clementina Marsico, and Isabella Walser-Bürgler. 2019. 'Contesting Europe: Comparative Perspectives on Early Modern Discourses on Europe, 1400–1800 – an Introduction', in *Contesting Europe: Comparative Perspectives on Early Modern Discourses on Europe, 1400–1800*, ed. by Nicolas Detering, Clementina Marsico, and Isabella Walser-Bürgler, Intersections, 67 (Leiden: Brill), pp. 1–10.

Detering, Nicolas and Dennis Pulina. 2019. 'Rivalry of Lament: Early Personifications of Europe in Neo-Latin Panegyrics for Charles V and Francis I', in *Contesting Europe: Comparative Perspectives on Early Modern Discourses on Europe, 1400–1800*, ed. by Nicolas Detering, Clementina Marsico, and Isabella Walser-Bürgler, Intersections, 67 (Leiden: Brill), pp. 13–38.

Dibon, Paul. 1978. 'Communication in the *Respublica Litteraria* in the 17th Century', *Res publica litterarum*, 1: 43–56.

Duchhardt, Heinz. 1979. *Studien zur Friedensvermittlung in der frühen Neuzeit*, Schriften der Mainzer Philosophischen Fakultätsgesellschaft, 6 (Wiesbaden: Steiner).

Duchhardt, Heinz. 1997. *Balance of Power und Pentarchie, 1700–1785* (Paderborn: Schöningh).

Duchhardt, Heinz. 2000. 'Europa-Diskurs und Europa-Forschung: Ein Rückblick auf ein Jahrhundert', *Jahrbuch für Europäische Geschichte*, 1: 1–14.

Durkheim, Emile. 1974 [1898]. *Sociology and Philosophy*. Transl. by David F. Pocock. With an Introduction by John G. Peristiany (New York: The Free Press).

Duroselle, Jean-Baptiste. 1965. *L'idée d'Europe dans l'histoire* (Paris: Denoël).

Edwards, John R. 2009. *Language and Identity: An Introduction* (Cambridge: Cambridge University Press).

Eisenstein, Elizabeth L. 1979. *The Printing Press as an Agent of Change: Communications and Cultural Transformations in Early Modern Europe, Vol. 1* (Cambridge: Cambridge University Press).

Enenkel, Karl A.E. 2014. 'Neo-Latin Erotic and Pornographic Literature (*c.* 1400–*c.* 1700)', in *Brill's Encyclopaedia of the Neo-Latin World. Vol. 1: Macropaedia*, ed. by Philip Ford, Jan Bloemendal, and Charles Fantazzi (Leiden: Brill), pp. 487–501.

Epperlein, Siegfried. 1971. 'Zur Bedeutungsgeschichte von *Europa, Hesperia* und *Occidentalis* in der Antike und im frühen Mittelalter', *Philologus*, 115: 81–92.

Fantazzi, Charles (ed.). 2008. *A Companion to Juan Luis Vives*, Brill's Companions to the Christian Tradition, 12 (Leiden: Brill).

Fauque, Danielle M.A. 2010. 'La correspondance Jérôme Lalande et Nevil Maskelyne: Un exemple de collaboration internationale au XVIIIᵉ siècle', in *Jérôme Lalande (1732–1807): Une trajectoire scientifique*, ed. by Guy Boistel, Jérôme Lamy, and Colette Le Lay (Rennes: Presses universitaires de Rennes), pp. 109–28.

Feuchter, Jörg. 2014. 'Der Reichstag im 15. Jahrhundert – ein europäisches Forum?', in *Europa, das Reich und die Osmanen: Die Türkenreichstage von 1454/55 nach dem Fall von Konstantinopel*, ed. by Marika Bacsóka, Anna-Maria Blank, and Thomas Woelki, Zeitsprünge. Forschungen zur Frühen Neuzeit, 18 (Frankfurt a.M.: Klostermann), pp. 30–43.

Fischer, Jürgen. 1957. *Oriens, Occidens, Europa: Begriff und Gedanke 'Europa' in der späten Antike und im frühen Mittelalter*, Veröffentlichungen des Instituts für Europäische Geschichte Mainz, 15 (Wiesbaden: Steiner).

Fleming, David A. 1966. 'John Barclay: Neo-Latinist at the Jacobean Court', *Renaissance News*, 19: 228–36.

Flemming, Gerd. 2002. 'Latein in Fernost: Die Verträge von Nerčinsk (1689) und Kjachta (1727)', in *Weltbild und Weltdeutung*, ed. by Peter Neukam and Bernhard O'Connor,

Dialog Schule – Wissenschaft. Klassische Sprachen und Literaturen, 36 (Munich: Bayerischer Schulbuch-Verlag), pp. 7–48.

Fritzemeyer, Werner. 1931. *Christenheit und Europa: Zur Geschichte des europäischen Gemeinschaftsgefühls von Dante bis Leibniz*, Historische Zeitschrift. Beihefte, 23 (Munich and Berlin: Oldenbourg).

Fuhrmann, Manfred. 1981. *Europa: Zur Geschichte einer kulturellen und politischen Idee*, Konstanzer Universitätsreden, 121 (Konstanz: Universitätsverlag).

Fumaroli, Marc. 2018. *The Republic of Letters*. Transl. from the French by Lara Vergnaud (New Haven, CT: Yale University Press).

Gale, George. 2005. 'Leibniz, Peter the Great, and the Modernization of Russia: Or Adventures of a Philosopher-King in the East', *Divinatio*, 22: 7–36.

García, D. José 2012. 'La *Europa* de Andrés Laguna', *Anales de la Real Academia de Doctores de España*, 16: 145–53.

Gehler, Michael. 2010. *Europa – Ideen – Institutionen – Vereinigung* (Munich: Olzog).

Ginzburg, Carlo. 2000. *Rapporti di forza: storia, retorica, prova* (Milan: Feltrinelli).

Girault, René. 1995. 'Das Europa der Historiker', in *Europa im Blick der Historiker: Europäische Integration im 20. Jahrhundert. Bewusstsein und Institutionen*, Historische Zeitschrift. Beihefte, 21, ed. by Rainer Hudemann, Hartmut Kaelble, and Klaus Schwabe (Munich: Oldenbourg), pp. 55–90.

Glei, Reinhold F. 2016. 'Die Polemik des "Christlichen Abendlandes" gegen Judentum und Islam', in *Pluralistische Identität: Beobachtungen zu Herkunft und Zukunft Europas*, ed. by Dirk Ansorge (Darmstadt: Wissenschaftliche Buchgesellschaft), pp. 68–83

Gollwitzer, Helmut. 1951. *Europabild und Europagedanke: Beiträge zur deutschen Geistesgeschichte des 18. und 19. Jahrhunderts* (Munich: Beck).

González Manjarrés, Miguel Ángel. 2000. *Andrés Laguna y el humanismo medico: Estudio filológico* (Salamanca: Junta de Castilla y León).

Goodman, Dena. 1996. *The Republic of Letters: A Cultural History of the French Enlightenment* (Ithaca, NY: Cornell University Press).

Grafton, Anthony. 2009. *Worlds Made by Words: Scholarship and Community in the Modern West* (Cambridge, MA: Harvard University Press).

Halkin, Léon-E. 1994. *Erasmus: A Critical Biography*. Transl. by John Tonkin (Cambridge, MA: Blackwell).

Hall, Jonathan M. 2002. *Hellenicity: Between Ethnicity and Culture* (Chicago: Chicago University Press).

Hankins, James. 1995. 'Renaissance Crusaders: Humanist Crusade Literature in the Age of Mehmed II', *Dumbarton Oaks Papers*, 49: 111–207.

Hansen, Rainer. 1992. 'Martin Mair: Ein gelehrter Rat in fürstlichem und städtischem Dienst in der zweiten Hälfte des 15. Jahrhunderts' (unpublished doctoral thesis, University of Kiel).

Hartmann, Andreas. 2003. 'Im Osten nichts Neues: Europa und seine Barbaren seit dem V. Jahrhundert v. Chr.', in *Blicke auf Europa: Kontinuität und Wandel*, ed. by Andreas Michler and Waltraud Schreiber (Neuried: ars una), pp. 31–69.

Hay, Denys. 1957. *Europe: The Emergence of an Idea* (Edinburgh: Edinburgh University Press).

Hazard, Paul. 1935. *La crise de la conscience européenne (1680–1715)* (Paris: Boivin et Cie).

Healy, Margaret. 2001. *Fictions of Disease in Early Modern England: Bodies, Plagues and Politics* (Basingstoke: Palgrave).

Heinen, Ulrich. 2019. 'Rubens' Europe and the *Pax Hispanica*', in *Contesting Europe: Comparative Perspectives on Early Modern Discourses on Europe, 1400–1800*, ed. by Nicolas Detering, Clementina Marsico, and Isabella Walser-Bürgler, Intersections, 67 (Leiden: Brill), pp. 104–45.

Helmig, Jan. 2007. 'Geopolitik – Annäherung an ein schwieriges Konzept', *Aus Politik und Zeitgeschichte*, 20/21: 31–37.

Helmrath, Johannes. 2000. 'Pius II. und die Türken', in *Europa und die Türken in der Renaissance*, ed. by Bodo Guthmüller and Wilhelm Kühlmann, Frühe Neuzeit, 54 (Tübingen: de Gruyter), pp. 79–137.

Helmrath, Johannes. 2004. 'The German *Reichstage* and the Crusade', in *Crusading in the Fifteenth Century: Message and Impact*, ed. by Norman Housley (Basingstoke: Palgrave Macmillan), pp. 53–69.

Helmrath, Johannes. 2005. 'Enea Silvio Piccolomini (Pius II.) – Ein Humanist als Vater des Europagedankens?', in *Europa und die Europäer: Quellen und Essays zur modernen europäischen Geschichte*, ed. by Rüdiger Hohls, Iris Schröder, and Hannes Siegrist (Stuttgart: Steiner), pp. 361–69.

Hentze, Wilhelm (ed.). 1999. *De Karolo rege et Leone papa: Der Bericht über die Zusammenkunft Karls des Großen mit Papst Leo III. in Paderborn 799 in einem Epos für Karl den Kaiser*, Studien und Quellen zur westfälischen Geschichte, 36 (Paderborn: Bonifatius).

Housley, Norman (ed.). 2004. *Crusading in the Fifteenth Century: Message and Impact* (Basingstoke: Palgrave Macmillan).

IJsewijn, Jozef. 1990. *Companion to Neo-Latin Studies. Part I: History and Diffusion of Neo-Latin Literature*, Supplementa Humanistica Lovaniensia, 5, 2nd edn (Leuven: Leuven University Press).

IJsewijn, Jozef and Dirk Sacré. 1993. 'The Ultimate Efforts to Save Latin as the Means of International Communication', *History of European Ideas*, 16: 51–66.

Janson, Tore. 2004. *A Natural History of Latin*. Transl. and adapted into English by Merethe Damsgård Sørensen and Nigel Vincent (Oxford: Oxford University Press).

Jax, Karl. 1938. 'Johannes Putschius: Ein Tiroler Heimatdichter (1516–1542)', *Veröffentlichungen des Museums Ferdinandeum*, 18: 334–47.

Jones, Priska. 2009. *Europa in der Karikatur: Deutsche und britische Darstellungen im 20. Jahrhundert* (Frankfurt a.M.: Campus).

Jouanna. Danielle. 2009. *L'Europe est née en Grèce: La naissance de l'idée d'Europe en Grèce ancienne* (Paris: L'Harmattan).

Kaelble, Hartmut. 1994. 'L'Europe vécue et l'Europe pensée au XXᵉ siècle: Les spécifités sociales de l'Europe', in *Identité et conscience européennes au XXᵉ siècle*, ed. by René Girault (Paris: Hachette Littératures,), pp. 27–45.

Kaiser, Ronny. 2014. 'Antiketransformationen in Enea Silvio Piccolominis *Clades*-Rede (15. Oktober 1454)', in *Europa, das Reich und die Osmanen: Die Türkenreichstage von 1454/55 nach dem Fall von Konstantinopel*, ed. by Marika Bacsóka, Anna-Maria Blank, and Thomas Woelki, Zeitsprünge. Forschungen zur Frühen Neuzeit, 18 (Frankfurt a.M.: Klostermann), pp. 87–109.

Kaiser, Ronny. 2019. '*Tota caduca et dehiscens* – Europe's Critical Condition in Andrés Laguna's *Europa* (1543)', in *Contesting Europe: Comparative Perspectives on Early Modern Discourses on Europe, 1400–1800*, ed. by Nicolas Detering, Clementina Marsico, and Isabella Walser-Bürgler, Intersections, 67 (Leiden: Brill), pp. 39–53.

Kajanto, Iiro. 1979. 'The Position of Latin in Eighteenth-Century Finland', in *Acta Conventus Neo-Latini Amstelodamensis: Proceedings of the Second International Congress of Neo-Latin Studies, Amsterdam, 19–24 August 1973*, ed. by Eckhard Kessler, Peter Tuynman, and Gerdina C. Kuiper (Munich: Fink), pp. 93–106.

Kampers, Franz. 1925. 'Rex et sacerdos', *Historisches Jahrbuch*, 45: 495–515.

Kampmann, Christoph. 1994. 'Universalismus und Staatenvielfalt: Zur europäischen Identität in der Frühen Neuzeit', in *Europa – aber was ist es? Aspekte seiner Identität in interdisziplinärer Sicht*, ed. by Jörg A. Schlumberger and Peter Segl, Bayreuther historische Kolloquien, 8 (Cologne: Böhlau), pp. 45–76.

Kjaer, Poul F. and Niklas Olsen. 2016. 'Introduction: European Crises of Public Power from Weimar until Today', in *Critical Theories of Crisis in Europe: From Weimar to the Euro*, ed. by Poul F. Kjaer and Niklas Olsen (London and New York: Rowman & Littlefield), pp. xi–xx.

Kläger, Florian and Gerd Bayer (eds.). 2016. *Early Modern Constructions of Europe: Literature, Culture, History*, Routledge Studies in Renaissance Literature and Culture, 29 (New York: Routledge).

Kläger, Florian and Gerd Bayer. 2016. 'Introduction: Early Modern Constructions of Europe', in *Early Modern Constructions of Europe: Literature, Culture, History*, ed. by Florian Kläger and Gerd Bayer, Routledge Studies in Renaissance Literature and Culture, 29 (New York: Routledge), pp. 1–23.

Kofler, Wolfgang and Martin Korenjak. 2012. 'Dichtung', in *Tyrolis Latina: Geschichte der lateinischen Literatur in Tirol. Bd. 1: Von den Anfängen bis zur Gründung der Universität Innsbruck*, ed. by Martin Korenjak and others (Vienna: Böhlau), pp. 225–65.

Kohler, Alfred. 2003. *Ferdinand I., 1503–1564: Fürst, König und Kaiser* (Munich: Beck).

Korenjak, Martin. 2016. *Geschichte der neulateinischen Literatur: Vom Humanismus bis zur Gegenwart* (Munich: Beck).

Koschorke, Albrecht and others. 2007. *Der fiktive Staat: Konstruktionen des politischen Körpers in der Geschichte Europas* (Frankfurt a.M.: Fischer).

Kousoulis, Antonis A., Marianna Karamanou, and George Androutsos. 2011. 'Andrés Laguna: A Great Medical Humanist (1499–1559)', *História da Medicina*, 24: 671–74.

Kreis, Georg. 2012. 'Das Europäische Haus', in *Europäische Erinnerungsorte. Bd. 2: Das Haus Europa*, ed. by Pim den Boer and others (Munich: Oldenbourg), pp. 577–85.

Lacoste, Yves. 1990. *Geographie und politisches Handeln: Perspektiven einer neuen Geopolitik*, Kleine kulturwissenschaftliche Bibliothek, 26 (Berlin: Wagenbach).

Lee, Alexander. 2018. *Humanism and Empire: The Imperial Ideal in Fourteenth-Century Italy* (Oxford: Oxford University Press).

Leerssen, Joep. 2006. *National Thought in Europe: A Cultural History* (Amsterdam: Amsterdam University Press).

Leonhardt, Jürgen. 2013. *Latin: Story of a World Language*. Transl. by Kenneth Kronenberg (Cambridge, MA: Belknap Press of Harvard University Press).

Lesaffer, Randall. 2007. 'Peace Treaties from Lodi to Westphalia', in *Peace Treaties and International Law in European History: From the Late Middle Ages to World War One*, ed. by Randall Lesaffer (Cambridge: Cambridge University Press), pp. 9–44.

Levinson, Stephen C. 1997. 'From Outer to Inner Space: Linguistic Categories and Non-Linguistic Thinking', in *Language and Conceptualization*, ed. by Jan Nuyts and Eric Pederson (Cambridge: Cambridge University Press), pp. 13–45.

Li, Wenchao. 2000. *Die christliche China-Mission im 17. Jahrhundert: Verständnis, Unverständnis, Missverständnis. Eine geistesgeschichtliche Studie zum Christentum, Buddhismus und Konfuzianismus*, Supplementa Studia Leibnitiana, 32 (Stuttgart: Steiner).

Li, Wenchao. 2015. 'Un commerce de lumière – Leibniz' Vorstellungen von kulturellem Wissensaustausch', in *Umwelt und Weltgestaltung: Leibniz' politisches Denken in seiner Zeit*, ed. by Friedrich Beiderbeck, Irene Dingel, and Wenchao Li (Göttingen: Vandenhoeck & Ruprecht), pp. 293–306.

Lučin, Bratislav. 2007. 'Introduction', in *The Marulić Reader*, ed. by Bratislav Lučin (Split: Književni krug), pp. 7–31.

Lučin, Bratislav. 2009. 'Marko Marulić: Kroatischer Dichter und europäischer Humanist', *Colloquia Maruliana*, 18: 349–55.

Lützeler, Paul Michael. 2016. 'The European Imaginary in the Discourse on Peace', in *Early Modern Constructions of Europe: Literature, Culture, History*, ed. by Florian Kläger and Gerd Bayer, Routledge Studies in Renaissance Literature and Culture, 29 (New York: Routledge), pp. 194–210.

Lyons, Justin D. 2004. 'The Temple and the Tower: Winston Churchill on the Political Language of Peace', *Perspectives on Political Science*, 33: 30–39.

Mackey, William F. 2001. 'Conflicting Languages in a United Europe', *Sociolinguistica. International Yearbook of European Sociolinguistics*, 15: 1–17.

Mader, Eric-Oliver. 2011. 'Das Europabild in der politischen Theorie des 16. und 17. Jahrhunderts', in *Departure for Modern Europe: A Handbook of Early Modern Philosophy (1400–1700)*, ed. by Hubertus Busche (Hamburg: Meiner), pp. 823–39.

Malcolm, Noel. 2019. *Useful Enemies: Islam and the Ottoman Empire in Western Political Thought, 1450–1750* (Oxford: Oxford University Press).

Malettke, Klaus. 1994. 'Europabewusstsein und europäische Friedenspläne im 17. und 18. Jahrhundert', *Francia*, 21: 63–94.

Malitz, Jürgen. 2003. 'Imperium Romanum und Europagedanke', in *Blicke auf Europa: Kontinuität und Wandel*, ed. by Andreas Michler and Waltraud Schreiber (Neuried: ars una), pp. 79–103.

Margolin, Jean-Claude. 1970. 'Erasme et la psychologie des peuples', *Revue d'ethnopsychologie*, 25: 373–424.

Marsh, David. 1998. *Lucian and the Latins: Humor and Humanism in the Early Renaissance*, (Ann Arbor, MI: University of Michigan Press).

Matar, Nabil. 2016. '*Ūrubba* in Early Modern Arabic Sources', in: *Early Modern Constructions of Europe: Literature, Culture, History*, ed. by Florian Kläger and Gerd Bayer, Routledge Studies in Renaissance Literature and Culture, 29 (New York: Routledge), pp. 41–56.

Maurer, Michael. 1993. '"Nationalcharakter" in der frühen Neuzeit: Ein mentalitätsgeschichtlicher Versuch', in *Transformationen des Wir-Gefühls: Studien zum nationalen Habitus*, ed. by Reinhard Blomert, Helmut Kuzmics, and Annette Treibel (Frankfurt a.M.: Suhrkamp), pp. 45–81.

Meierkord, Christiane. 2007. 'Lingua Franca Communication in Multiethnic Contexts', in *Handbook of Intercultural Communication*, ed. by Helga Kotthoff and Helen Spencer-Oatey, Handbooks of Applied Linguistics, 7 (Berlin: de Gruyter), pp. 199–218.

Meserve, Margaret. 2004. 'Italian Humanists and the Problem of the Crusade', in *Crusading in the Fifteenth Century: Message and Impact*, ed. by Norman Housley (Basingstoke: Palgrave Macmillan), pp. 13–38.

Meurer, Peter. 2008. '*Europa Regina*: 16th Century Maps of Europe in the Form of a Queen', *Belgeo*, 3–4: 355–70 <https://doi.org/10.4000/belgeo.7711>.

Mitterauer, Michael. 2003. *Warum Europa? Mittelalterliche Grundlagen eines Sonderwegs* (Munich: Beck).

Mudrov, Sergei A. 2016. 'Religion in the Treaty of Lisbon: Aspects and Evaluation', *Journal of Contemporary Religion*, 31: 1–16.

Müller, Heribert. 2014. 'Europa, das Reich und die Osmanen. Die Türkenreichstage von 1454/55 nach dem Fall von Konstantinopel, oder: Eine Hinführung zu Großem und Kleinem im Spiegel der Deutschen Reichstagsakten', in *Europa, das Reich und die Osmanen: Die Türkenreichstage von 1454/55 nach dem Fall von Konstantinopel*, ed. by Marika Bacsóka, Anna-Maria Blank, and Thomas Woelki, Zeitsprünge. Forschungen zur Frühen Neuzeit, 18 (Frankfurt a.M.: Klostermann), pp. 9–29.

Müller, Klaus. 1991. 'Die Idee des europäischen Gleichgewichts in der Frühen Neuzeit', in *Europa – Begriff und Idee: Historische Streiflichter*, ed. by Hans Hecker, Kultur und Erkenntnis, 8 (Bonn: Bouvier), pp. 61–74.

Müller, Renate. 1994. 'Europa in der Antike: Mythos und Toponym', *Traverse. Zeitschrift für Geschichte / Revue d'histoire*, 3: 195–210.

Oddy, Niall. 2017. '"Europe" in Renaissance France: The Word, Its Uses and Contexts (*c.* 1540–1620)' (unpublished doctoral thesis, University of Durham).

Oschema, Klaus. 2001. 'Der Europa-Begriff im Hoch- und Spätmittelalter: Zwischen geographischem Weltbild und kultureller Konnotation', *Jahrbuch für europäische Geschichte*, 2: 191–235.

Oschema, Klaus. 2013. *Bilder von Europa im Mittelalter* (Ostfildern: Thorbecke).

Oz-Salzberger, Fania. 2015. 'Languages and Literacy', in *The Oxford Handbook of Early Modern European History. Vol. 1: 1350–1750: Peoples and Place*, ed. by Hamish Scott (Oxford: Oxford University Press), pp. 192–213.

Pagden, Anthony. 2002. 'Europe: Conceptualizing a Continent', in *The Idea of Europe: From Antiquity to the European Union*, ed. by Anthony Pagden (Cambridge: Cambridge University Press), pp. 33–54.

Parker, Geoffrey. 2008. 'Crisis and Catastrophe: The Global Crisis of the Seventeenth Century Reconsidered', *American Historical Review*, 113: 1053–79.

Pérez Fernández, José María. 2012. 'Translation and the Early Modern Idea of Europe', *Translation and Literature*, 21: 299–318.

Piechocki, Katharina N. 2019. *Cartographic Humanism: The Making of Early Modern Europe* (Chicago: The University of Chicago Press).

Piirimäe, Pärtel. 2007. 'Russia, the Turks and Europe: Legitimations of War and the Formation of European Identity in the Early Modern Period', *Journal of Early Modern History*, 11: 63–86.

Pocock, J.G.A. 2002: 'Some Europes in Their History', in *The Idea of Europe: From Antiquity to the European Union*, ed. by Anthony Pagden (Cambridge: Cambridge University Press), pp. 55–71.

Poeschel, Sabine. 1985. *Studien zur Ikonographie der Erdteile in der Kunst des 16.–18. Jahrhunderts* (Munich: Scaneg).

Posset, Franz. 2009. 'Open Letter of a Croatian Lay Theologian to a "German" Pope: Marko Marulić to Adrian VI', *Colloquia Maruliana*, 18: 135–57.

Reckwitz, Andreas. 2000. *Die Transformation der Kulturtheorien: Zur Entwicklung eines Theorienprogramms* (Weilerswist: Velbrück).

Reinhardt, Volker. 2013. *Pius II. Piccolomini: Der Papst, mit dem die Renaissance begann. Eine Biographie* (Munich: Beck).

Reuter, Timothy. 1992. 'Medieval Ideas of Europe and Their Modern Historians', *History Workshop*, 33: 176–80.

Ribhegge, Wilhelm. 1998. 'Erasmus und Europa: Studien zur Korrespondenz des Erasmus von Rotterdam', *Zeitschrift für Historische Forschung*, 25: 549–80.

Riethmüller, Albrecht. 2012. 'Die Hymne der europäischen Union', in *Europäische Erinnerungsorte. Bd. 2: Das Haus Europa*, ed. by Pim den Boer and others (Munich: Oldenbourg), pp. 89–96.

Romberg, Marion. 2017. *Die Welt im Dienst des Glaubens: Erdteilallegorien in Dorfkirchen auf dem Gebiet des Fürstbistums Augsburg im 18. Jahrhundert* (Stuttgart: Steiner).

Rougemont, Denis de. 1961. *Vingt-huit siècles d'Europe: La conscience européenne à travers les textes – d'Hésiode à nos jours* (Paris: Bartillat).

Saitta, Armando. 1948. *Dalla Res Publica Christiana agli Stati Uniti di Europa: sviluppo dell'idea pacifista in Francia nei secoli XVII–XIX* (Rome: Storia e Letteratura).

Schlumberger, Jörg A. and Peter Segl (eds.). 1994. *Europa – aber was ist es? Aspekte seiner Identität in interdisziplinärer Sicht*, Bayreuther historische Kolloquien, 8 (Cologne: Böhlau).

Schmale, Wolfgang. 2000. 'Europa – die weibliche Form', *L'Homme: Zeitschrift für feministische Geschichtswissenschaft*, 11: 211–33.

Schmale, Wolfgang. 2000. *Geschichte Europas* (Vienna: Böhlau).

Schmale, Wolfgang. 2004. 'Europa, Braut der Fürsten: Die politische Relevanz des Europamythos im 17. Jahrhundert', in *Europa im 17. Jahrhundert: Ein politischer Mythos und seine Bilder*, ed. by Klaus Bußmann and Elke A. Werner (Wiesbaden: Steiner), pp. 241–67.

Schmale, Wolfgang and others. 2004. *Studien zur europäischen Identität im 17. Jahrhundert: Mit 28 Abbildungen und 72 Tabellen*, Herausforderungen, 15 (Bochum: Winkler).

Schmidt, Helmut D. 1966. 'The Establishment of "Europe" as a Political Expression', *The Historical Journal*, 9: 172–78.

Schulze, Winfried. 1998. 'Die Entstehung des nationalen Vorurteils: Zur Kultur der Wahrnehmung fremder Nationen in der europäischen Frühen Neuzeit', in *Menschen und Grenzen in der Frühen Neuzeit*, ed. by Wolfgang Schmale and Reinhard Stauber (Berlin: Spitz), pp. 23–49.

Schusterová, Magda. 2016. *Der Friedensvertrag Georgs von Podiebrad von 1464 vor dem Hintergrund der spätmittelalterlichen Vertragspraxis*, Osnabrücker Schriften zur Rechtsgeschichte, 17 (Göttingen: v&r unipress).

Scott, Hamish M. (ed.). 2015. *Oxford Handbook of Early Modern European History, 1350–1750*, 2 vols. (Oxford: Oxford University Press).

Segl, Peter. 1994. 'Europas Grundlegung im Mittelalter', in *Europa – aber was ist es? Aspekte seiner Identität in interdisziplinärer Sicht*, ed. by Jörg A. Schlumberger and Peter Segl, Bayreuther historische Kolloquien, 8 (Cologne: Böhlau), pp. 21–43.

Sheehan, Michael. 1996. *The Balance of Power: History and Theory* (London: Routledge).

Simek, Rudolf. 1997. 'Weltbild, geogr.', in *Lexikon des Mittelalters, Bd. 8*, ed. by Robert-Henri Bautier (Munich and Zurich: Artemis, 1997), coll. 2159–65.

Smith, David Baird. 1914. 'John Barclay', *The Scottish Historical Review*, 12: 37–59.

Spengler, Oswald. 1918/1922. *Der Untergang des Abendlandes: Umrisse einer Morphologie der Weltgeschichte, 2 Bde.* (Vienna: Braumüller / Munich: Beck).

Stevenson, Jane. 2005. *Women Latin Poets: Language, Gender, and Authority from Antiquity to the Eighteenth Century* (Oxford: Oxford University Press).

Stråth, Bo. 2000. 'Introduction: Europe as a Discourse', in *Europe and the Other and Europe as the Other*, ed. by Bo Stråth (Brussels: Lang), pp. 13–44.

Strieder, Friedrich Wilhelm. 1787. *Grundlage zu einer Hessischen Gelehrten und Schriftsteller Geschichte: Seit der Reformation bis auf gegenwärtige Zeiten, Bd. 7* (Kassel: Cramer), pp. 484–90.

Sutter Fichtner, Paula. 2003. *The Habsburg Monarchy, 1490–1848: Attributes of Empire* (New York: Palgrave).

Swedberg, Richard. 1994. 'The Idea of "Europe" and the Origin of the European Union – A Sociological Approach', *Zeitschrift für Soziologie*, 23: 378–87.

Tóth, István G. 2000. *Literacy and Written Culture in Early Modern Central Europe* (New York: Central University Press).

Townson, Michael. 1992. *Mother-Tongue and Fatherland: Language and Politics in German* (Manchester: Manchester University Press).

Trunk, Achim. 2008. *Europa, ein Ausweg: Politische Eliten und europäische Identität in den 1950er-Jahren*, Studien zur Internationalen Geschichte, 18 (Munich: Oldenbourg).

Valéry, Paul. 1957. 'Note (ou L'Européen)', in *Oeuvres: Vol. 1*, ed. by Jean Hytier (Paris: Gallimard), pp. 1000–14.

Vielemeier, Ludger. 1991. 'European Union in Public Opinion Polls, 1945–50', in *Documents of the History of European Integration: Vol. 4: Transnational Organizations of Political Parties and Pressure Groups in the Struggle for European Union, 1945–1950*, ed. by Walter Lipgens and Wilfried Loth (Berlin: de Gruyter), pp. 574–626.

Vogel, Christian Daniel. 1839. 'Nachrichten über das Leben und die Schriften des ehemaligen Professors und Nassauischen Historiographen Cyriacus Lentulus', *Annalen des Vereins für Nassauische Alterthumskunde und Geschichtsforschung*, 3: 111–16.

Wagner, Fritz. 1974. 'Europa um 1700 – Idee und Wirklichkeit', *Francia*, 2: 295–308.

Walser, Isabella. 2017. '*Unitas multiplex*: John Barclay's Notion of Europe in His *Icon animorum* (1614)', *History of European Ideas*, 43: 533–46 <https://doi.org/10.1080/0 1916599.2017.1309673>.

Walser-Bürgler, Isabella. 2017. 'Europa und europäische Identität(en) in der neulatei-
    nischen Literatur: Neue Wege und Perspektiven in Forschung und Unterricht',
    Ianus. Informationen zum Altsprachlichen Unterricht, 38: 56–72.

Walser-Bürgler, Isabella. 2018. '*Europa Exultans*: The Personification of Europe as
    a Representation of the Habsburg Universal Monarchy in Johann Lauterbach's
    Pastoral Poem *Europa Eidyllion* (1558)', *Lias. Journal of Early Modern Intellectual
    Culture and Its Sources*, 45: 1–43.

Walser-Bürgler, Isabella. 2018. 'Europe without the Bull? Reflections on the Absence of
    the Ancient Myth of Europa in the Neo-Latin Discourse on Europe', *Medievalia et
    Humanistica*, 44: 81–103.

Walser-Bürgler, Isabella. 2019. 'Andrés Laguna, *Europa heautentimorumene* (1543):
    Europas Klage im Kontext europapolitischer Bewusstseinsbildung', *Latein Forum*,
    97/98: 6–24.

Walser-Bürgler, Isabella. 2019. 'Continuities of Historical Crises and Discourses of
    Europe from the Neo-Latin Past to the 21st Century', *International Relations and
    Diplomacy*, 7: 549–63 <https://doi.org/10.17265/2328-2134/2019.12.001>.

Walser-Bürgler, Isabella. 2019. 'Geopolitical Instruction and the Construction of
    Europe in Seventeenth-Century Neo-Latin Texts', in *Contesting Europe: Comparative
    Perspectives on Early Modern Discourses on Europe, 1400–1800*, ed. by Nicolas
    Detering, Clementina Marsico, and Isabella Walser-Bürgler, Intersections, 67
    (Leiden: Brill), pp. 317–46.

Walser-Bürgler, Isabella. 2020. 'Staging Oratory in Renaissance Germany: The Delivery
    of Andrés Laguna's *Europa heautentimorumene* (1543)', *Rhetorica. A Journal of the
    History of Rhetoric*, 38 (2020), 84–117 <https://doi.org/10.1525/rh.2020.38.1.84>.

Walser-Bürgler, Isabella. 2021. 'Reflections of "Europe" and Continental Thinking? The
    Language of Inclusion in the *Instrumenta Pacis Westphalicae* (1648)', *The Seventeenth
    Century*, 36: 3–31 <https://doi.org/10.1080/0268117X.2019.1704852>.

Waquet, Françoise. 1989. 'Qu'est-ce que la République des Lettres? Essai de sémantique
    historique', *Bibliothèque de l'école des chartes*, 147: 473–502.

Waquet, Françoise. 1998. *Le Latin ou l'empire d'un signe: XVIᵉ–XXᵉ siècle* (Paris: Albin
    Michel).

Waquet, Françoise (ed.). 2000. *Mapping the World of Learning: The* Polyhistor *of Daniel
    Georg Morhof*, Wolfenbütteler Forschungen, 91 (Wiesbaden: Harrassowitz).

Waquet, Françoise. 2017. 'The Republic of Letters', in *A Guide to Neo-Latin Literature*,
    ed. by Victoria Moul (Cambridge: Cambridge University Press), pp. 66–80.

Werner, Elke A. 2015. 'Anthropomorphic Maps: On the Aesthetic Form and Political
    Function of Body Metaphors in the Early Modern Europe Discourse', in *The
    Anthropomorphic Lens: Anthropomorphism, Microcosmism and Analogy in Early
    Modern Thought and Visual Arts*, ed. by Walter S. Melion, Bret Rothstein, and Michel
    Weemans, Intersections, 34 (Leiden: Brill), pp. 251–72.

White, Hayden. 2000. 'The Discourse of Europe and the Search for a European Identity', in *Europe and the Other and Europe as the Other*, ed. by Bo Stråth (Brussels: Lang), pp. 67–86.

Wilson, Peter H. 2010. *Europe's Tragedy: A New History of the Thirty Years' War* (London: Penguin).

Wintle, Michael. 1999. 'Renaissance Maps and the Construction of the Idea of Europe', *Journal of Historical Geography*, 25: 137–65.

Wintle, Michael. 2009. *The Image of Europe: Visualizing Europe in Cartography and Iconography throughout the Ages* (Cambridge: Cambridge University Press).

Wintle, Michael. 2016. 'Islam as Europe's "Other" in the Long Term: Some Discontinuities', *History*, 101: 42–61.

www.ingramcontent.com/pod-product-compliance
Lightning Source LLC
Chambersburg PA
CBHW050454110726
47899CB00003B/937